The ... and The Press
in Canada

YOUR RECEIPT
THANK YOU

16-02-78

5 • • • • 3.75
5 • • • • 4.95
* • • • 8.70Ca

0063A002

The Law
and The Press
in Canada

Wilfred H. Kesterton

The Carleton Library No. 100
Published by McClelland and Stewart Limited in
association with the Institute of
Canadian Studies, Carleton University

The Carleton Library
A series of Canadian reprints, new titles,
and new collections of source material relating to
Canada, issued under the editorial supervision
of Carleton University, Ottawa.

© *1976 McClelland and Stewart Limited*

ISBN 7710-9800-6

ALL RIGHTS RESERVED

The Canadian Publishers
McClelland and Stewart Limited
25 Hollinger Road, Toronto

Printed and bound in Canada

TABLE OF CONTENTS

Chapter I

Introduction

Under the libertarian press system, the system which prevails in Canada, the twin qualities desired for the media are freedom and responsibility. That truism envisages persons of the press doing their work freely, unhampered by governmental controls and regulatory bodies.[1] Ideally the only check imposed on media performance is the journalist's sense of what is true, fair and socially desirable, operating under the due process of law.

It is with that due process of law that this study is concerned. That concern is justified because, when the journalist's own good judgment fails and he behaves irresponsibly, the laws of libel, contempt of court and obscenity, as well as lesser known laws, will restrain him and protect society. Not that when law and press conflict, it is always the media which are in the wrong. Sometimes journalists will risk the penalties of the law in order to perform a duty to the public. But whether they be responsible or irresponsible there will be times when journalists will become intimately involved with the law.

If that involvement be granted, it seems obvious that media practitioners will need some knowledge of the law as it affects the press. Expertise in this area is comparable to the athlete's familiarity with the rules of the games he plays. If the journalist is to become truly professional, he will need to add at least a basic grounding in press law to his skill as an investigative reporter, to the deep and wide learning in the subject matter of his reports and to the other qualifications of his calling.

Such legal "competence" should not be confined to a few specialists on a newspaper, magazine or broadcasting station. This fact was pointed up for the writer a few years ago when a journalism student asked, "Why should we study the law of the press?" Said the student: "I intend to become a newspaper reporter. My newspaper will have a lawyer to read its stories. He will tell us when we run the risk of committing libel, contempt of court and other legally dangerous offences. Why should I spend time learning the law when the law will be somebody else's worry?"

Such undergraduate ingenuousness runs counter to the experience of a publisher friend of the writer. A few years ago the publisher's newspaper had been plunged into a potentially crippling libel suit.

When the libel action had first threatened, the newspaper engaged legal counsel not only to fight that action, but to provide continuing legal advice to keep libel out of future stories.

Such continuing legal service did not end the publisher's troubles, however. He soon learned that it was impractical to bring dozens of small, daily, routine news stories to the lawyer for scrutiny, even though several were not free of some libel or contempt danger. And, in the larger news accounts, the editor-in-chief, made gun-shy by early sad experience, was calling for legal advice so often that he was running up lawyers' bills that were a serious financial burden to the newspaper. Because of this the publisher became convinced that his editors and reporters too must learn more press law. In that way the risk of further costly legal actions would be lessened, and the expense of retaining standby legal aid would be reduced.

Traditionally the city editor and news editor are regarded as the first line of defence against libel and other legal dangers. Yet, because editors are at least one stage removed from the source of news, they cannot be aware of all the hazards of every story that comes across their desks. Sometimes it is only the alertness of the reporter on the spot that can direct attention to legal risks. If the reporter is insensitive, inattentive or ignorant, he may neglect to tell his editors of circumstances which editors should but cannot know about and which might involve the newspaper in litigation. The editors are in a situation akin to that of the generals who cannot direct the action of the platoon when it comes under fire in a local skirmish.

It is with the foregoing idea in mind that this book will approach the problem of the law of the press as it relates to the Canadian journalist. It will emphasize rudimentary concepts, practices and prohibitions that the ''front-line'' journalist should know about. Here a word of caution is called for. This study does not claim to replace the professional advice certain media situations imperatively call for. In the life of the newspaper, magazine or broadcasting station, there will undoubtedly be occasions when it would be utter folly for the editorial office ''amateur'' to play around with such legal matters as libel and contempt of court. The golden rule here is this: ''in times of legal danger, take professional advice.'' At best, what this book, for its part, purports to do is to serve as a rough guide for the journalist-reader. Its aim is to give him a ''feel'' for the law of the press. What it may help him to realize is that there will be times when the journalist can go further, in safety, than he might otherwise suppose, and that, in other circumstances, he should in prudence stop and consider the consequences before taking a dangerous course of action.

To this end some emphasis will be placed on general precepts. At the same time this book will not neglect a background consideration of media law. It is hoped that the study will also provide historical "context" for the ideas presented, and that it will also furnish guidance useful to media people whose place in the news conveying process is somewhat removed from the reporter's "front-line" involvement.

Some History

Historically the development and transformation of the law as it affects the press relate to the change from an authoritarian to a libertarian system of government in England and Canada. Under authoritarianism, the state, whether personified by the king or the ruling authorities, was sacrosanct. The law was designed to protect the state from the individual instead of the other way about. Soon after the beginning of printing in England, the king exercised strict control over the press through the Court of Star Chamber. Beginning with the reign of Elizabeth all books were required to be licensed before publication. The London Stationers' Company enjoyed a monopoly of printing. Censorship outlived the Star Chamber and did not expire until 1695. However, the liberty gained was extremely limited. In the mid-1700's it was still considered contempt of court to publish, without permission of the judges, reports of legal proceedings. It was not until 1771 that Parliament finally gave up attempts to prevent the publication of reports of its debates.

During the eighteenth century, the press faced innumerable prosecutions for treasonable, seditious or libellous publications. Criminal law predominated over the civil law. In the realm of defamation, it was criminal law that was used against the journalist who offended the ruling establishment. It was an aphorism of criminal libel that the greater the truth the greater the libel. This meant that when the newsman criticized the government, he could not plead truth in his own defence because truth was considered to aggravate the crime with which he was charged. Penalties for crimes were more severe than those for civil offences. Even when civil law was resorted to, reliance was heavily on common law rather than on statute law. Punishments for common law offences were also severe.

Over the years changes have been made. "General warrants" authorizing officers of the government to search for and seize the author of a libel or his papers had been used to persecute the press, but in 1765 they were declared illegal. John Peter Zenger in the British colony of New York in 1735 and Joseph Howe in Nova Scotia in 1835 won their cases despite the fact that they were prosecuted rather than sued. But their victories did not alter the law. In 1792 Fox's Libel Act empowered the jury to decide both whether matter complained of as libel had been published and whether that matter was libellous, whereas formerly the jury had been entitled to decide only the fact of publication. Yet it was several years after this before the courts ceased to return many verdicts automatically supportive of the establishment. This outcome was partly due to the French Revolution and the ferment of ideas characteristic of the times. The fears and prejudices produced by the disturbing movements and writings of the day were translated into verdicts against the press. Public opinion was as effective as the government and judges had been before in placing restraint on the journalist.[3] Prosecutions for blasphemous libel were frequently resorted to. It took the conflicts between the authorities and William Cobbett, Jonathan Wooler, William Hone, Sir Francis Burdett, and Richard Carlile to put the government on the defensive and to make criminal libel an unpopular weapon in the struggle between the establishment and its critics.

The Libel Act, 1843, (Lord Campbell's Act), permitted a defendant in a libel prosecution to plead truth in justification of what he had published provided that he had written the matter complained of without malice and for the public benefit. The plea of truth was already allowable as a defence in a legal suit, without the provisos of public benefit and absence of malice.

The Newspaper Stamp duties, first instituted in 1712, had been a device for harassing the press, but they were finally abolished in 1855. The Newspaper Libel and Registration Act, 1881, outlined provisions allowing courts of summary jurisdiction to deal with libel proceedings. If after the hearing of evidence the court of summary jurisdiction was of the opinion that the libel alleged was of a trivial nature, and that a penalty not exceeding fifty pounds would adequately punish the offence, then it was empowered to give the option of electing a summary trial. In this case the severest penalty to be expected was the fifty pounds specified. In 1888, the Law of Libel Amendment Act set forth the condition that reports of law court sittings and of public meetings were to be made privileged.

Such legislative acts encompassed changes that were later to be adopted in Canada, notably during the last part of the nineteenth century when much of the press law was placed on Canadian statute books. Together with common law derived chiefly from England, such borrowings from the basis of the law of the press on which contemporary Canadian press law has been built.

Some Concepts and Definitions

Before attention is directed to what that contemporary press law is, it seems essential to consider some of the basic concepts and definitions necessary to an understanding of that law. A certain vocabulary is needed before the rudiments of defamation, contempt of court, blasphemy and obscenity can be comprehended.

The most immediate distinction that needs to be grasped is that between crimes and civil wrongs, and, by extension, between criminal and civil law. P. G. Osborn says:

> A crime may be described as an act, default or conduct prejudicial to the community, the commission of which by law renders the person responsible liable to punishment by fine or imprisonment in special proceedings, normally instituted by officers in the service of the Crown. Crimes are divided into treasons, felonies and misdemeanours, in that order of seriousness.[4]

A crime is *not* distinguishable from a civil wrong by reason of any difference to be found in the nature of the wrongful act itself. The distinction resides in the legal consequences that may follow the act. A crime is a wrongful act capable of being followed by criminal proceedings. A civil wrong is a wrongful act capable of being followed by civil proceedings.[5] Glanville Williams clarifies the matter:

> Criminal and civil proceedings are (in the normal case) easily distinguishable; they are generally brought in different courts, the procedure is different, and the terminology is different.
>
> In criminal proceedings the terminology is as follows. You have a *prosecutor prosecuting a defendant* and the result of the prosecution if successful is a *conviction,* and the defendant is punished by a variety of punishments ranging from life imprisonment to a fine, or else is released on probation or discharged without punishment.
>
> Turning to civil proceedings, the terminology is that the *plaintiff sues* (i.e. brings an *action* against) a *defendant.* The proceedings if successful result in *judgment for the plaintiff,* and the judgment may order the defendant to pay the plaintiff money, or to transfer property to him, or to do or not to do something (injunction), or to perform a contract (specific performance.)[6]

The defendant loser in a civil action is said to be ''liable''; the defendant loser in a criminal proceeding is said to be ''guilty.''

Criminal law deals with violations of the law considered to be so serious that they cause *society* to institute proceedings against the wrongdoer. Proceedings may be of two main kinds. They may be summary proceedings or indictments. Indictable offences are of the graver kind and are triable by judge and jury. Summary offences, sometimes called petty offences, are triable without a jury by courts of summary jurisdiction.

A civil law term deserving definition is *tort*. It derives from the French word for a "wrong" and the Latin word for "crooked" or "winding." Quoting Sir F. Pollock, Osborn describes a *tort* as "[a]n act which causes harm to a determinate individual whether intentionally or not, being the breach of a duty arising out of a personal relation or contract, and which is either contrary to law, or an omission of a specific legal duty, or a violation of an absolute right.'"[7]

Just as it is essential to distinguish between criminal and civil law, it is necessary to distinguish between common law and other kinds of law. The meaning of the term "common law" varies according to what it is contrasted with. Originally common law meant law common to the whole of England, and as such it is in contradistinction to the local law. In another sense common law is law which is not equity, a concept which need not detain us here. Common law may mean law which is not foreign law, not Roman law for example. More generally, common law means the law that is not the result of legislation. It is this meaning which, unless otherwise stated, this book will attach to the phrase.

An important ingredient of common as non-statute law is what is known as the "precedent." A precedent is a court decision which creates the law which will be applied in subsequent legal judgments. This differs from the *"obiter dictum."* The *obiter dictum* is a chance remark, a saying by the way, which is not binding on future courts, although it may be later quoted with a certain measure of respect according to the reputation of the judge who made the *dictum* and to other factors. An *obiter dictum* may perhaps be better contrasted with the *ratio decidendi* of a case, which Glanville Williams defines as "the part of the case that is said to possess authority."[8]

Because of their heavy reliance on the common law inherited from England, all Canadian provinces except Quebec are known as "common law" provinces. Quebec is known as a "civil law" province. Theoretically civil law is written, with rules contained in a code enacted by a legislature; common law is unwritten, its source being judicial decisions. Quebec's civil law derives from the *Code Napoléon*, said to be the prototype of all civil codes.

Finally, two concepts which will be used later in this book require definition. One is "preliminary inquiry." This term is used in connection with criminal proceedings. What it involves is the calling of evidence by the prosecution, before a defendant is brought before a jury, to establish a *prima facie* case of guilt. Unless such a *prima facie* case is made the defendant will not be committed to trial. A second concept that will be referred to later is "examination for discovery." It refers to civil actions. It entails a delineation of the case which is to be tried. It involves a determination by means of questions put to the contending parties of the issues which the court will later be required to resolve, and production and examination by both parties to the action of the documents related to the case.

Chapter II

Contempt of Court

An area of the law which the journalist, through the nature of his calling, may become involved with is contempt of court. According to the Hon. J. C. McRuer contempt may be criminal or civil.[1] He distinguishes between the two by saying that "contempts which tend to bring the administration of justice into scorn, or which tend to interfere with the due course of justice, are criminal in their nature, but a contempt in disregarding the orders of a judge of a civil court is not criminal in its nature."[2] It is with criminal contempt that this chapter will mainly concern itself.

According to Sir John C. Fox, the phrase "contempt of court" has been used in English law since the twelfth century.[3] The Canadian law derives from English common law. In Canada contempt is the only criminal offence not included in the Criminal Code or other federal statutues.[4] This does not mean that the Code says nothing concerning some of the conditions related to contempt of court proceedings, as witness Sections 8 and 9 of the Criminal Code, to be considered later.

P. G. Osborn defines contempt of court as "(1) Failure to comply with an order of a superior court, or an act of resistance or insult to the court, or the judges. (2) Conduct likely to prejudice the fair trial of an accused person; punishable by fine or commital to prison."[5] Contempt may be classified as occurring "in the face of the court" or "not in the face of the court." The journalist is rarely cited for contempt committed in the court (*coram curia*). He stands in greater danger of committing contempt outside the court through publication or comment. Such contempt is known as "constructive" contempt. What D. A. Schmeiser calls "the classical definition of contempt and the reason for its existence"[6] was provided by Chancellor Hardwicke in 1742. The Lord Chancellor said contempt of court might consist of "scandalizing the court itself," of "abusing parties who are concerned in causes here," or of "prejuding mankind against persons before the cause is heard."[7]

Speaking about the situation in England, Thomas Dawson has said, "In modern times the second sort of contempt [abusing parties who are concerned in causes here] appears to have been merged with the third [the prejudicing of mankind against persons before the cause is heard], at least as far as contempt by printed publications is concerned."[8] Contempt of court through abusing parties to an action has virtually disappeared from Canada in modern times. L. A. Powe, Jr. says, "Although Lord Hardwicke . . . announced three categories of constructive contempt, today there are only two: prejudicing a case by denial of a fair trial and scandalizing the court."[9] Professor Atkey points out that there is only one reported Canadian case of the offence of abusing parties to an action, this occurring in 1934 when Charles E. Campbell, publisher, and J. S. Cowper, writer, for the *Edmonton Bulletin* were fined after publishing two articles prejudicial to the interest of a litigant in a civil action.[10]

The offence of scandalizing the court is not dormant in Canada. Two or three examples will illustrate its nature. (In order to avoid digressions these and subsequent examples will be referred to only briefly in the main text. But a more detailed account of each case will be found in Appendix A. The Appendix describes cases in the order in which they appear in the text.)

In 1954 Eric Nicol and the Vancouver *Province* were fined as a result of Nicol's column in which he used a specific case to criticize capital punishment. (*See Case No. 1*) In 1962 Philip Glanzer received the same kind of treatment as Nicol, after Glanzer had written several articles critical of York County Court judges. (*See Case No. 2*) Tom Murphy offended similarly in 1968 when he commented adversely on the Supreme Court of New Brunswick's handling of the Strax case. (*See Case No. 3*)

It should not be inferred from these examples that the press is forbidden in all circumstances to criticize the courts. Schmeiser points out that "When a case is over and the right of appeal has elapsed, however, the right then exists fairly to criticize the parties involved, the administration of justice, or even the actions of particular judges."[11] But this must be done with caution. The philosophical basis for this right of criticism was suggested by Lord Atkin:

> But whether the authority and position of an individual judge, or the due administration of justice, is concerned, no wrong is committed by any member of the public who exercises the ordinary right of criticizing, in good faith, in private or public, the public act done in the seat of justice. The path of criticism is a public way: the wrong headed are permitted to err therein: provided that members of the public abstain from imputing improper motives to those taking part in the administration of justice, they are immune. Justice is not a cloistered virtue: she must be allowed to suffer the scrutiny and respectful, even though outspoken, comments of ordinary men.[12]

It is worth reemphasizing that *wrong motives must not be attributed* to those who administer justice.

Professor Atkey says, "Contempt convictions for scandalizing the court have generally been reluctantly imposed on the mass media."[13] He speaks of the situation as "allowing reasonable criticism of the administration of justice where the public good has demanded it, but standing in readiness where acute circumstances require it."[14]

There is a body of opinion which feels that, even sparingly used, contempt citations for scandalizing the court are uncalled for. This was the contention of the defendant in the Murphy case referred to as Case 3 above. Reference was made to *Macleod* v. *St. Aubyn*, [1899] A. C. 549 (P.C.) where the Privy Council stated at page 561 that contempt convictions had become obsolete in England as courts were satisfied to leave to public opinion attacks or comment derogatory or scandalous to them.

An opinion consonant with that expressed by the defence in the Murphy case has been developed by L. A. Powe, Jr.[15] While inveighing against the conviction of *Georgia Straight* for defamatory libel, he said, "Stripped of technicalities scandalizing the court is a milder form of seditious libel."[16] After making strictures about the narrowness of the Atkin *dictum (supra)* Powe says, "The Canadian position is thus much less tolerant than the English on scandalizing the court but no reasons for this are articulated in the decisions."[17]

Some students of the law maintain that the third of Hardwicke's categories of contempt—the prejudicing of mankind against persons before the cause is heard—is the only kind that should be punished. The result of such contempt can be the subversion of justice. By published criticisms or comments on contemporary litigation it may influence the minds of those responsible for deciding the facts or the law, jurors or judges, with the result that the litigants are prejudiced.

J. J. Robinette subdivides matter which may result in a citation for this kind of contempt under the headings: "any false statement of fact which would tend to influence the results of the trial; any comment, argument or suggestion calculated or tending to influence the result of a trial, which the juryman may read; and even perfectly true matters, not argument, because some of the facts that you are publishing may not be admissible in court, and the juryman or potential juryman in the community will be reading in the newspaper something that they are not by law entitled to hear or know."[18]

A 1951 Ottawa trial of a Mrs. Sullivan is illustrative of any false statement of fact which tends to influence the result of a trial. (*See Case No. 4*) Robinette's second sub-category of constructive contempt—any comment, argument or suggestion calculated or tending to influence the result of a trial—may be exemplified by the 1962 trial of members of the Sons of Freedom sect in Nelson, British Columbia.[19] A case in which the plaintiff alleged both sub-categories of constructive contempt involved a 1915 editorial by John Lewis Lewis about the Meriden Britannia Co. suit against Mayor Walters of Hamilton. (*See Case No. 5*)

As Robinette says, the publishing of perfectly true matters which are not admissible in court and which jurors and newspaper readers are not by law entitled to know may constitute contempt. Such a contempt occurred in 1966 when Rudy Platiel, *Globe and Mail* reporter, was covering the courts of Halton County Courthouse. (*See Case No. 6*)

Despite the convictons returned in all but one of the examples referred to, the journalist should be aware that the law of contempt is usually not allowed, through its narrow and literal interpretation, to override other important interests of society. How the application of the law was tempered by relevant circumstances was well illustrated in 1956 in a case involving the Hon. R. E. Sommers, former Minister of Lands and Forests for British Columbia. (*See Case No. 7*)

A facet of the law of contempt that may be of concern to the journalist has to do with procedure for appeal from contempt citations. Section 9(1) of the Canadian Criminal Code deals with contempt *in the face of* the court, and Section 9(2) with contempt *not in the face of* the court. Section 9(2) says, "Where a court or judge summarily convicts a person for contempt of court not committed in the face of the court and punishment is imposed in respect thereof, that person may appeal from the conviction, or against the punishment imposed."[20] Until a Code amendment in 1970, Section 9(1) allowed an appeal from the punishment imposed only, but in that year an amendment brought treatment of appeals against summary convictions for contempt *in the face of the court* into conformity with the treatment of appeals arising out of contempt *not in the face of the court.* Now Section 1 of the Code reads, "Where a court, judge, justice or magistrate summarily convicts a person for contempt of court committed in the face of the court and punishment is imposed in respect thereof, that person may appeal from the conviction, or against the punishment imposed."[21] Section 9(3) says, "An appeal under this section lies to the court of appeal of the province in which the proceedings take place. . . ."[22]

The reader must not infer from the foregoing discussion of summary convictions that the provisions of the Code have destroyed the power of common law to punish contempt. Section 8 of the Criminal Code says, "but nothing in this section affects the power, jurisdiction, or authority that a court, judge, justice or magistrate had, immediately before the coming into force of this Act, to impose punishment for contempt of court.''[23] A contempt case dealt with in the summary fashion referred to arose out of a strike at Tilco Plastics Company, Peterborough, in late 1965. (*See Case No. 8*)

Now that the ambit and categories of contempt have been delineated and a word has been said about appeals from contempt convictions, it seems useful to look a little more closely at specific restrictions, the disregarding of which might constitute contempt.

A question may be raised about the propriety of reporting, at the time an offence is committed and before anyone is charged with that offence, eye witness and other details of the event. The thought is that matter which might be considered prejudicial to a fair trial if reported while that trial is taking place would, because of its effect on potential jurors who read newspaper accounts, be equally prejudicial if reported even before charges have been laid. It might be, for example, that a quarrel occurs in a tavern and a man is shot and killed. Although the newspaper reporting the incident is properly circumspect in not associating the events described with the man being held by the police on a coroner's warrant, the news account may present in minute detail and with quotations, eye-witness descriptions of the affair. Does this sort of reporting constitute contempt?

In this context Professor Atkey has said,

the very task of determining the 'higher rights of the courts' involves an exercise of judicial discretion not always consistent in its application and depending in each case upon the particular facts and circumstances, the time of publication, the causes leading to publication, and the tenor of what is published. In short there are no clear and easily defined guidelines for the press to follow.[24]

J. J. Robinette indicated the uncertainty involved in this area of reporting when he was asked:

What are the restrictions on interviewing eyewitnesses, victims, etc., in cases of major crimes, where those interviewed may be called to court as witnesses? Obviously the guilt of no specific person would be used or implied in stories resulting from interviews.[25]

Robinette answered:

The question is not directed to any contempt of court, but to just how far you are entitled to go out and talk to witnesses. Witnesses are members of the public. If they are willing to talk, you can talk to them. The courts have indicated though that they do not approve of newspapers conducting their own trial, that is, interviewing witnesses and then reporting what the witnesses have said. That is a different matter from the point raised in the question, where somebody was worrying, apparently about whether one could seek people out and talk to them. Certainly you are entitled to go out and talk to them.[26]

This must not be taken as a sanction to publish, with immunity from contempt of court danger, matter which would be *sub judice* once proceedings were begun. The prohibition applies both to preliminary inquiries, to be discussed later in this chapter, and to comment on interlocutory proceedings in a civil action.

After the trial proper is over and the judge has given his verdict, the newspaper may comment on the case even though an application for a new trial is pending, but when an order for a new trial has been definitely made, then comment should end. As Thomas Dawson says:

In regard to pending appeals, as these are held before judges, lords-justices, or law-lords, and witnesses are rarely examined thereon, it would not be considered so likely that comment on the merits of the case would tend to prevent a fair hearing of the appeal. However, judges have more than once frankly acknowledged that they cannot say that they are never influenced in some degree by what they read in the Press, and it is therefore safer to refrain from public discussion of a pending appeal. Then, too, it is always possible that an appeal will result in an order for a new trial before a jury, and this is an additional reason why a newspaper should avoid such a discussion. The mere fact, however, that a losing party announces, through his counsel at the trial, that he intends to appeal, does not prevent comments and criticisms being made on the case. An appeal is not pending until formal written notice of appeal has been served.[27]

Nothing in the foregoing must be taken to mean that a reporter may, with impunity, impute a crime to anyone involved in a criminal event. It is no protection to say, "Police believe Mr. X killed Mr. Y." There is no magic in the word "alleged." Indeed, to say, "*It is alleged* that Mr. X was seen near the spot where the shooting occurred . . ." suggests to the reader that the writer knows he is skirting libel or contempt and hopes that the word "alleged" will keep him out of trouble. If Mr. X is to be connected directly with the event at all, about the only fact (assuming it to be true) that it is safe to report is, "Mr. X has been charged with . . ."

Photography and Contempt of Court

There seem to be two main ways in which press photography relates to contempt of court. Pictures taken outside the court may be of a *sub judice* nature, as when the picture of an accused man may imply guilt, particularly in respect to aiding in the identification of suspects, before the person on trial has been found guilty. Or pictures taken within the courtroom may interfere with proceedings by disturbing the court or by making witnesses or defendants nervous or confused.

Typical of the first sort of contempt was that which resulted in the fining in 1961 of Thomson Newspapers for publishing *sub judice* pictures and articles by the Timmins *Press* and Kirkland Lake *Northern News* in connection with a murder trial.[28]

In circumstances unconnected with law cases newspapers are entitled to take pictures of person in public places. An incident which illustrates what newspapers may or may not do occurred in 1965 in Milton, Ontario.[29]

In Canada, magistrates and judges have the say as to whether they will allow photographers to enter their courtrooms or its precincts to take pictures. The definition of precinct may be wide or narrow depending on the judge involved. In general agreement with the restrictions outlined in Canon 35 of the American Bar Association, they have not often done so. (Canon 35, adopted in 1937 and later revised to take account of developments in the electronic media, states that the taking of photographs in the courtroom and the broadcasting or televising of court proceedings are calculated to detract from the essential dignity of the proceedings, distract the witness in giving testimony, degrade the court and create misconceptions in the mind of the public and should not be permitted.) One exception to the characteristic ban has been provided on the rare occasions when courts have been moved to hospital bedsides to take evidence from witnesses unable to go to court. Similarly excepted are naturalization proceedings which are, however, quite different in nature from trials designed to determine guilt or innocence, liability or non-liability.

Before his retirement in 1966, the late Hon. Mr. Justice J. H. Sissons had long permitted picture taking in his North West Territories courts, his reasoning being that courts in which Eskimo women breast-feed their babies are much more informal than courts in more southerly parts of Canada.

Canadian members of the press have agitated to widen the privilege of newspapers to take pictures in courtrooms. They claim that improved equipment and "available light" techniques make it possible to take photographs without disturbing the court. However, the prevailing practice has not been changed. A restriction comparable to the ban on photographs was illustrated in 1964 when the Ontario Court of Appeal dismissed an appeal by Radio Station CHUM.[30]

Other Contempt of Court Restrictions

Many, perhaps most, prohibitions for the journalist-related contempt of court are matters of common law. In addition there are several restrictions on the press set forth in Canadian statutes.

Two of these concern the reporting of preliminary inquiries. In 1969 the Criminal Code was amended to allow the accused person to apply to have newspapers and broadcasts restrained from publishing evidence given at such inquiries. The presiding justice may then prohibit such publication until the accused has been discharged, or, if the accused is committed for trial or ordered to stand trial, until the trial is ended. If the accused is unrepresented by counsel, the justice is required, before evidence taking begins, to tell the accused of his right to apply for a restraining order. Failure to comply with the order might result in punishment on summary conviction.[31]

Even if the accused does not take advantage of this new section (Section 467) of the Code there is still an area of preliminary inquiries which the media may not report. Here no application for a prohibition need be made and the restriction is an automatic one. By a 1959 amendment, the Criminal Code (Section 470) prohibits media references to confessions made at preliminary hearings. The prohibition applies until the accused is discharged or until the subsequent trial is over.[32]

Two members of the media that ran afoul of this law were the Winnipeg *Tribune* in 1962[33] and radio station CJOB in 1966.[34]

One of the reasons for putting a curb on the reporting of preliminary hearings is that, inasmuch as such hearings are designed to determine whether the prosecution has gathered enough *prima facie* evidence to justify a trial, it is only the prosecution which is required to present a case and the defence is almost never presented. This means that the full reporting of a preliminary inquiry is almost certain to be one-sided. Such reporting is likely, therefore, to be unfair to the defendant. It may later prejudice his trial. The prohibition against reporting of evidence, particularly of confessions, is thus in keeping with a wish to keep such prejudice to a minimum. No restraints, comparable to those imposed in connection with preliminary inquiries are imposed, under Canadian law, on the reportage of coroners' inquests. But because there are similar reasons for having restraints similar to those on preliminary inquiries, there is some current agitation to have the reporting of such inquests similarly curtailed.

Section 162 (1)(a) of the Criminal Code says ''a proprietor, editor, master printer or publisher commits an offence who prints or publishes in relation to any judicial proceedings any indecent medical, surgical or physiological details, being matter or details that, if published, are calculated to injure public morals.''[35] This section of the Code does not apply to *bona fide* law reports or *bona fide* medical journals.[36]

The comment just made about Section 162 (1)(a) of the Criminal Code applies equally to Section 162 (1)(b). This part of the Code says that:

A proprietor, editor, master printer or publisher commits an offence who prints or publishes in relation to any judicial proceedings for dissolution of marriage, judicial separation or restitution of conjugal rights any particulars other than
(I) the names, addresses and occupations of the parties and witnesses,
(II) a concise statement of the charges, defences and countercharges in support of which evidence has been given,
(III) submissions on a point of law arising in the course of proceedings, and the decision of the court in connection therewith, and
(IV) the summing up of the judge, the finding of the jury and the judgment of the court and the observations that are made by the judge in giving judgment.[37]

The Criminal Code states that the trial of juveniles is to be without publicity. According to Section 441, ''Where an accused is or appears to be under the age of sixteen years, his trial shall take place without publicity, whether he is charged alone or jointly with another person.''[38]

Before the Criminal Code amendment which forbids publication of evidence given at preliminary hearings, the intention of Section 441 was sometimes thwarted by a provision of the Juvenile Delinquents Act. Section 9(1) says that

Where the act complained of is, under the provisions of the Criminal Code or otherwise, an indictable offence, and the accused child is apparently or actually over the age of fourteen years, the Court may, in its discretion, order the child to be proceeded against by indictment in the ordinary courts in accordance with the Criminal Code in that behalf; but such course shall in no case be followed unless the Court is of the opinion that the good of the child and the interest of the community demand it.[39]

In 1970 an attempt was made to repeal the Juvenile Delinquents Act and replace it with the Young Offenders Act, but the new bill was allowed to die on the order paper, and as this chapter was being written the old legislation was in force. Before the 1969 Criminal Code Amendment, which was discussed earlier in this chapter, placed restrictions on the reporting of evidence at preliminary inquiries, a juvenile whose case was transferred to the ordinary criminal courts might find that he faced a preliminary inquiry the factual details of which could be legitimately reported by the press. He might then encounter the prejudicial treatment inherent in the one-sided reporting to which preliminary inquiries lend themselves.[40]

Section 442 of the Criminal Code deals with the exclusion of the public from courts in certain cases. The section states:

> The trial of an accused that is a corporation or who is or appears to be sixteen years of age or more shall be held in open court, but where the court, judge, justice or magistrate, as the case may be, is of opinion that it is in the interest of public morals, the maintenance of order or the proper administration of justice to exclude all or any members of the public from the court room, he may so order.[41]

Because the concept of the "open court" is a highly regarded tradition of Canadian justice this section is rarely invoked.

In addition to the restrictions on the press so far discussed, there are numerous prohibitions related to civil or administrative proceedings. These exclusions of the press are generally governed by the statute law of the province where the proceedings are being conducted. In general the law is most explicit in debarring the press in proceedings dealing with mental incompetents, deserted wives' and children's maintenance, and other matters of the family court.

Chapter III

Free Press—Fair Trial

A major purpose, perhaps the major purpose, of the law of contempt of court is to ensure that trials shall be fair. To protect the rights of litigants, the contempt law imposes prohibitions which, among other things, restrict the perfect freedom of the press. In a less than utopian society, trials cannot be absolutely fair if reporting of those trials is to be absolutely free. Free press and fair trial cannot coexist as absolutes.

In practical terms there must be compromise between press freedom and trial fairness. In Canada, as in the United Kingdom, the considerations of a fair trial prevail over considerations of a free press. That is not to say that, in these countries, the press is in large measure unfree. What is implied is simply that the press is restrained in most cases when unfairness in a trial seems likely to result.

In the United States, with its First Amendment, the scales are weighted much more in favor of a free press. The principle which governs the reporting of trials is known as the "clear and present danger" test. It derives from the *Schenck* case, which said, "The question in every case is whether the words used are used in such circumstances and are of such a nature as to create a clear and present danger that they will bring about the substantive evils that Congress has a right to prevent."[1] D. A. Schmeiser[2] cites three American contempt cases in which verdicts of guilty were reversed by the Supreme Court of the United States. He quotes the third decision, *Craig* v. *Harney*[3] as restating the "clear and present danger" test in even stronger language: "The vehemence of the language used is not alone the measure of the power to publish for contempt. The fires which it kindles must constitute an imminent, not merely a likely, threat to the administration of justice. The danger must not be remote or even probable; it must immediately imperil."[4] Schmeiser's opinion is that "In view of this conclusion it is difficult to conceive of any publication which might be classed as contemptuous."[5]

For debaters of the "free press—fair trial" issue the American situation provides the widest scope for heated controversy. The United States furnishes far "worse" examples of "trial by newspaper" than does Canada. For this reason, despite the fact that this book deals primarily with the Canadian experience, it is probably instructive to devote a little attention to some of the American instances which thrust themselves on public notice. These and others have had the effect of placing proponents of the extreme free press viewpoint on the defensive in the debate.

Many members of the American bar have demanded severe limitations on press coverage of crime ever since the sideshow antics of the trial in 1935 of Bruno Richard Hauptmann, who was charged with the kidnapping of the Lindbergh baby. But it was news reporting of the John F. Kennedy assassination and its aftermath that brought interest in "trial by newspaper" to its highest pitch. In particular, the presumed effect of media publicity on a trial of Lee Harvey Oswald had he survived to be tried gave special impetus to the "free press—fair trial" debate. Of the affair Alfred Friendly and Ronald L. Goldfarb have said:

> The case against the press, made in various forms by the American Bar Association, local bar groups, law school faculties, and others, as well as the Warren Commission, came in its most concise form in a declaration by the American Civil Liberties Union: "It is generally conceded that as a result of the conduct of the Dallas police and communications media when Oswald was taken into custody, he could not have had a fair trial anywhere in the United States".[6]

The trial of Jack Ruby, Lee Harvey Oswald's killer, received coverage marked by a sensationalism which also earned strictures from media critics.

Another notable case was that of Dr. Sam Sheppard of Cleveland, Ohio. He came to national prominence after July 4, 1954, when his wife, Marilyn, was bludgeoned to death in their suburban home. Sheppard, a well-to-do osteopath, was convicted of murder in the second degree and sentenced to life imprisonment. He made many appeals to the Ohio courts to set him free on the grounds that reportage of his arrest and trial had prejudiced the jurors against him. After the Ohio Supreme Court rejected his appeal, he turned to the federal courts. Ten years after his conviction U. S. Judge Carl A. Weinman freed him. But in May 1965 the U. S. Court of Appeals in Cincinnati reversed the Weinman decision. Sheppard then appealed to the United States Supreme Court. In 1966 the Court gave judgment in favor of Sheppard.[7] The Court ordered Sheppard freed, and ruled that the state could try him again after a reasonable time. At his second trial he was acquitted on November 16, 1966. He enjoyed his freedom for less than four years. He died in April 1970.

In its 1966 decision the United States Supreme Court reviewed the circumstances surrounding Sheppard's first trial. Singled out for stern condemnation was the behavior of the media. Newspapers had carried stories under such headlines as "Getting Away With Murder," "Get

That Killer," "Why Don't Police Quiz Top Suspect?" "Why Isn't Sam Sheppard In Jail?" "Quit Stalling—Bring Him In," "But Who Will Speak For Marilyn?" and "Sam Called A 'Jekyll-Hyde' By Marilyn, Cousin To Testify." The press gave Judge Edward Blythin, who was up for re-election, pointed advice on how to conduct the trial. It condemned Sheppard for refusing to take lie detector or truth serum tests, even though many authorities have no faith in the accuracy of either test. It censured the accused man for failing to submit to questions except when his family and his lawyer agreed he might, forgetting that the function of the lawyer is to protect his client, to see that he is guaranteed due process of law.

The Coroner's inquest which preceded the trial was conducted in a circus atmosphere, to which the press contributed. In the trial proper, a long table was placed for the press before the bar of the court, so that witnesses and accused were exposed to the close, unnerving scrutiny of reporters. The goings and comings of the press, and the flashing of flashbulbs, the grinding of television cameras and the questioning by reporters just outside the courtroom caused the presiding judge to lose effective control over the trial he was conducting.

In a radio broadcast Bob Considine compared Sheppard, irrelevantly, with Alger Hiss; Judge Blythin took no steps to find out whether any of the jurors had heard the broadcast. The trial judge also overlooked evidence that two jurors had heard a broadcast by Walter Winchell in which Winchell said that Carole Beasley, under arrest in New York for robbery, had told him that, as Sheppard's mistress, she had borne him a child.

Both newspapers and broadcasters were guilty of publishing material during the trial which was never heard from the witness stand. Such matter included charges that Sheppard had purposely hindered the murder investigation and must be guilty because he had hired a prominent criminal lawyer; that he was a perjurer; that before her death, his wife had called him a "Jekyll-Hyde"; and that he was a "bare-faced liar" because of his testimony as to police treatment. During the trial the newspapers drew inferences which the evidence that was given did not warrant. In particular they interpreted evidence, unjustifiably, in a way which would incriminate Sheppard. It is little wonder that Judge Weinman, who termed the trial a "mockery of justice," said, "If ever there was a trial by newspaper, this was the perfect example."[8]

It is significant that, despite the flagrant abuse of its communication role of which the American press was guilty, the courts which heard the Sheppard case on appeal did not regard the media as being primarily responsible for a fair trial for Dr. Sheppard. As Gillmor and Barron point out:

In their arguments before the Supreme Court on February 28, 1966, Sheppard's attorney, F. Lee Bailey, and Ohio's Attorney-General, William B. Saxbe, differed in their views of the effects of press coverage on the trial, but they did agree that the responsibility for preventing "trial by newspaper" from contaminating juries should be borne by judges, prosecutors and policemen and not by the press.[9]

Nothing could point up more clearly Canadian-American differences in attitude towards the "free press—fair trial" issue.

It is important that the Canadian journalist be aware of the differences. There is a built-in situation which could blur the distinction in his mind. Canadian newspapers, usually via wire copy, customarily carry accounts of the more noteworthy American criminal cases. They give those cases the sort of treatment which is perfectly legal under the American law. They operate under the more lenient libel and contempt laws which prevail in the United States. And it is quite safe to do so. But if, through unthinking habit developed in the coverage of international crime news, Canadian newspapers applied the American ground rules to Canadian, particularly *local* Canadian stories, those papers could get into serious legal trouble. The moral for the Canadian journalist is to remember that Canadian law applies to Canadian stories of Canadian events and to act accordingly.

The Sheppard decision, discussed above, was followed shortly by the report of the American Bar Associations's Advisory Committee on Fair Trial and Free Press, better known as the Reardon Report.[10] It had been given impetus by the recommendation of the Warren Commission that efforts be made "to bring about a proper balance between the right of the public to be informed and the right of the individual to a fair and impartial trial." The Reardon Report led to the approval of standards relating to Fair Trial and Free Press by the American Bar Association House of Delegates at its mid-winter meeting in February 1968. The primary emphasis of those standards was on the restrictions imposed on officers of the court to restrain them from communicating to the press matter which would impair a fair trial. It was only in Part IV, Recommendations Relating To The Exercise Of The Contempt Power, that a large measure of responsibility for a fair trial was assigned to the press. That section read:

4.1 Limited use of the contempt power.
It is recommended that the contempt power should be used only with considerable caution but should be exercised under the following circumstances:

(a) Against a person who, knowing that a criminal trial by jury is in progress or that a jury is being selected for such a trial:
(i) disseminates by any means of public communication an extrajudicial statement relating to the defendant or to the issues in the case that goes beyond the public record of the court in the case, that is wilfully designed by that person to affect the outcome of the trial, and that seriously threatens to have such an effect; or
(ii) makes such a statement intending that it be disseminated by any means of public communication.
(b) Against a person who knowingly violates a valid judicial order not to disseminate, until completion of the trial or disposition without trial, specified information referred to in the course of judicial hearing closed pursuant to sections 3.1 or 3.5(d) of these recommendations.[11]

It is interesting to note, regarding the Reardon Report, as the London *Economist* does, that:

> The committee's major proposal, however, was the very one that the press had piously urged: a set of rules for courts, the police and Bar Associations to prevent agents of the law from making known before a trial anything except the identity of the accused (not including his prior criminal record), the charge, the circumstances of the crime and arrest and the nature of the evidence seized.
> Predictably, the reaction of the press was a shrill scream of protest, the common denominator of which was that the Reardon report was an invitation to the secret administration of justice.[12]

The fairness of a trial is not determined exclusively by the manner in which the media report that trial. In both Canada and the United States there are legal safeguards designed to protect the interests of litigants. With reference to the American situation, Howard Felsher and Michael Rosen list these as 1) change of venue, 2) change of venire, 3) continuance, 4) severance, 5) *voir dire* examination, 6) challenges, 7) isolation of the jury; and 8) instructions to the jury.[13] The only one of these which does not seem to apply to Canada is the change of venire. But in the case of Canada the contempt law may be added as a distinctive safeguard.

A change of venue involves a shifting of the trial from the locality where the crime was committed. It is usually asked for on the grounds that local opinion has become so inflamed over the issues of the trial that the defendant is unlikely to receive fair treatment at the hands of the court. For this reason it is usually the defence which asks for the trial to be moved, although the motion for a venue change may come from the prosecution. The Honorable J. C. McRuer points to cost as a factor discouraging the transfer of a trial from one county to another.[14] It is likely, however, that a change of venue is a remedy limited in effectiveness by the fact that it is only the minor crimes which do not get bruited about by the omnipresent media from community to community. Communities are no longer so isolated that a change of trial venue is apt to provide the remedy sought.

A safeguard of a fair trial which is available in six of the 50 American states[15] is a change of venire. This is the converse of a change of venue in the sense that, instead of changing the location of the trial, jurors are brought in from a different community. The presumption is that strange jurors from a strange city will be free of the prejudices which pre-trial publicity has stirred up in the community where the crime is committed. For the same reasons that a change of venue is likely to be ineffective, it is questionable whether a change of venire can accomplish what it purports to do.

Continuance is another device designed to help to make a trial more fair. It involves postponing a trial until the emotions aroused by the crime for which the accused is on trial can subside. Again it is a remedy of limited value in the case of major crimes, the details of which have been imprinted on the readers' minds by excessive newspaper, radio and television coverage. Interest in the case might die down during the postponement, but once the case again came before the courts, interest is likely to be revived again.

Severance is the term which refers to the separation of the trials of two or more defendants in a joint crime. The rationale for using the device is that it shields one co-defendant from the effects of the adverse publicity suffered by another co-defendant. The safeguard is considered valuable for the protection it gives to the defendant who did not get the unfavorable publicity, but it does little for the defendant who was unfavorably reported in the first place. As Felsher and Rosen point out, ''Obviously the motion of severance does not help the man who really needs the help.''[16]

Voir dire examination before the trial begins may be used by a judge to determine whether prospective jurors have preconceptions or prejudices about the case. Such prejudicial opinions may cause the judge to disqualify the potential jurors who hold them. Or the judge may ask candidates for jury service whether they believe they can set aside such prejudgments and adjudicate the case on the basis of the facts brought out in the trial alone. Assured that they can, the judge may accept such persons as jurymen. It is to be noted that the process is one based on faith.

Justice McRuer is of the opinion that this faith is justified. He sees the safeguard as being tied in with the strength of the jury system. His remarks, while perhaps not applicable as to detail to all of Canada, are applicable in spirit and tenor to the whole nation, and not just to Ontario alone:

> In this Province there are twelve jurors in all criminal cases tried by jury. They are selected by lot from a panel consisting of about sixty or more jurors, which has likewise been chosen by lot. In a case of great importance and public interest the panel is usually larger . . .
>
> When jurors are selected they are required to take an oath ''to give a true verdict according to the evidence.'' Judges in charging juries invariably caution them to put out of their minds anything they have learned about the case, except that which is revealed in the evidence. Nothing has been brought to the attention of this Commission to suggest that jurors do not take their oaths seriously. If jurors cannot be depended upon to adhere to their oaths as jurymen, the whole jury system loses its fundamental strength as a protection of the rights of the individual.
>
> The requirement that the verdict of a jury must be unanimous constitutes a very real safeguard against bias or prejudice. There may be some risk that one or two jurors may allow their preconceived notions to deflect them from the requirement of their oaths as jurymen, but that twelve jurors will be derelict to the sanctity of their oaths is very remote.[17]

Associated with the matter of selecting jurymen is the right of counsel to challenge prospective jurors. Attorneys may question jury panel members to determine whether they have a bias in the case. Questioning may delve into the background, work, education or anything else which may adversely affect the trying of the case. If counsel is dissatisfied with the answers given he may challenge the would-be jurors and thereby disqualify them. Such a challenge is said to be a challenge ''for cause.'' In addition, counsel is allowed a certain number of challenges for which no reason need be given. Such a challenge is known as a ''peremptory'' challenge.

Justice McRuer thus describes the procedure, set forth in the Criminal Code of Canada, Section 562 and 567(b), by which challenges are made:

> . . . If an offence is punishable with death, the accused has twenty peremptory challenges, that is, without assigning a reason; where the offence is not punishable with death but the punishment may be imprisonment for more than five years, the accused has twelve

peremptory challenges; in other cases, the accused has four peremptory challenges.

In addition, the accused is entitled to challenge any number of jurors on the ground that the "juror is not indifferent between the Queen and the accused." This is a right that is frequently exercised in our courts. In such cases, the prospective juror may be, and usually is, examined under oath as to his previous knowledge of the case, what he has read about it, and whether he feels that he can give a true verdict based on the evidence. Two triers are selected for the purpose of determining whether the juror "stands indifferent." This procedure is a very real safeguard.[18]

Isolation of the jury is a measure taken to shield a jury from media accounts of a trial while that trial is in progress. The safeguard is sometimes called sequestration. It involves locking up the jurors and denying them access to radio, television and newspaper accounts of the trial. Those who deny the effectiveness of the device claim that pre-trial publicity will have done a damage to the impartiality of the jury which cannot be repaired by the late quarantine which isolating the jury imposes.

The judge's instructions to the jury include directions as to what are matters of law and matters of fact. They include orders to the jury to render the verdict only on the basis of the evidence presented in the courtroom, and not to read or listen to stories concerning the case. Again there is a fairly wide difference of opinion regarding the efficiency of this safeguard.

This brings us to Canadian contempt law as safeguard of a fair trial. Perhaps this device can best be characterized by the words of Justice McRuer, particularly since he couples his description with a recognition of the role of the media in helping to ensure that justice shall be open and thereby fair:

> The law of contempt of court gives the accused . . . a considerable protection against unfair reporting. Judges have taken a stern view of lurid, inaccurate or inflammatory reporting, and have suppressed comment on evidence until a final verdict is given. Where there has been unfairness, exemplary punishment has followed. The responsible press has supported the courts in their efforts to make the law of contempt of court function as an effective protection of the right of the individual to a fair trial.

> We have come to the conclusion that the fundamental principle that the courts of justice should be open to the public not only in name, but in reality is essential to a free society. To preserve the

openness of the courts, the news media must be permitted to carry to the public what goes on in the courts. Justice administered under public and fair scrutiny will be better justice, whether it is at a preliminary inquiry or at a trial, and confidence in its administration will be enhanced if justice in all its stages is administerd openly, subject to the exceptions now recognized by law.[19]

Chapter IV

The Revealing of Sources

An element of press activity which may give rise to a contempt of court situation involves the question of whether reporters should be made to reveal the source of news stories which they write or broadcast. The pro and con arguments about confidentiality are as persistent as the free press-fair trial debate.

Journalists of both the libertarian and social responsibility schools would agree that in the triangular relationship involving press, government, and people, it must be the interests of the people which are paramount. Obviously there will be situations in which the public will be best served by allowing the journalist to keep his sources confidential. Otherwise those sources will quickly dry up, and the journalist will be unable to pass along information essential to the reader's or listener's or viewer's participation in the democratic process, and to his playing of a meaningful role in the society of which he is a part. On the other hand there may be occasions when it will injure a segment of society or individual members of that society if the journalist is allowed to keep silent about his informants. Situations in which a community's safety is threatened or in which property or human life is in danger or a man is suing for libel are cases in point.

Canadian law tries to take account of such countervailing interests. Although in an overwhelming majority of cases the journalist is not called upon to disclose the origin of the reports he writes or broadcasts, there are three circumstances in which his sources may come under investigation. These are: 1) where he appears to have information pertinent to a public inquiry by a Commission or Board acting under statutory or special powers conferred by parliament, or the legislature of a province, or by a committee of parliament or a legislature; 2) where he publishes information that a crime has been committed which appears pertinent to the determination of the guilt of particular persons; and 3) where he is accused of libel in criminal or civil proceedings as a result of publication of information, and bases his defence on an assertion of honest belief in the truth of the matter published.[1]

In the named circumstances the public interest in disclosure is considered to outweigh the journalist's professional interest in confidentiality. In the second instance the rationale for disclosure is that when life or property is endangered, anyone may reasonably be expected to help lessen that danger by providing information which will enable authorities to counteract that danger.

The reason for requiring a journalist to name sources when he is a defendant in a libel action is rather different but equally persuasive. A fictional example will illustrate. A journalist may write a column in which he says that the treasurer of the Anytown Agricultural Society has used the club's funds to bet on the horses. The journalist says that for several months the treasurer has lost money through his gambling. He also says that during that time the Society's treasury could not have stood up to an auditor's inspection. Later, says the columnist, the treasurer started to win so that he was able to replace the money before any shortage could be discovered. Following this report the treasurer files a libel suit against the journalist. The journalist defends himself by saying his story is true. What proof do you have that it is true? asks the treasurer. I know it to be true because I got the story from absolutely unimpeachable sources, says the journalist. What are those sources? counters the treasurer. I cannot tell you, says the journalist, because I promised confidentiality to my sources.

To take the journalist's word that his criticism is true without requiring him to document that criticism by naming names would obviously be unfair. It would clearly violate the principle in law that every man is entitled to know the name of his accuser.

The example cited points up a curiously anomalous situation in libel suits. On the face of it, when the treasurer filed suit he became the plaintiff and the journalist became the defendant. The journalist was sued for libel. Theoretically he should be assumed to be non-liable (c.f. innocent) until proved liable (c.f. guilty.) Therefore, again theoretically, the burden of proof should be laid on the plaintiff, that is, the treasurer. But the matter is more complex than that. When the journalist used his column to charge the treasurer with financial misbehavior, the journalist became, in a non-legal but perhaps more serious sense, the complainant, the accuser. The treasurer became, "in the court of public opinion," the defendant. As such he too is entitled to be considered innocent until proved guilty. Because, in relation to the grave accusations the columnist has made (if not in relation to the actual libel suit that has been launched), the treasurer is the "defendant" and the journalist the "plaintiff," then the onus of proof should be on the journalist. The law takes account of this inherent dilemma by placing the burden of proof on the plaintiff (treasurer) in establishing a *prima facie* case of libel, but, once the trial proper begins, placing the burden of proof on the defenant journalist. Under such circumstances it seems only just that the advantage of disclosure of sources should be awarded the possibly libelled plaintiff rather than giving the advantage of confidentiality to the defendant journalist.

If a journalist refuses to name sources in the situation just described, the usual penalty is that the court will disregard the defence he offers. In the first two instances previously listed (i.e. public inquiry and alleging of a crime) the punishment may be a fine or jail sentence or both. Theoretically an unco-operative journalist might be imprisoned until he decided to disclose his sources, thereby purging the contempt.

The privilege of confidentiality in Canada derives from common law observance of Wigmore's four canons. Such privilege is granted only if all of four conditions are satisfied: 1) the communication originates in a confidence that the source will not be disclosed; 2) the element of confidentiality is essential to the relationship between the two parties; 3) the relationship is one which, in the view of the community, ought to be fostered; 4) the injury done by disclosure would be greater than the benefit derived from correct disposal of the litigation.[2]

Apparently the journalist-interviewer relationship is not considered to fulfill the Wigmore criteria, at least in the three circumstances cited. Confidentiality is respected in all ten provinces of Canada only in the solicitor-client and husband-wife relationship. In Quebec and Newfoundland, the priest-penitent relationship is also similarly protected, but as D.A. Schmeiser[3] is at pains to point out, in Newfoundland the priest-penitent relationship is ambiguous and might be interpreted as meaning the confession as heard by a Roman Catholic priest. Only in Quebec is the doctor-patient relationship a privileged one.

Nor is the privilege of confidentiality which is extended in the solicitor-client, doctor-patient, priest-penitent, husband-wife relationship situation of a kind envisaged by journalists claiming a like treatment. As Gillmor and Barron point out:

The difference is that in the above cases [*viz* solicitor-client etc.] both parties are generally known, their communication is confidential and the privilege belongs to the client or patient who alone can waive it. Shield laws are for the benefit of the newsman alone; and he may assert privilege in connection with any information furnished him, whether confidential or not.[4]

In the newsman's case, the informant knows and intends that the news will be published, but intends that his identity shall be kept secret. In the other cases, the reverse is true.[5] This difference gives further support to a treatment of a journalist-informant situation that is different from that accorded in a solicitor-client, doctor-patient, husband-wife and penitent-priest situation.

The Canadian practice of requiring disclosure of sources conforms with that of a majority of the American states rather than with the sixteen states which have statutes intended to guarantee confidentiality. The latter states are Alabama, Alaska, Arizona, Arkansas, California, Indiana, Kentucky, Louisiana, Maryland, Michigan, Montana, New Jersey, New Mexico, Ohio, Pennsylvania[6] and New York.[7] Only the Alaska, Arkansas, Louisiana and New Mexico statutes qualify the privilege granted,[8] but that the protection offered in the other states with so-called shield laws is not as complete as it seems is indicated by at least some of the examples which follow. In the first of these the test occurred before the state of New York enacted a law to protect the journalist.

In 1957 Judy Garland filed a $1,393,333 breach of contract suit against the Columbia Broadcasting System. Reporter Marie Torre, writing in the New York *Herald-Tribune,* said that a CBS official had told her about a dispute between Miss Garland and the broadcasting company. In the examination for discovery before the breach of contract trial, Miss Torre was asked to name the executive who had furnished the information. This she refused to do. Although threatened with a thirty day contempt sentence, she remained adamant in her refusal. She was then sentenced to ten days in jail. Miss Torre appealed the sentence, but in September 1958 the conviction was upheld unanimously, and she served her time in prison. In the verdict rendered, Circuit Judge Stewart voiced the unanimous decision of the U. S. Court of Appeals. In his judgment, "[F]reedom of the press, precious and vital though it is to a free society is not an absolute."[9] He asserted that "The concept that it is the duty of a witness to testify in a court of law has roots fully as deep in our history as does the guarantee of a free press."[10] Although he did not give an opinion as to whether the power to enforce disclosure was to be considered an element of Fifth Amendment due process, it seems evident that the court had made Fifth Amendment considerations to prevail over First Amendment considerations.

That shield laws do not operate automatically to protect journalists was demonstrated by *In Re Taylor.*[11] The appeal was from a contempt conviction against the general manager and city editor of the Philadelphia *Bulletin.* The two men had refused to reveal to a Philadelphia grand jury investigating crime and corruption in city government documentary evidence relating to news stories dealing with the situation. They gave as grounds for their refusal the fact that notes, tape recordings, medical records, expense records and so on could identify their sources. The journalists were sentenced to five days imprisonment and fined $1,000 each. The rationale for the contempt citation was that the Pennsylvania law protecting news stories did not extend to compulsory disclosure of documents and other inanimate objects. The Supreme Court of Pennsylvania reversed the orders of the grand jury and the sentences were vacated, Mr. Justice Cohen dissenting.

Another state with a statutory provision to protect journalists is California. On June 20, 1966 *Newsweek* reported an instance of the invoking of such protection. CBS newsman Bill Stout had interviewed a teenager for television and had asked him about his part in the Watts riots during the previous August. All camera-shots of the interviewee were either out of focus or taken from the rear or above. Because a ring and watch he was wearing were similar to those worn by the subject of the interview, a young Negro who had been arrested on a narcotics charge was suspected of being the sought-for teenager. Summoned before a grand jury, Stout, as he was entitled to do, refused to confirm that the arrested youth was the man he had interviewed. But his refusal did not help his informant. The voice prints of the black interviewed on television were compared with those of the youth in custody. The prints matched. Despite certain expert evidence to the contrary, the authorities considered voice prints to be as reliable as finger prints for identification purposes. They therefore concluded that the man they were holding was the suspect they had been seeking, and they arraigned him on four charges of arson.[12]

New Jersey is also a state with a "shield" law. Despite this, in May, 1972, after Peter Bridge had written a story for the *Newark Evening News* in which it quoted Pearl Beatty, Housing Authority Commissioner, as saying she had been offered a bribe, Bridge was brought before the grand jury and directed to name the "briber." He refused to do this. He also refused to answer five of 85 questions put to him because he said the answers would reveal other confidential sources. Bridge's case worked its way up to the United States Supreme Court, which in October ruled by an 8 to 1 vote against keeping him from being jailed on a civil contempt charge. By that time his newspaper had ceased to publish.[13] He was jailed for 20 days.[14]

For refusing to surrender WBAI-FM tapes of a prison riot, Edwin Goodman served 44 hours of a 30-day sentence.[15]

Nor did the so-called "shield" law of California serve as a shield to William T. Farr, Los Angeles *Herald-Examiner* reporter. In the fall of 1970 he had obtained and published details from the pretrial statement of a prosecution witness in the Charles Manson murder trial, despite the fact that Trial Judge Charles H. Older had previously forbidden lawyers and others involved to divulge information about the case. Judge Older decided to punish the person who had leaked the story. He therefore called on Farr to name his sources. The reporter refused. He claimed that Section 1070 of the California Evidence Code, which purports to protect newsmen from contempt citations for keeping sources confidential, exempted him from having to make disclosure. His contention was apparently accepted.

However, seven months later, when Farr resigned from his newspaper to take a public relations job, Judge Older claimed that the reporter had lost the protection of Section 1070, subpoenaed him, and again called upon him to name his informant or informants. The judge also maintained that Farr was an accessory to the violation of the court's "gag" law. The reporter said his source was among six attorneys whose names he submitted. But he refused to be more specific than that and his "nominees" denied on oath that they had been involved in the leak.

Judge Older ordered the reporter jailed until he made disclosure. Farr was allowed to go free while his appeal was being heard. Section 1070 was amended in December 1971 to give protection to *former* newsmen, but that same month a state appeals court upheld the judge's decision. It also ruled that if the Evidence Code interfered with the power of the court to control its own proceedings and officers, the code would be unconstitutional. In November the United States Supreme Court refused to review Farr's case. The reporter was jailed temporarily three hours later while the state appeal court considered a petition for a permanent stay of sentence.[16] The petition was denied and Farr again went to jail from November 27, 1972 to January 11, 1973, when he was again released while further consideration was given to his appeal.[17]

Despite the fact that Canada has no shield laws, there have been few harassments of journalists by the law in Canada. Incidents have been widely spaced. In 1952 Jacqueline Sirois (later Jacqueline Sirois Moore) wrote an article for *Weekend* magazine in which she said certain informants had told her they had paid protection money on account of illegal activities. Mr. Justice François Caron, who was the Commissioner inquiring into vice conditions in Montreal, summoned her to one of his hearings. She was asked to name the sources of her story but refused to do so. The justices then said: "I hold you in contempt. Come back at 10:15 tomorrow and if you don't change your mind, I will be obliged to sentence you." She did come back, did divulge sources, and so purged her contempt.

A Canadian case in which refusal to divulge sources was not found to be legally acceptable involved Blair Fraser and *Maclean's* magazine. (*See Case No. 9*) A contrary legal verdict during examination proceedings was given in 1961 in a case in which Toronto *Telegram* reporter Frank Drea was a defendant. (*See Case No. 10*)

Probably no incident in recent times has aroused so much Canadian debate on the subject of confidentiality of sources as a 1969 event.

Early that year the CBC public affairs show, "The Way It Is," prepared a film report on the city of Montreal. As part of this offering, John Smith, a member of the CBC unit, interviewed a man who claimed to be an FLQ terrorist. The man told Smith that it was his job to teach others how to make and set off bombs. Feeling that this sort of information was important to authorities concerned with protecting life and property, the CBC told the police. But the corporation did not name the man who had been interviewed because Smith had promised not to disclose his identity.

Smith was soon summoned to appear before the Montreal Fire Commission, the body chosen to investigate the bombings which had been taking place. By now Smith had come to believe the interview had been a hoax. Believing also that it was necessary to protect his sources, Smith refused to be sworn before the Fire Commission. Lawyers Marcel Beauchemin and Marcel Côté asked Fire Commissioner John McDougall to cite the CBC reporter-researcher for contempt of the hearing.

Summoned again, Smith again refused to be sworn. In doing so he read from a prepared text which said, "I know full well that the law obliges me to answer the questions of this Commission . . . but nevertheless I will not testify." He contended that "it is the job of the journalist to inform his public of the state of society" and that he "is continuously privy to confidential information." He maintained that giving assurances that information divulged confidentially will be so treated was as much a part of the journalist's function as it was a lawyer's. "If my refusal to testify is illegal," he said, "then it is illegal to have a free press and an informed public, because a press cannot be free and a public cannot be informed if journalists cannot give assurances . . . confidentiality will be kept confidential."[18]

Reaction to the Smith incident was sharp and categorical. Predictably, many journalists condemned the sentencing and imprisonment of the CBC reporter-interviewer. Some editors and commentators demanded shield laws to protect journalists from having to divulge the sources of the stories they write or broadcast. Some claimed that denial of confidentiality might lead to the state of affairs existing in South Africa. They were afraid that an insistence on disclosure might help to bring about a situation in which papers could not print anything detrimental to the government.[19] Others, believing that Canada should follow the example of the American shield law states, raised the question of whether courts should not be required to show that a matter was in the public interest before they could compel a journalist to reveal his sources.[20]

The Toronto *Gobe and Mail* editorialized about Bill 79, the Fire Investigations Act under which Smith had been summoned to the

Commission hearing. The editorial said, "Bill 79 has . . . harshly bruised the legitimate rights of John Smith."[21] It contended that "Bill 79 springs, not just from the dark waters through which Quebec is now passing, but from the style in which Canadian law, both inside and outside Quebec, has evolved."[22] It also quoted approvingly—and attempted to apply to the Smith case—the words of Justice Oliver Wendell Holmes, in reference to another, American court: "To declare that the government may commit crimes in order to secure the arrest of private individuals—this would bring terrible retribution. Against that pernicious doctrine, this court should resolutely set its face."[23]

Was the John Smith case as significant as such commentators seemed to think? Was it a *cause célèbre?* Did it pose a real threat to the freedom of Canada's mass media? Should the journalist be given the blanket right to preserve the anonymity of the sources of his reports? Attempts made by many media professionals to answer such questions were not reassuring. Many editorial writers made errors in their assessment of the John Smith affair. Many were singularly uninformed about the law of the press in the area of contempt of court and the revealing of sources. Many seemed unaware of any underlying philosophy designed to reconcile the interests of the journalist with the interests of the society he serves.

Some critics of the Smith imprisonment made the issue of revealing of sources unnecessarily confusing by coupling it with an account of what the police were reported to have done to the prisoner. As Warren Davis described it, on the CBC television program, "The Way It Is," "[Smith] is then shackled, chained at the ankle, handcuffed to a guard and taken to Bordeaux jail, where, before a group of watching guards, he is stripped, given forms to sign, and in prison clothes put in a solitary cell in the punishment block, the hole."[24] With similar emphasis Doug Collins asked whether the Oliver Wendell Holmes stricture previously quoted did not apply "if, under the Fire Investigation Act, they can hold people . . . without right of consulting counsel."[25] On the same program, other panelists hastened to point out that they too did not approve of any denial of the right of an arrested person to receive the advice of his solicitor at any time.[26] But they were equally firm in pointing out that the iniquitous things which were alleged to have happened to Smith were an issue quite separate from his refusal to testify.[27] Quite clearly it is possible to condemn the rather high-handed treatment which Smith was reported to have received and still favor the requirement that the journalist name his sources in appropriate situations.

Some critics[28] made the mistake of regarding the Montreal incident as introducing a new threat, one perhaps unique to Quebec. In doing so they showed ignorance of Canadian contempt citation precedents. The fact is, of course, that Wigmore's four canons, discussed earlier in this chapter, apply equally throught Canada. People knowledgeable in the law thought it a mistake to regard the Quebec contretemps as unique. The Quebec legislation was not a piece of isolated legislation, they said, since there were a similar act at the federal level and an Inquiry Act in each of the provinces. They called attention to the fact that any Supreme Court judge could commit reporters for refusal to disclose. Indeed, some felt that any Supreme Court judge in Canada might have imposed a longer sentence than the Montreal Fire Investigation Commission did.[29]

Many journalists, in a spontaneous reaction to a situation about which they were not too knowledgeable, seemed to regard the controversy as a contest between an all embracing requirement of disclosure under all circumstances and a complete and absolute protection of journalists under all circumstances. As a result they conceived the defencelessness of the journalist to be far greater than it actually is; and they called for an absolute protection which could not, under the free press-fair trial philosophy which prevails in Canada, be justified. The fact is that the media enjoy a degree of protection far greater than generally realized. As has been indicated earlier, it is also true that to grant the media the absolute privilege of keeping their sources secret might produce injustices that would outweigh any hardships imposed on the press by the requirement to name sources.

Related to the average journalist's ignorance about his obligation to disclose was a comparable ignorance about the previously discussed privileges of others involved with the law: husband and wife; solicitor and client; penitent and priest; doctor and patient. Such faulty knowledge was typified by John Smith when he claimed for the journalist the lawyer's privilege of confidentiality on the grounds that such confidentiality was as essential to the journalist's function as it was to the lawyer's. In doing so he showed no awareness of the difference between the lawyer-client and journalist-informant relationships—a difference which has already been examined.[30]

There was still another facet of the John Smith affair about which commentators and editorialists were not too clear. Many discussed the CBC journalist's citation for contempt as though he had been punished for refusing to name sources, when, in point of fact, his offence had been to decline to answer any questions put to him by the Commission. Both Hyliard Chappell and Bruce Phillips on the "Something Else" program commented more knowledgeably. They were exceptional in realizing, as not too many journalist commentators did, that what Smith had done was, in fact, to say, "I refuse to give any evidence whatsoever;"[31] they felt that Smith should have accepted the summons and then decided what answers to give after the questions were put. As Bruce Phillips commented, "It's pretty hard for him to defend not turning up at the hearing at all. If, on the other hand, he went and they demanded discolosure of sources he would have been on an entirely different wicket. He doesn't even know . . . for sure . . . what questions were going to be put to him. I think it's better to go to court and make a case there.''[32]

In his statement to justify his refusal to testify before the Montreal Fire Commission, John Smith protested that he was being required to reveal sources *even though he had not been charged with a criminal offence.* In doing so he implied that the requirement of disclosure was an exceptional one. The *Globe and Mail* editorial previously cited[33] and Doug Collins in the program already referred to[34] also gave the impression that they thought it remarkable that Smith should be so dealt with even though he was not arraigned under criminal proceedings. Yet there was nothing abnormal in what the Fire Commissioner had done, as was illustrated by the previously considered Blair Fraser, Jacqueline Sirois and Marie Torre cases, three earlier precedents which did not involve criminal prosecutions.

Perhaps the most influential journalist to speak out against the treatment of the CBC staffer and in favor of protection of sources was Gérard Pelletier. Interviewed[35] by Patrick Watson, the Secretary of State took the view that under appropriate conditions, the most notable being that the privileged reporter be a *bona fide* journalist investigating stories in the performance of his professional duties, ''the public interest will be best served'' by granting him immunity. Mr. Pelletier made it clear that he felt that the decision for or against disclosure should be in the hands of the press rather than of the judiciary. The decisiveness of his answer was perhaps partially accounted for by the form used by Watson in one of his questions. After describing a hypothetical situation in which, through interview, a newspaper had learned that someone had been responsible for separatist violence, the CBC interviewer asked, ''You would not feel obligated to go to the police and say, 'Here's how we got this story'?'' Naturally enough, perhaps, Pelletier remarked in the course of his answer, '' . . . we are not police informers, we are informers of the public . . .'' Yet the picture thus conjured up hardly represents the disclosure vs. anonymity issue. There is a world of difference between (on the one hand) running to the police every time the press gets information that might conceivably affect public security, and (on the other) writing news stories based on such information and being willing to divulge sources on those rare occasions when the journalist is summoned to appear before a properly constituted court or commission.

An objection to the Pelletier assessment of the disclosure question is that it leaves it to the journalist exclusively to weigh the countervailing considerations of public and press interest, and to decide whether sources are to be divulged. Part of the argument against the granting of such a privilege arises out of the uncertainty of the status of journalism. It is not a profession, has no code of ethics, is not subject to self-regulation as is the case with law or medicine, and in Canada is just beginning to face the gentle and by no means ubiquitous scrutiny of press councils. Both its failure to achieve professional status and the unwisdom of setting up press councils with anything more than the power to admonish derives from the nature of the freedom it claims. It is a platitude that freedom of the press is no different in kind or degree than the freedom to which any citizen in the country is entitled. It might be argued that both the working journalist and the casual "man in the street" correspondent should be subject to the same type of Press Council supervision. The same line of reasoning suggests that if the press were granted the privilege of unvarying confidentiality so too should any member of the public be granted that privilege.

Mr. Chappell stated an opinion widely held by thoughtful students of the question when he said that he could not see how the privilege of confidentiality could be granted to the journalist without granting the same privilege to doctors, psychiatrists, social workers, probation officers and religious people. To extend the privilege that far, he thought, would seriously impair the ability of the courts to function.[36] Others have made the same point about stockbrokers, accountants, detectives and officials of banks and trust companies, for which the right of confidentiality has sometimes been claimed.

Several commentators have expressed scepticism of the press in claiming privilege. They contend that if the journalist can repeat stories but conceal their source, he can invent stories and use privilege to conceal the pretense. They feel that the real motive for privilege is not zeal for the public good, but the desire for prestige or readership attention. Mr. Chappell felt that under the guise of confidentiality the newspaper might perpetrate a simple hoax.[37] Desmond Morton, Osgoode Hall law school professor, considered the public interest not to be served by keeping confidentiality. He called attention to the fact that newspapers publish for a wide variety of reasons, one of which is to sell copies and make money, and that many journals, while speaking of the public interest at a high level of abstraction, were really concerned with their own private interest of trying to get a headline. While conceding that there might be occasions when such headlines might incidentally serve the public interest where a creative piece of journalism was involved, he felt that all too often such stories were only marginal to the public interest. Thus he did not believe journalism was justified in asking for a *generalized* (italics mine) protection when the value of non-disclosure was by no means proved.[38]

All four legal authorities interviewed by Patrick Watson on the program, "The Way It Is," (Morton; Maxwell Cohen, dean of the McGill Law School; Michel Côté, legal adviser to the Montreal Police Department; and Joseph Sedgwick, a distinguished practising lawyer with 46 years' experience refused to accept Watson's suggestion that the law should require the court to show that it was in the public interest before it could compel a journalist to reveal his sources.[39] Even Maxwell Cohen, who seemed most aware of the journalist's watch-dog role in exposing public acts to public scrutiny, felt that, in terms of Wigmore's fourth canon, ". . . the onus is really on the journalists to prove that they are on balance hampered in their job by the general duty to disclose."[40]

When Watson persisted and questioned what public interest would be served by putting Smith in jail, Morton replied readily that Smith's punishment fulfilled the *pour encourager les autres* principle. He felt that what was done to Smith would encourage reporters not to rely on their unnamed sources but to go out and verify their information with evidence they could expose to public scrutiny.[41]

Mr. Sedgwick supplemented the Morton answer by saying that, unless contumacious journalists were to be punished for defiance of the courts, the courts would be effectively amending the law, and that they would be implying that journalists have a protection which they do not, in fact, have.[42]

All four legal authorities were at pains to point out that the law lays no heavy hand on the press through indiscriminate contempt citations. They firmly rejected Watson's implications that the fact that two *La Presse* reporters had just been excused from testifying in a Montreal trial indicated that the treatment of John Smith had somehow gone beyond what was right and proper.[43] Mr. Sedgwick felt that "In the case of Mr. Smith it was thought that the public interest demanded that he should disclose [his source]. In the case of the two *La Presse* reporters it was thought that it didn't." He took this to show that the law as it stands is able to settle such questions with wisdom and discretion.[44]

While there seemed to be a consensus that the power to punish contempt was needed to check irresponsibility and to protect the private and public interest, Professor Cohen at least showed an awareness of journalism's praiseworthy role in combatting government secrecy. He said, "Where you are dealing with an enormously complex series of relationships of the state to the individual, and where the state is still in many respects highly secrecy-oriented . . . journalism becomes a kind of countervailing power to unloosen the congealed secrecies that don't make the democratic process perhaps as loose-limbed as it ought to be." He believed that one of the prices society should be prepared to pay for the loosening process which the journalist helps to accomplish might be an increase in the area of insecurity resulting from an increased confidentiality of sources. But he felt that any changes in this direction should be made with "a certain sense of the other price we're paying for it, namely that you may be providing new privileges, the total consequences of which you cannot foresee."[45] It is less a matter of irony and more an illustration of the intricacy of the revealing of sources question that journalists should claim the privilege of secrecy in order to help them thwart government secrecy.

Canadian journalists seem aware that the laws of contempt hold hazards.[46] Bruce Phillips perhaps typified such a viewpoint when he said, speaking of the John Smith case, "I'm quite prepared to live with [the] situation and refuse to divulge sources and take the consequences. My view is that Smith and any other newspaperman worth his salt would behave that way. If he is given information in confidence he has his own bond upon it, and unless it is something affecting the security of the country or a matter of that character, he has no choice if he wishes to go on being a journalist except to defend the confidence that he has been given . . . I think the press is able to take care of itself in cases like this. I think that we've got to accept the fact there are going to be situations where the court's requirement for information is going to directly conflict with the reporter's obligation to his source of information . . . Sometimes [journalists] are going to land in jail because of it, but it wouldn't be the first time a journalist went to jail."[47]

Journalists who did go to jail under the conditions described by Mr. Phillips would at least have been dealt with under the well-understood concept of "due process" of law, with the requirement to divulge being exacted only by a properly constituted court or commission. If the Alberta Press Act of 1937 had not been ruled *ultra vires* the government itself would have been empowered to compel disclosure without the journalist enjoying any of the protections built into the procedures which make up "due process." One of its harsh terms was that it would have required any newspaper "to name within twenty-four hours sources of any statement" made by that paper "within sixty days of the making of an order so to do." Failure to comply would have brought dire punishments. Journalists all across Canada recognized in the Bill a genuine threat to freedom and reacted with anger. Both the principles involved in the successful fight against the enactment and the public reaction to the measure made the affair a true Canadian *cause célèbre*.

By the Alberta Press Bill yardstick, the John Smith affair was not a *cause célèbre*.

CRIMINAL LAW	CIVIL LAW
Seditious libel	_____
Blasphemous libel (or blasphemy)	_____
Obscene libel (or obscenity)	_____

	DEFAMATION
Defamatory libel	Libel
_____	Slander

Chapter V

Civil Defamation

It is appropriate, after the foregoing rather extended discussion of contempt of court and its "corollaries", to turn attention to the subject of libel. The term "libel" itself is a somewhat confusing one. Although it may be used in a generic sense to include all four kinds of criminal libel and the one kind of civil libel, it usually refers simply to that civil libel alone.

In order to distinguish among the various kinds of libel with which the law deals, the *schema* (page 40) is offered.

As seen from the above chart, criminal libel may be seditious, blasphemous, obscene or defamatory. The only libel dealt with by civil law is libel as a form of defamation. This type of libel is referred to without any accompanying adjective, so that when the simple term "libel" is used, civil libel is usually understood. When the words "defamatory libel" are employed, criminal libel is the sense intended. Slander is a form of defamation which is dealt with by civil law only.

Defamatory libel, seditious libel and blasphemous libel will provide the subject matter of chapter six. Obscene libel, or "obscenity" as it is now called, will be considered in chapter seven. The present chapter will concern itself with civil defamation, that is, libel and slander.

Definitions, Concepts and General Observations Related to Libel and Slander

Gatley says that "a defamatory imputation is one to a man's discredit, or which tends to lower him in the estimation of others, or to expose him to hatred, contempt or ridicule, or to injure his reputation in his office, trade or profession, or to injure his financial credit."[1] Libel and slander are torts characterized by the publication of matter which conveys a defamatory imputation. Libel and slander are usually expressed in words, but, as Gatley points out, "[s]tatues, waxworks, pictures, photographs (particularly in collocation with words), cartoons, cinema or television pictures, marks on a pavement, burning a man in effigy, hanging a sign outside his house or hissing him, signs and gestures have all been capable of conveying a defamatory imputation."[2]

There are many definitions of libel. A textbook definition in current vogue reads: "Any written or printed words which tend to lower a person in the estimation of right-thinking men, or cause him to be shunned or avoided, or expose him to hatred, contempt or ridicule, constitute a libel."[3] In 1882, what Mr. (now Ontario Supreme Court Justice) Alexander Stark has called "surely the neatest and best and the most accurate definition of all"[4] was provided by Mr. Justice Cave: "A libel is a false statement about a man to his discredit."[5]

A prevalent misconception is that it is still possible to distinguish between libel and slander on the basis of whether the defamation is oral or written. At one time, it *was* possible to do this, but the advent of talking pictures, radio and television has blurred the distinction. Today a more accurate statement would be as follows: Libel involves publication of defamatory matter in permanent form; slander involves publication of defamatory matter in transitory form. Thus, although spoken defamation, uttered over the back fence, constitutes slander, broadcast defamation constitutes libel.[6]

A case in which the plaintiff brought a successful action for libel (rather than slander even though the words used were mainly oral rather than printed) was *Youssoupoff* v *Metro-Goldwyn-Mayer*.[7] In this case Princess Youssoupoff alleged that she was portrayed in the talking picture entitled "Rasputin, the Mad Monk" in the character named Princess "Natasha" as having been seduced by Rasputin. On the grounds that she had been defamed she was awarded damages of $125,000. The lower court verdict was sustained on appeal.

It should be noted that, except under certain special circumstances to be considered later, it is immaterial to the fact of libel whether it was the intention of the alleged libeller to commit libel or not. According to Gatley:

> Even a *bona fide* belief that the words are true will afford no defence in the absence of privilege, though such belief may be urged in mitigation of damages. "A man in good faith may publish a libel believing it to be true, and it may be found by the jury that he acted in good faith, believing it to be true, and reasonably believing it to be true, but that in fact the statement was false. Under those circumstances he has no defence to the action, however excellent his intention."[8]

A classic illustration of the irrelevance of intention to the fact of libel occurred in 1910. As a result of the case[9] which provides the foregoing quotation, it has been said that the ghost of Artemus Jones has haunted English newspapers ever since. The affair started in July 1908 when the Paris correspondent of the *Sunday Chronicle* was told to write a feature piece on the subject of the French resort, Dieppe, and its coming Motor Week. In his account headed "Motor-Mad Dieppe," the reporter said:

Upon the terrace marches of the world, attracted by the motor races—a world immensely pleased with itself, and minded to draw a wealth of inspiration—and, incidentally, of golden cocktails—from any scheme to speed the passing hour . . . "Whist! There is Artemus Jones with a woman who is not his wife, who must be, you know—the other thing!" whispers a fair neighbour of mine excitedly in her bosom friend's ear. Really, is it not surprising how certain of our fellow-countrymen behave when they come abroad? Who would suppose, by his goings on, that he was a churchwarden in Peckham? No one, indeed, would assume that Jones in the atmosphere of London would take on so austere a job as the duties of churchwarden. Here, in the atmosphere of Dieppe, on the French side of the Channel, he is the life and soul of a gay little band that haunts the Casino and turns night into day, besides betraying a most unholy delight in the society of female butterflies.[10]

Artemus Jones, like the incident described, was a creation of the reporter's overfertile imagination. For this reason the reporter and the officers of the newspaper were disagreeably startled when a real Thomas Artemus Jones first demanded a retraction and apology and then, dissatisfied with the newspaper's ungenerous disclaimer, filed a libel suit on account of the offending article. The plaintiff was not married, he did not live in Peckham and he was not a churchwarden. The defence emphasized these facts and the fact that the correspondent and *Sunday Chronicle* had no intention of libelling anyone. The reaction of the Court was this: "What does intention matter?" This was in accord with the maxim that a man is presumed to intend the consequences of his actions. And certainly, since the real-life Artemus Jones was thought by some readers to be the Artemus Jones referred to and others teased him for his supposed indiscretions, the damage was done whether the defendants intended the damage or not. The trial court found the defendants liable and awarded the plaintiff £1,750 damages. The case was appealed, first to the Court of Appeal, and then to the House of Lords. Both appeals were denied and the original award was allowed to stand.

The law distinguishes between statements which are defamatory and those which are merely injurious. Both are falsehoods told by one man to the prejudice of another. Both are punishable. The merely injurious falsehood does not affect a man's reputation. A defamatory statement does. To wrongly say a tradesman has ceased to carry on business is an injurious falsehood; if it causes actual damage and the falsehood was wilful the statement is actionable. To wrongly say the same man is incompetent or dishonest is a defamatory statement; it is usually actionable also.[11]

The law distinguishes between defamation *per se* and defamation *per quod*. In defamation *per se* no special (in contrast to general) damage has to be proved. According to Salmond, the special damage required to support the case in defamation proceedings actionable *per quod* must be the loss of some definite material advantage.[12] The damage, which Salmond suggests might more accurately be called "actual" rather than "special," must not consist merely of the loss of reputation itself. Loss of the voluntary hospitality of friends and a resulting separation of a husband and wife are cited as examples of such special damage. A comparable damage is to be seen in the following sort of newspaper error which could result in a successful action for defamation:

> The social pages of a newspaper may carry an *erroneous* story to the effect that Dr. X attended a party on a certain evening. That same evening one of Dr. X's patients phones to say she is quite ill and needs his medical services at once. But the telephone answering service handling his calls says that Dr. X cannot attend her because the doctor himself is ill. When she later reads the newspaper account of the party, the patient concludes that the doctor was lying about his illness and angrily gets herself a different doctor.

By showing how he has lost his reputation—indeed, by showing how he lost specifically *one* patient—the doctor might win his libel action.

Not all libel is direct and explicit. Sometimes statements which are innocuous on the surface carry a second and defamatory meaning. This is known as an *innuendo*. In the language of Gatley, "words may convey a defamatory imputation only by reason of some special knowledge available to those to whom they were published, of the circumstances of publication, or of some special meaning or inference to be attached to or drawn from the words."[13] According to Harry Street, "To put a top-flight singer's name third, instead of first, on an advertising bill for a concert was actionable; a caption under a newspaper photograph to the effect that it was Mr. C. and his fiancée was defamatory of the plaintiff, the wife of Mr. C; to include a cartoon of an amateur golfer in an advertisement for chocolate implied that he was prostituting his amateur status."[14] The plaintiff who alleges innuendo often runs the danger that the defendant may plead that the innuendo is true. This permits the defendant to put on the record damaging facts against the plaintiff to support his plea.

In Canada libel actions are tried by both a judge and jury (consisting of six persons). The law lays down this requirement except where parties to the action agree that the trial shall be held before the judge alone. In practice they almost never do so agree.[15] The first task of the judge is to decide whether the words complained of are capable of constituting libel; and then the jury determines whether in fact there was a libel.

It is also necessary to point out that, in the words of Ronald G. Atkey, "Libel is, technically, an every day occurrence in most Canadian newspapers, yet few actions are ever commenced because of the limited likelihood of the person 'libelled' being able to prove substantial damages thus making the suit worth while."[16]

And finally, it is to be noted by way of general observation, that it is legally impossible to libel the dead.[17] Gatley says on the subject:

> [D]efamatory words published of a deceased person are not deemed to inflict on the surviving relatives any such legal damage as will sustain an action if *their* reputation is not affected. Libel and slander are essentially personal wrongs, and the right of action, therefore, dies with the person defamed. But it is a criminal offence to write and publish defamatory words of any deceased person if it be done with intent to injure and bring contempt on his family, and so provoke them to a breach of the peace.[18]

A Canadian case illustrative of the fact that libel is a personal wrong was *Knox* v. *Spencer*. (*See Case No. 11*)

Legislation Providing Canada's Present Civil Law of Defamation

Libel is dealt with in Canada by both statute law and common law. Because each Canadian province has its own statute dealing with defamation, civil law, unlike the criminal law of libel, varies from province to province. Quebec legislation, being based on the *Code Napoléon*, is the most different from the general pattern. The most skimpy statute is that of Newfoundland, which deals with slander only. As a result, Newfoundland relies even more heavily on common law than do her sister provinces.

At the time this book was being written the following provincial defamation and other related civil law statutes were in effect:

(British Columbia) Libel and Slander Act, R.S.B.C. 1969, c. 218
(Alberta) The Defamation Amendment Act, S.A. 1972, c. 105
(Saskatchewan) The Libel and Slander Act, R.S.S. 1965, c. 107
(Manitoba) The Defamation Act, R.S.M. 1970, C. D20, The Newspapers Act, R.S.M. 1970, c. N90

(Ontario) The Libel and Slander Act, R.S.O. 1970 c. 243
(Quebec) Newspaper Declaration Act, R.S.Q. 1964, c.49, Press Act,
       R.S.Q. 1964, c. 48
(New Brunswick) Defamation Act, R.S.N.B. 1952, c.58
(Nova Scotia) Defamation Act, R.S.N.S. 1967, c.72
(Prince Edward Island) The Defamation Act, R.S.P.E.I. 1952, c.41
(Newfoundland) The Slander Act, R.S.Nfld. 1970, c.352.

Journalists are advised to consult library holdings of provincial
statutes to keep themselves abreast of any amendments or statute
revisions of the defamation law for the province in which they are
practising.

Statute Definitions and Preconditions

Unlike the Criminal Code, the various provincial statutes do not define
libel. Therefore, the courts trying civil actions are governed by
common law interpretations.

In many cases the defences open in law against libel suits depend
upon the publication's fulfilling the definition of a "newspaper" as set
down in the appropriate defamation act. The Libel and Slander Act of
Ontario reads as follows:

> "[N]ewspaper" means a paper containing public news, intelligence,
> or occurrences, or remarks or observations thereon, printed for sale
> and published periodically, or in parts or numbers at intervals not
> exceeding thirty-one days between the publication of any two such
> papers, parts or numbers, and includes a paper printed in order to be
> made public weekly or more often or at intervals not exceeding
> thirty-one days and containing only, or principally, adver-
> tisements.[19]

Rather similar definitions appear in the Acts of British Columbia,
Alberta, Saskatchewan, Manitoba, Quebec, New Brunswick, Nova
Scotia and Prince Edward Island. The Newfoundland Act contains no
such definition.

Licensing of newspapers in the sense written about by Milton in his
Areopagitica is not part of the Canadian experience, although several
provinces do require that newspapers be registered. In such cases the
requirement is another precondition of some of the protections provided by appropriate defamation acts. Provinces which provide for
registration (or annual "returns" or "particulars of ownership" or

"filing of affidavits" or "declarations") are Saskatchewan, Manitoba, and Quebec. Such provisos are connected with court proof of publication of matter complained about. Many provinces have ruled that the identification of responsible publishers will be furnished by requiring that the name of the proprietor and publisher and address of the publication be stated in a conspicuous place in the newspaper. Alberta, Saskatchewan, Manitoba (with variations), Ontario, Quebec (printer and publisher), New Brunswick, Nova Scotia and Prince Edward Island legislation spells out requirements of this kind. Many provinces couple with this the provision that production in evidence of a printed copy of a newspaper is *prima facie* proof of the publication of the matter specified in the legal case. Alberta, Saskatchewan, Manitoba, Ontario, New Brunswick, Nova Scotia and Prince Edward Island are so served.

Unlike the Criminal Code, civil law in Canada does not define publishing, although the Manitoba Defamation Act defines "publication" as "any words legibly marked upon any substance or any object signifying the matter otherwise than by words, exhibited in public or caused to be seen or shown or circulated or delivered with a view to its being seen by any person."[20]

Provincial legislation which deals with broadcast defamation in the same way as written defamation is that of British Columbia, Alberta, Manitoba, Ontario, New Brunswick, Nova Scotia and Prince Edward Island. The Ontario and B. C. Acts explicitly call broadcast defamation "libel," both saying defamatory words in a broadcast shall be deemed to be published and constitute libel.[21] The Ontario Act says words shall be construed as including a reference to pictures, visual images, gestures or other methods of signifying meaning. The Nova Scotia Defamation Act (which says that "words" include pictures, visual images, gestures or other methods of signifying meaning) further stipulates that "the broadcasting of words shall be treated as publication in permanent form."[22] As has been pointed out, it is permanence which is the quality which distinguishes libel from slander. The statutes of Alberta, Manitoba, New Brunswick and Prince Edward Island are less explicit than those of Ontario, British Columbia and Nova Scotia in treating broadcasting as libel, but they do deal with it as libel by imposing similar conditions on the defences of privilege and fair comment. They also make similar concessions and exact similar penalties in their treatment of publishing and broadcasting. Five of the seven provinces mentioned use, with or without slight modification, the following definition of "broadcasting":

the dissemination of any form of radio-electric communication, including radiotelegraph, radio-telephone and the wireless transmission of writing, signs, signals, pictures and sounds of all kinds, by means of Hertzian waves intended to be received by the public directly or through the medium of relay stations.[23]

Alberta and British Columbia speak of electromagnetic waves and gigacycles rather than Hertzian waves.

Provinces which treat broadcasting libel in the same way as printed libel (British Columbia, Alberta, Manitoba, Ontario, New Brunswick, Nova Scotia, Prince Edward Island) lay down stipulations which entitle the broadcaster to the benefits of the Act. These conditions are comparable to those laid down for the registration of newspapers, publication of the names of newspaper personnel and their addresses on the newspaper masthead, and production of a printed copy of a newspaper as *prima facie* evidence of publication. Representative of the seven statutes is section 8(3) of the Ontario Act:

> Where a person, by registered letter containing his address and addressed to a broadcasting station, alleges that a libel against him has been broadcasted from the station and requests the name and address of the owner and operator of the station sections 5 and 6 [sections which give certain benefits to the publisher or broadcaster] do not apply with respect to an action by such person against such owner or operator for the alleged libel unless the person whose name and address are so requested delivers the requested information to the first-mentioned person, or mails it by registered mail addressed to him, within ten days from the date on which the first-mentioned registered letter is received at the broadcasting station.[24]

Defences Available in Libel Actions

There are three main defences which may be resorted to in a libel action: the plea of truth; the plea of privilege; the plea of fair comment.

1. Truth

The plea of truth is known in law as a plea of justification. If a defendant pleads and proves that a defamatory statement is true, no libel action will lie for the publication of that statement. This condition seems evident from the definition of libel quoted *supra,* that "a libel is a false statement about a man to his discredit," wherefrom falsehood is seen to be an essential ingredient of libel. This fact suggests why it is said that truth is a *complete* defence against a libel action.

Of course it must be forgotten that what is needed is not merely truth but *provable* truth, and it is not always easy to prove truth. The burden of proof rests with the defendant; it is for him to prove that the statement is true, not for the plaintiff to prove that it is false.[25] According to Gatley, "Where the defendant pleads justification *simpliciter* the burden lies on him to prove the truth of the words in their natural and ordinary meaning."[26] Citing "*Per* Collins M. R. in *Digby* v. *Financial News Ltd.* [1907] 1 K. B. at p. 509" and related judgments, Gatley also says, " 'A plea of justification means that all the words were true and covers not only the bare statements of fact in the alleged libel but also any imputation which the words in their context may be taken to convey'."[27]

It perhaps needs to be added, as various provincial statutes specify, that the mere fact that a statement is proved does not make the defendant immune from legal penalty if the publication or broadcast complained of is blasphemous, seditious or indecent;[28] but in this case the offence is that of blasphemy, sedition or obscenity rather than of defamation.

J. J. Robinette, Q. C., when answering questions put to him at a legal-journalism seminar of Thomson Newspapers Limited, illustrated the situation in which a plea of truth might be offered in defence of a libel action. The question he was asked was this:

In the "Many Long Years Ago" column here, a reporter one day last year described the shenanigans of a man he presumed to be by this time long since dead. The man had struck someone and had been found guilty in court. Now forty years later the report had come back to haunt him. He claimed he almost lost his job through the story. Is there any cause for action?[29]

Mr. Robinette answered:

In my opinion, no, because what the newspaper was publishing was the truth. He had in fact been convicted forty years ago and there was no untrue statement. The newspaper can carry history, it can carry something that has happened one hundred years ago. It may be very uninteresting history, it may have been very unfair and not the right thing to have done from a moral standpoint, to drag up a conviction of forty years ago against a man; but if in fact he was convicted and the newspaper publishes it, the defence is simply truth. He was convicted. So there would be no cause for action.[30]

Although, as we have said, proved truth provides a perfect defence in a libel action, an unsuccessful plea of truth may be considered to be an aggravation of the libel. As Gatley says, "A defendant should never place a plea of justification on the record unless he has clear and sufficient evidence of the truth of the imputation, for failure to establish the defence at the trial *may* properly be taken in aggravation of the damages."[31]

Several Canadian provinces have adopted some of the provisions of the British Defamation Act of 1952. Of these provisions the Nova Scotia and Ontario statutes have borrowed one of particular benefit to defendants using justification as a plea in libel actions. In almost identical words the two acts state the following:

> In an action for libel or slander for words containing two or more distinct charges against the plaintiff, a defence of justification shall not fail by reason only that the truth of every charge is not proved if the words not proved to be true do not materially injure the plaintiff's reputation having regard to the truth of the remaining charges.[32]

The implication here, according to Robinette, is that ". . . although prior to 1958 you had to prove the substance or the gist of every allegation, today that is not strictly true. If you prove the truth of one, which destroys reputation for all practical purposes, it is not injurious to the plaintiff to call him something else when he has really not much reputation left."[33]

2. Privilege, qualified and absolute

Canadian law allows the plea of privilege as a defence in libel proceedings. Privilege may be absolute or qualified, Absolute privilege may be defined as relating to a statement that is of such a nature that it is not actionable, no matter how false and defamatory it may be, and even though it is published with malice. Malice, in its legal context, is not to be confused with spite or ill-will; it relates rather to the purpose for which the publication is made, a malicious statement being one published for some purpose other than the purpose for which the law confers the priviliege of making it. Gatley[34] describes malice in the following terms:

> The malice essential to support the action is some dishonest or otherwise improper motive. Such a motive will be inferred on proof that the words were calculated to produce actual damage, and that the defendant knew that they were false when he published them, or was recklessly indifferent as to whether they were false or not. "The publication of a statement which to the defendant's knowledge is false and calculated to injure is malicious, and is treated as intended to injure."[35] "A statement made by a man who knows that it is false,

is made maliciously. So also if he knows that it is likely to injure and has no belief whether it is true or false, and makes it recklessly, not caring whether it is true or false.''[36] But mere negligence is not malice. A statement false in fact and calculated to produce actual damage will therefore not support such an action if it was made in the belief, even the careless belief, that it was true. Again, ''the mere absence of just cause or excuse is not of itself malice. Malice in its proper and accurate sense is a question of motive, intention, or state of mind''[37]

Of the seven cases of absolute privilege applicable in Great Britain, six would seem to apply in Canada:

1. Any statement made in the course of and with reference to judicial proceedings by any judge, juryman, party, witness, or advocate;
2. Fair, accurate, and contemporaneous reports of public judicial proceedings published in a newspaper;
3. Any statement made in Parliament by a member of either House;
4. Parliamentary papers published by the direction of either House, and any republication thereof by any person in full;
5. Any statement made by one officer of State to another in the course of his official duty;
6. Communications between husband and wife.[38]

The only instances applicable to newspapers and broadcasting seem to be 2 and possibly 4. Thus the Alberta, Saskatchewan, Manitoba, Ontario, New Brunswick and Prince Edward Island statutes speak of proceedings publicly heard before any court as being *absolutely* privileged. The British Columbia, Quebec and Nova Scotia acts use the word ''privileged'' only, without the adjective ''absolute'' with regard to court proceedings. The British Columbia, Alberta, Manitoba, New Brunswick and Prince Edward Island Acts are the only provincial statutes to deal with Salmond's fourth instance of absolute privilege cited above (that is, ''Parliamentary papers published by direction of either House.'') The B. C. statute talks of ''publication at the request of any Government office or department,'' but it is clear that only qualified privilege is intended since it specifies that publication must be without malice. The Alberta, Manitoba, New Bruswick and Prince Edward Island statutes use the expression ''privileged'' without an accompanying adjective.

In the provincial statutes, conditions laid down for the reporting of courts, where absolute privilege is claimed, are more stringent than those concerning other meetings. The Ontario Libel and Slander Act, which may be taken as representative, specifies the following:

4 (1) A fair and accurate report without comment in a newspaper or in a broadcast of proceedings publicly heard before a court of justice, if published in the newspaper or broadcast contemporaneously with such proceedings is absolutely privileged unless the defendant has refused or neglected to insert in the newspaper in which the report complained of appeared or to broadcast, as the case may be, a reasonable statement of explanation or contradiction by or on behalf of the plaintiff.[39]

It is to be noted that not only must reports be fair and accurate but they must be made without comment and issued contemporaneously with court proceedings. (Some Acts permit reportage up to thirty days after the trial.[40]) Apparently to be "fair" a report does *not* have to be *verbatim et seriatim*. That is, a summary which does not adhere to the strict chronology and exact language of what is reported is acceptable so long as that summary does not distort what it purports to report. To comment on *sub judice* matter is to invite contempt of court citations, of course.

An occasion of qualified privilege is one in which a person, provided he is not actuated by malice, is entitled to make defamatory statements about another. Statements, to enjoy qualified privilege, must be made honestly and without any indirect or improper motive. The privilege given is given for some reason, and the defendant forfeits the protection of the privilege if he uses the occasion for a different and wrong reason. If a defendant does not genuinely believe in the truth of a statement he makes, the law regards that fact as conclusive proof of malice and of improper motive. But the converse is not necessarily true. It does not necessarily mean that if a defendant genuinely believes in the truth of his statement he is devoid of malice or that his motive is a proper one.

The foregoing are some of the considerations which apply to occasions of qualified privilege. Salmond lists the chief instances of qualified privilege as follows:

1. Statements made in the performance of a duty;
2. Statements made in the protection of an interest;
3. Reports of parliamentary, judicial and certain other public proceedings;
4. Professional communications between solicitor and client.[41]

Obviously the fourth instance does not apply to newspapers. Statutory protection, in all provinces except Newfoundland, is given for fair and accurate reports of situations of which those specified in the Ontario Act may again be taken to be typical: proceedings of Parliament or any legislative or administrative body or public commission of inquiry or of any organization whose members represent a public authority[42]; public meetings[43]; reports, bulletins, notices or other documents publicly issued by government[44]; and findings or decisions of certain specified associations in reference to persons who are members of or contractually subject to such associations.[45]

In those statutes which go into detail there is little variation from province to province. Reportage of public meetings, for example, is an occasion of qualified privilege the conditions of which are remarkably uniform. Many statutes specifically define "public meetings." The British Columbia Libel and Slander Act describes the public meeting as "any meeting *bona fide* and lawfully held for a public purpose, and for the furtherance or discussion of any matter of public concern, whether the admission thereto be general or restricted."[46] Similar definitions are to be found in the Alberta, Saskatchewan, Manitoba, New Brunswick, Nova Scotia, and Prince Edward Island statutes. Even statutes which do not define a "public meeting" spell out conditions under which reports of meetings enjoy qualified privilege, and also enumerate related and comparable privileged events and subjects. Several provincial statutes have adopted the restriction that public meetings have to be lawfully convened for a lawful purpose and have to be open to the public; the report of the meeting has to be fair and accurate; publication of the matter at issue must be for the public benefit; and the person against whom complaint is made must "publish in a conspicuous place in the newspaper a reasonable explanation or contradiction by the person defamed in respect of the defamatory matter."[47] The provincial statutes lay down the condition, as they do with defamation of a less specific nature, that reports must not contain malice. They also specify, almost as an automatic reminder, the "co-conditions" which the defendant must observe if he is to avoid not only action for defamation, but for related criminal offences as well: his reports or broadcasts must be free of seditious, blasphemous and indecent matter. In any case, unwillingness to publish the explanatory statement referred to earlier may be taken as evidence of malice on the part of the defendant. The converse is also true. Many acts extend these same conditions to all sorts of matters such as proceedings of Senate, Commons, legislatures, parliamentary committees, municipal councils, school boards and boards of education.

As Ronald G. Atkey says, "The common law . . . provides a number of forms of qualified privilege which are useful to newspapers."[48] He continues:

For example, statements made by a newspaper in discharging some moral, social or legal duty are protected. An erroneous news story reporting someone as missing might qualify for this protection if it is not made maliciously. Again, statements made to a person who has a common interest in a subject with the person who makes them provides another instance of qualified privilege. If one newspaper in a chain unjustly criticizes another newspaper in the same chain by way of an open letter to that other newspaper, the privilege might well be invoked. Statements made in self-defence can also claim qualified privilege as well. For example, if one man attacks another in the public press, the latter may make a reply, and the reply may contain countercharges against his assailant, if they form a reasonably necessary part of his defence.[49]

Professor Atkey also makes the following useful observation:

The difference between qualified and absolute privilege, i.e. the waiver of the immunity if the publication is made maliciously in the case of qualified privilege, is a difference more apparent than real. Most Canadian newspapermen in their day-to-day operations regard the rules of qualified privilege as their primary "rules of thumb" in potentially libellous situations, and there have been few cases in which a newspaper has been alleged to have maliciously published otherwise privileged reports.[50]

A case illustrating the conditions under which a plea of privilege may or may not be made was tried on appeal in Manitoba in 1950. (*See Case No. 12*) Another interesting case followed publication in the Toronto *Globe and Mail* of an editorial entitled "Mission Accomplished." (*See Case No. 13*)

3. Fair Comment

As defence in an action for defamation, a defendant may plead that the matter complained of is fair comment on a matter of public interest. According to Salmond, the requirements to be fulfilled are that the matter must on the face of it appear to be comment, that it must be fair, and that it must be a matter of public interest. Related conditions are that the facts on which the comment is based must be truly stated, that comments must be honestly believed to be true, and therefore not motivated by malice, and that any imputations of corrupt motives must either be proved true or else be a correct inference from the facts commented upon. The privilege of fair comment as being on matters of public interest extends also to comments on matters submitted to public criticism by the persons concerned. Criticisms of dramatic performances, books, musical concerts and so forth fall into this category.[51]

In the light of the foregoing it is apparent that a newspaper may deal with a man's public conduct much more severely than with his private conduct, particularly if that private conduct has no connection with the public good. A man who runs for public office, an author who publishes a book, an artist who paints a picture, an actress who goes on the stage are usually fair game for a kind of criticism which could not with legal safety be levelled against a private person. Thus, as Alexander Stark implies in *Dangerous Words*, it was because the Cherry sisters, attempting a theatrical comeback, had offered themselves for public judgment that they were unable to win a legal action against the *Des Moines Leader* after the newspaper had written the following description of their performance:

Effie is an old jade of fifty summers, Jess is a frisky filly of forty, and Addie, the flower of the family, a capering monstrosity of thirty-five. Their long skinny arms equipped with talons at the extremities, swung mechanically, and anon waved frantically at the suffering audience. The mouths of their rancid features opened like caverns and sounds like the wailings of damned souls issued therefrom. They pranced around the stage with a motion that suggested a cross between the *danse du ventre* and a fox trot—strange creatures with painted faces and hideous mien. Effie is spavined, Addie has stringhalt and Jessie, the only one who showed her stockings, has legs with calves as classic in their outline as the curves of a broom handle.[52]

It is most unlikely that the same newspaper would find it legally safe to use the same language to describe a private citizen. Nor would it safely so characterize a painter or an author, since the physical appearance of such men would be unrelated to what they are offering for public approval. Another illustration of what may or may not be subject of fair comment is to be found in what one might say about a public building, for example. The value judgment that that building is an architectural monstrosity is certainly not actionable; the false statement that its ceilings and floors are unsafe and persons entering the building run the grave risk of being killed is certainly actionable.

A defence plea which combines both truth and fair comment is known in law as a "rolled-up plea." It is frequently used because editorials in newspapers usually combine facts and comments closely intertwined. According to Gatley, the form the pleading takes is this: "In so far as the words complained of consist of statements of fact, they are true in substance and in fact; and in so far as the said words consist of expressions of opinion, they are *bona fide* and fair comment made in good faith and without malice on the said facts which are matters of public interest.''[53]

R. F. V. Heuston says there is considerable judicial opinion supporting the view that fair comment differs in its nature from qualified privilege even though Salmond himself believed that fair comment was simply an instance of qualified privilege.[54] Heuston points out that the defence of fair comment is a denial of the libel but that the defence of privilege is an admission of the libel along with the claim that the libel was published in circumstances giving the defendant an immunity not available to persons who were not operating within the area of privilege.[55] Anyone in the country may make fair comment on a work of art. But it would take such an instance as the press's reporting of a member of parliament's remarks during a sitting of the house to enjoy the qualified privilege of uttering, with legal immunity, the falsehood that ''Mr. X. is a convicted criminal.'' Hueston says:

. . . There are two admitted differences between the defence of fair comment and the defence of qualified privilege. If the publication was upon a privileged occasion, the burden is upon the plaintiff to prove express malice; the defendant, on the other hand, has first the burden of showing that a comment is fair before the burden of proving malice is cast back upon the plaintiff. On the other hand, the plaintiff who has submitted his work or his acts for public criticisms bears the onus of proving a *prima facie* protected occasion is not in fact protected, whereas the defendant who relies upon qualified privilege has affirmatively to prove the existence of the privilege.[56]

In their provincial statutes, Nova Scotia and Ontario, as in the case with regard to partial proof in justification, have copied the British Defamation Act of 1952 with regard to fair comment. Both acts say, in almost identical language:

In an action for libel or slander in respect of words consisting partly of allegations of fact and partly of expressions of opinions, a defence of fair comment shall not fail by reason only that the truth of every allegation of fact is not proved if the expression of opinion is fair comment having regard to such of the facts alleged or referred to in the words complained of as are proved.[57]

An example of an unsuccessful plea of fair comment is provided by the 1970 libel suit against Judy LaMarsh. (*See Case No. 14*) The offence described on page 9, which resulted in a contempt citation, also caused Eric Nicol and his employers to be found liable for a civil defamation. (*See Case No. 15*) A case which illustrates that a defamation imputing a criminal offence is actionable *per se* was tried in Alberta in 1964. A "rolled up plea" was also an ingredient of the trial. (*See Case No. 16*)

A significant precedent to allow wider latitude in comments on political matters was provided by an English case in 1968. What gave rise to it was the publishing of letters to the editor of *The Daily Telegraph* in which it was alleged that a solicitor who had formerly been Town Clerk and then legal advisor to a private company with property interests contrary to those of the town had been dishonest. The letter writer implied that the solicitor had used "back door influence" with Town Council employees to gain concessions for the company. The solicitor and his firm sued both the letter writer and *The Daily Telegraph* for libel. Lord Denning, Master of the Rolls, ruled that the letters were fair comment on a matter of public interest and gave the following significant *ratio decidendi* in deciding the case:

> If he was an honest man expressing his genuine opinion on a subject of public interest, then no matter that his words conveyed derogatory imputations: no matter that his opinion was wrong or exaggerated or prejudiced; and no matter that it was badly expressed so that other people read all sorts of innuendoes into it; nevertheless, he has a good defence of fair comment. His honesty is the cardinal test. He must honestly express his real view. So long as he does this, he has nothing to fear, even though other people may read more into it . . . I stress this because the right of fair comment is one of the essential elements which go to make up our freedom of speech. We must maintain that right intact. It must not be whittled down by legal refinements. When a citizen is troubled by things going wrong, he should be free to "write to the newspaper": and the newspaper should be free to publish his letter. It is the only way to get things put right. The matter must, of course, be one of public interest. The writer must get his facts right: and he must honestly state his real opinion. But that being done, both he and the newspaper should be clear of any liability. They should not be deterred by fear of libel actions.[58]

Other Features of Statute Law of Benefit to Journalists Including Procedural Defences

Although not a complete defence, the offer or making of an apology may be given in evidence to mitigate damages against the defendant.

Various Canadian civil statutes lay down the conditions under which damages against the defendant may be mitigated. To receive such consideration the defendant may plead that he published or broadcast the libel without malice and without gross negligence, and that, before commencement of the action or at the earliest opportunity, he published or broadcast full apology. The Alberta Act is fairly typical of what the civil law says about the conditions which make possible the lesser punishment of special damage.

"Special" damage is defined in terms which contrast it with "general" damage. According to Salmond,

> General damage is that kind of damage which the law presumes to follow from the wrong complained of and which, therefore, need not be expressly set out in the plaintiff's pleadings. Special damage, on the other hand, is damage of such a kind that it will not be presumed by the law and therefore must be expressly alleged in those pleadings so that the defendant may have due notice of the nature of the claim—otherwise the plaintiff will not be permitted to give evidence of it nor will the jury be at liberty to award compensation in respect of it.[59]

Section 18(1) of the Alberta Act says the plaintiff shall recover only special damage if it appears on the trial

a) that the alleged defamatory matter was published in good faith,
b) that there was reasonable grounds to believe that the publication thereof was for the public benefit,
c) that it did not impute to the plaintiff the commission of a criminal offence,
d) that the publication took place in mistake or misapprehension of the facts, and
e) that

i) where the alleged defamatory matter was published in a newspaper, a full and fair retraction of and a full apology for any statement therein alleged to be erroneous

A) were published in the newspaper before the commencement of the action, and

B) were so published in as conspicuous a place and type as was the alleged defamatory matter,

OR

ii) where the alleged defamatory matter was broadcast, the retraction and apology were broadcast from broadcasting stations from which the alleged defamatory matter was broadcast, on at least two occasions on different days and at the same time of day as the alleged defamatory matter was broadcast or at a time as near as possible to that time.[60]

Provinces which deal with the matter in a similar way are British Columbia, Saskatchewan, Manitoba, Ontario, New Brunswick, Nova Scotia and Prince Edward Island. The Quebec Act has substantially the same provisions but they are not spelled out in such detail. It is to be noted that in this part of the various statutes the Alberta, Manitoba, New Brunswick, Nova Scotia, and Prince Edward Island acts speak of "special" damages. The British Columbia, Saskatchewan and Ontario acts speak of "actual" damages. The Quebec statute deals with "actual and real" damages.

In most libel actions the best tactic for reducing the damages the newspaper will be required to pay is to apologize, promptly, ungrudgingly and fully. Anomalous though it may seem, it is possible for a defendant to plead both justification and publication of a retraction. This contention was upheld in a 1963 action involving the Toronto Star. (*See Case No. 17*) In British Columbia in 1970 a case heard on appeal involved the defendants' failure to apologize, their unsuccessful plea of fair comment, and the court's acceptance of the plaintiff's claim of innuendo. (*See Case No. 18*)

An apology is likely to be more effective where the plaintiff has launched his suit in order to clear his name and reputation rather than to win money damages in compensation. Indeed, in such cases there is often a good likelihood that the apology will dissuade the plaintiff from continuing with his action, with the result that the suit does not come to trial. The apology does not exculpate the newspaper from all liability, of course, and sometimes it may constitute an admission of the libel. Occasionally, where apologies are insincere or a subterfuge for inflicting a further but "disguised" libel, such apologies may aggravate rather than mitigate damages. A suit by a union official against a union-published newspaper in British Columbia illustrated just such a "spurious" apology. (*See Case No. 19*)

Most civil statutes outline requirements which plaintiffs must fulfill to support a libel action. For example, the Alberta statute requires the plaintiff to give seven days' notice of his intention to bring action in the case of a daily newspaper and fourteen days' notice in the case of any other newspaper or of a broadcasting station. That notice has to specify the defamatory matter complained of, and it has to be delivered within three months after the defamatory matter has come to the plaintiff's notice or knowledge. Most provincial defamation laws limit the time after which a libel action may be brought against newspaper or against broadcasting personnel. Such laws also require that plaintiffs observe certain formalities in bringing action against defendants. The statutes also stipulate the time which has to elapse between the giving of notice of the legal action and the filing of the suit against the defendant. Perhaps the New Brunswick statute (section 18) may be taken as representative of this area of the law. Here notice of intention to begin the libel action must be delivered within three months after the alleged defamatory matter has been published or has come to the attention of the plaintiff. The notice must specify the defamatory matter complained of. In the case of the daily newspaper the notice must be given at least seven days before the suit is launched, and, in the case of any other newspaper or of a broadcast, at least fourteen days before. The purpose of the "buffer" period set down is to give the newspaper or broadcaster an opportunity to publish or broadcast the apologies, retractions or corrective statements which may help to mitigate the damages subsequently assessed. There is also a "statute of limitations" implication in section 14 of the New Brunswick law which stipulates that actions for defamation must be commenced within six months after publication of the defamatory matter has come to the attention of the person defamed. A modification of this provision says that any action brought and maintainable for defamation published within that period may include "a claim for any other defamation published against the plaintiff by the defendant in the same newspaper or from the same station within a period of one year before the commencement of the action."[61] British Columbia and Newfoundland are the only provinces with legislation deficient in this area of the libel law.

Many provincial defamation statutes specifically empower juries to give their verdicts not merely on the *fact of publication*, but on the defamatory *content* of the published matter complained of as well. Legislation which is specific on this point (and which empowers the jury to decide both general and special damages) is that of British Columbia, Alberta, Saskatchewan, Manitoba, Ontario, New Brunswick, Nova Scotia and Prince Edward Island.

The stipulation perpetuates a benefit conferred in England by Fox's Libel Act of 1792. It means, in effect, that if a plaintiff is to win a legal case he must receive the favorable "vote" of both judge and jury; to win his case the defendant needs *only* to win the favor of *either* judge *or* jury. Harry Street, in reference to the English situation, is of the opinion that the scales are weighted in favor of the defendant in a libel action. His remarks seem equally applicable to Canada:

It is often said proudly that in England the jury decides whether a statement is defamatory. But if the judge rules that the statement is not capable of being defamatory the jury never has the chance to decide the point. And even if the trial judge does let the jury decide, the Court of Appeal can still overrule the jury's verdict that the statement was libellous by holding that the trial judge should never have left the issue to the jury because the statement could not be defamatory.[62]

Of importance to defendant as well as to plaintiff is the place where actions for defamation are tried. Where the subject is covered by provincial statute, the law is quite uniform. The acts stipulate that the action shall be tried in the judicial district where the chief office of the newspaper is, or wherein the plaintiff resides at the time the action is brought. However, provision is made to change the trial venue on application of either plaintiff or defendant if the change appears to be in the interests of justice or seems necessary to promote a fair trial. British Columbia, Alberta, Saskatchewan, Manitoba, Ontario, New Brunswick, Nova Scotia and Prince Edward Island make the foregoing provision. All except Saskatchewan include broadcast libel under the "place of trial" stipulations of their Act. They speak of the "judicial district" [or "centre" or "county"] where the owner or operator of the broadcasting station is situated or of the judicial district or centre in which the plaintiff resides as the place where the case may be tried if the actionable libel is a broadcast libel.

Another provision which benefits newspaper and broadcast personnel who might be defendants in libel actions has to do with the posting of security for costs. This is the requirement that the plaintiff, not possessing property sufficient to answer the costs of an action, post monies or make guarantees in other fashion satisfactory to the court so as to guarantee that, if required, the plaintiff will pay the costs of the case should the defendant win it. The effect of this law is to discourage frivolous, nuisance, or speculative suits that might otherwise be unfair to the newspapers or broadcasting stations against which they may be filed. The requirement is not unconditional, however. Security for costs is usually granted only if

a) the defendant has a good defence upon the merits of the case;
b) the statements complained of were published in good faith; and
c) the grounds of the action are trivial or frivolous.

Even these conditions are not sufficient to call for security for costs if the matter complained of imputes that the plaintiff has been convicted of a criminal offence; although special circumstances do permit even this exception to be overriden. Provinces with "security for costs" requirements are British Columbia, Saskatchewan, Ontario and Quebec. In Quebec "[t]he judge may . . . order the plaintiff to furnish security for costs provided that the defendant himself furnishes security to satisfy the judgment.''[63]

A feature of some statutes deals with newspaper headlines and captions. Where dealt with they are to be considered reports within the context of those sections of the statutes concerned with fair and accurate reports of matters subject to privilege. So considered, headlines and captions are subject to the same conditions of privilege as outlined in those parts of the statutes. Prince Edward Island, Manitoba, New Brunswick and Nova Scotia deal with this matter. Alberta relates headlines and captions to reports of court proceedings only.

All provincial statutes except those of Newfoundland and Saskatchewan deal more strictly with libelling of a candidate for parliamentary or municipal election than they do with plaintiffs who are not running for public office. Usually the mitigation of damages which the defendant may earn by retraction and tender of amends and by fulfilling other conditions is permitted in the libelling of a candidate only if the retraction of the charge against the candidate is made editorially or by broadcast in a conspicuous manner at least five days before the election. In the case of Quebec, ''[N]o newspaper may avail itself of the provisions of this Act . . . [w]hen the article complained of refers to a candidate and was published within the three days prior to the nomination-day and up to the polling-day in a parliamentary or municipal election.''[64]

Manitoba is unique in being the only Canadian province which permits legal action to be taken against persons accused of libelling a race or the adherents to a religious creed. Section 19 of its Defamation Act reads as follows:

1) The publication of a libel against a race or religious creed likely to expose persons belonging to the race or professing the religious creed to hatred, contempt or ridicule, and tending to raise unrest or disorder among the people, entitles a person belonging to the race, or professing the religious creed, to sue for an injunction to prevent the continuation and circulation of the libel; and Court of Queen's Bench may entertain the action.
2) The action may be taken against the person responsible for the authorship, publication, or circulation of the libel.[65]

As has been said, the Manitoba provision is exceptional. Elsewhere in Canada the common law prevails. This means that to sustain a libel action the plaintiff must show that the defamatory statement has been made about him. Outside of Manitoba the law is powerless to interfere with group libels. When no particular members of a group are specifically libelled, no individual can sue. Thus, for example, whereas attacks on Roman Catholics or Jews as a class are actionable in Manitoba, elsewhere they are not.[66]

A city or a municipal corporation or a government is not entitled to sue for libel.[67] The nature of this proposition is indicated by the 1921 judgment given by Judge Fisher of the Circuit Court of Cook County against the plaintiff City Corporation of Chicago which sued the *Chicago Tribune*. The case had arisen after the newspaper criticized Mayor "Big Bill" Thompson and his administration, using such statements as "The City is broke," "Bankruptcy is just around the corner for the City of Chicago," and "The City government has run on the rocks." Mayor Thompson persuaded the City Corporation to issue a writ claiming libel damages of ten million dollars. The City based its claim on the contention that the *Tribune*'s strictures had damaged its credit and prevented the sale of its bonds to the extent of the ten million dollars asked. Judge Fisher allowed a demurrer and gave judgment in favor of the newspaper. Clearly the remedy that was sought was not the right one; rather it should have been a libel suit brought by Thompson and his fellow officials on their own behalf as private individuals.[68]

Damages

Libel or slander may result in money awards by the defendant to the person defamed. Injunctions against the defendant may provide alternative and additional remedies. Damages may be compensatory, nominal or exemplary. According to P. G. Osborn, damages are

> [c]ompensation or indemnity for loss suffered owing to a breach of contract or tort. The principle is that the injured party should be put as nearly as possible in the same position, so far as money can do it, as if he had not been injured . . . Nominal damages are of a trifling amount awarded contemptuously, or for the mere invasion of a right without damage. Exemplary [also called "punitive"] damages are awarded not only by way of compensation, but as a punishment to the offender.[69]

In Canada punitive damages are awarded only reluctantly. The courts prefer to restrict libel awards to their primary purpose of compensating the plaintiff for his injuries. Only in occasional, extreme cases, where the media have acted recklessly, where they have unreasonably declined to apologize, or where the libel results in a profit to the media which is larger than the normal compensation awarded to the libel victim, have the courts awarded punitive damages.

Punitive damages were awarded by the Supreme Court of Ontario in *Platt* v. *Time International of Canada Ltd.* (*See Case No. 20*)

The apportionment of court costs in Canadian cases differs from that of most American jurisdictions. In the latter each party pays his own court costs whatever the outcome of the case. The plaintiff's lawyer takes a fixed percentage of the award as a contingent fee. In Canada the court costs of plaintiffs and defendants are separate items and must be borne by the losing party. Such costs include a large part of both lawyers' fees.

Slander

As has been indicated above, it is the transitoriness of slander which is the main quality which distinguishes it from libel. In common law, libel is always actionable *per se*, slander is always actionable *per quod*.[70] For slander to be actionable *per se* it is necessary for statute law to spell out the fact, which is what several Canadian statutes do for certain kinds of slander. Gatley, speaking of the English situation, says "[t]he cases in which an action for slander will lie without proof of special damage fall under four heads:

(1) Where the words impute a crime for which the plaintiff can be made to suffer physically by way of punishment.
(2) Where the words impute to the plaintiff a contagious or infectious disease.
(3) Where the words are calculated to disparage the plaintiff in any office, profession, calling, trade or business held or carried on by him at the time of publication.
(4) By the Slander of Women Act 1891, where the words impute adultery or unchastity to a woman or girl.[71]

Because, under common law, slander is defamation *per quod* rather than *per se*, it becomes necessary, in statute law, to specifically make slander actionable *per se* wherever it is intended that action for the slander shall lie without proof of actual or special damage. Thus in many provinces the imputing of unchastity or adultery to women in a slander is specifically described as being actionable *per se*. British Columbia, Saskatchewan and Ontario statutues say that special damage does not have to be proved when slander is alleged. The Newfoundland Slander Act does not restrict this provision to girls and women but includes "persons" in the protection provided.

The Ontario Act describes as slander *per se* spoken words calculated to disparage the plaintiff in any office, profession, calling, trade or business, and states that special damage does not have to be proved. Also in Ontario, action for slander of title, slander of goods or other malicious falsehood is handled in the same way as slander imputing unchastity, provided that certain conditions are fulfilled.

Chapter VI

Criminal Libel

As has been pointed out, criminal libel may be defamatory, blasphemous, seditious or obscene.

Defamatory Libel

Canada's law dealing with defamatory libel is provided by the Criminal Code, which, being an enactment of the federal parliament, has a uniform, Canada-wide application. The criminal law of defamation is set down in section 261 to 281 and 434, 513, 656 and 657.

Defamatory libel is defined by the Criminal Code of Canada as "matter published, without lawful justification or excuse, that is likely to injure the reputation of any person by exposing him to hatred, contempt or ridicule, or that is designed to insult the person of or concerning whom it is published."[1]

In the words of the Code, it "may be expressed directly or by insinuation or irony

(a) in words legibly marked upon any substance, or
(b) by any objects signifying a defamatory libel otherwise than by words."[2]

Criminal libel *may* involve only two persons, or as Halsbury has written, publication to the person defamed alone may support a libel *prosecution* [3] "provided," according to Gatley, "the words are of such a character as reasonably tend or are calculated to provoke a breach of the peace."[4] (A modification of this legal viewpoint is indicated in the Bankers' Toadies case, discussed in the appendix as *Case No. 21*.) This is in contrast to the civil law, where publication to support an action for libel must be to a third person.[5]

Defences in Defamatory Libel Prosecutions

As with civil libel, the main defences available in a defamatory libel prosecution are the plea of truth, the plea of fair comment, and the plea of privilege. The Criminal Code takes account of the plea of truth when it speaks of "true matter" and it refers specifically to "fair comment," but it avoids the word "privilege" completely. However, it includes a number of sections beginning "No person shall be deemed to publish a defamatory libel . . ." and specifies the situations which are non-defamatory. These include the same matters which are specifically designated as "privileged" in the provincial defamation statutes and others besides. Apparently it is privilege which is implied by the words "or excuse" in the statement, "A defamatory libel is matter published without lawful justification or excuse . . ."

1. Truth

Under proper conditions, truth is a defence under the criminal law governing defamatory libel. That this is so follows from the fact that the definition of defamatory libel, like that of civil libel cited in the previous chapter, makes falsehood an ingredient of the libel. In the Criminal Code definition it is the words "without lawful justification" which carry the sense of "false" as used in the Cave definition. As Salmond says, "The defence that a statement is true is termed a plea of justification, the defendant being said to justify the publication."[6]

It would seem that the defence of truth under criminal law is a more conditional defence than it is under civil law. This is suggested by section 275 of the Criminal Code which says: "No person shall be deemed to publish a defamatory libel where he proves that the publication of the defamatory matter in the manner in which it was published was for the public benefit at the time when it was published and that the matter itself was true."[7] In other words, truth is not a complete defence under criminal law. Public benefit has to be proved as well.

In view of section 275 of the Code it would seem that Mr. Robinette's "Many Long Years Ago" answer discussed in Chapter 5 (at page 49) would not apply to a prosecution for defamatory libel launched against the paper mentioned. Salmond says, "the publication of the truth, however defamatory, is no longer a criminal offence if the jury is of opinion that the publication of it was for public benefit."[8] The plea of truth would protect the newspaper only in the unlikely event that the paper could prove that the publication of the matter complained of was for the public benefit. If, for example, the complainant in the prosecution were a candidate for public office and the conviction reported by the paper related to his future competence in that office it seems likely that the paper could defend itself by pleading that the statement made had been true and in the public interest.

2. Fair Comment

The Criminal Code of Canada deals with fair comment in section 274, which reads as follows:

> No person shall be deemed to publish a defamatory libel by reason only that he publishes fair comments
> a) upon the public conduct of a person who takes part in public affairs, or
> b) upon a published book or other literary production, or any composition or work of art or performance publicly exhibited, or on any other communication made to the public on any subject, if the comments are confined to criticism thereof.[9]

3. Matters for Which the Criminal Code Provides a Defence Against Defamatory Libel Charges, Presumably on the Grounds of Privilege

In addition to the two defences discussed above, the Criminal Code sets forth certain saving provisions from defamatory libel which correspond to the usual defences in a civil action for libel. Cases in which a person is not deemed to publish a defamatory libel include: publishing proceedings of courts of justice;[10] publishing parliamentary papers;[11] publishing fair reports of parliamentary or judicial proceedings;[12] publishing fair reports of public meetings;[13] publishing matters of public interest for the public benefit;[14] publications invited or necessary in self-defence;[15] answers to inquiries;[16] giving information to persons having a common interest;[17] and publication in good faith for the redress of wrongs.[18]

Other Provisions of the Criminal Code

Secion 280 of the Criminal Code specifies that a person accused of publishing defamatory libel may successfully defend himself by proving that the matter complained of was contained in a paper published by order or under the authority of the Senate or House of Commons or a legislature.[19]

As they are under civil law, newspapers are entitled to certain protections against prosecution under the Criminal Code by virtue of the fact that they fulfill conditions laid down by the Code. One of these conditions is specified in the Code definition of a newspaper. Section 261 defines a ''newspaper'' as

any paper, magazine or periodical containing public news, intelligence or reports of events, or any remarks or observations thereon, printed for sale and published periodically or in parts or numbers at intervals not exceeding thirty-one days between the publication of any two such papers, parts or numbers, and any paper, magazine or periodical printed in order to be dispersed and made public, weekly or more often, or at intervals not exceeding thirty-one days, that contains advertisements exclusively or principally.[20]

Unlike the provincial statutes dealing with libel, the Criminal Code defines "publishing." Section 263 says:

A person publishes a libel when he
(a) exhibits it in public,
(b) causes it to be read or seen, or
(c) shows or delivers it, or causes it to be shown or delivered, with intent that it should be read or seen by the person whom it defames or by any other person.[21]

It is to be noted that the third part of the definition (re "the person whom it defames") conforms to the Halsbury statement that a criminal defamation may be published to the person defamed alone.

The Criminal Code contains valuable protection for newspaper proprietors and sellers of newspapers and books. A proprietor may avoid punishment for publishing defamatory matter if he can prove the matter was inserted in his newspaper without his knowledge and without negligence on his part. If his editor inserts such matter in his paper the publisher may successfully plead that he was not guilty of negligence, provided he can show that he did not give his editor general authority to insert such matter, or that, the nature of the matter having become known, he did not continue to confer such general authority. The relevant section of the Code is 267.[22] Section 268 provides, in similar fashion, that booksellers are not to be held responsible for knowing what their books, magazines, newspapers, "or other thing" contain, and they are not therefore to be considered guilty of publishing a libel unless any of the items complained about habitually contained such matter.[23]

Section 421(2) of the Criminal Code says, "Every proprietor, publisher, editor or other person charged with the publication of a defamatory libel or with conspiracy to publish a defamatory libel in a newspaper shall be dealt with, indicted, tried and punished in the province in which the newspaper is printed."[24] This regulation, with its provision for *conspiracy* to publish, was enacted as a result of the "Babies For Export" trial in 1948.

In keeping with Fox's Libel Act of 1792, the Criminal Code, as do some provincial statutes for civil libel, defines the powers and duties of judge and jury in determining a defamatory libel verdict. Section 281 of the Criminal Code says this:

> Where, on the trial of an indictment for publishing a defamatory libel, a plea of not guilty is pleaded, the jury that is sworn to try the issue may give a general verdict of guilty or not guilty upon the whole matter put in issue upon the indictment, and shall not be required or directed by the judge to find the defendant guilty merely on proof of publication by the defendant of the alleged defamatory libel, and of the sense ascribed thereto in the indictment, but the judge may, in his discretion, give a direction or opinion to the jury on the matter in issue as in other criminal proceedings, and the jury may, on the issue, find a special verdict.[25]

Punishment and Penalties

The Criminal Code deals with the use of defamation as a means of extortion. Section 266 provides the following:

(1) Every one commits an offence who, with intent
    (a) to extort money from any person, or
    (b) to induce a person to confer upon or procure for another person an appointment or office of profit or trust,
  publishes or threatens to publish or offers to abstain from publishing or to prevent the publication of a defamatory libel.
(2) Every one commits an offence who, as the result of the refusal of any person to permit money to be extorted or to confer or procure an appointment or office of profit or trust, publishes or threatens to publish a defamatory libel.[26]

Subsection (3) stipulates that every one who commits an offence under this section is guilty of an indictable offence and is liable to imprisonment for five years.[27]

Section 264 of the Criminal Code rules that:

> Every one who publishes a defamatory libel *that he knows to be false* [italics mine] is guilty of an indictable offence and is liable to imprisonment for five years.[28]

Section 265 of the Code provides that:

Every one who publishes a defamatory libel is guilty of an indictable offence and is liable to imprisonment for two years.[29]

Two Canadian Cases

Defamatory libel prosecutions in Canada have been infrequent. One of these was the "Bankers' Toadies" affair in 1938. (*See Case No. 21*) No Canadian defamatory libel cases were reported between this case and the *Georgia Straight* conviction of 1969. (*See Case No. 22*)

Seditious Libel

The Criminal Code defines seditious libel in terms of intention. Section 60(2) says, "A seditious libel is a libel that expresses a seditious intention."[30] Section 60(4) says, "Without limiting the generality of the meaning of the expression 'seditious intention', every one shall be presumed to have a seditious intention who . . .

   (b) publishes or circulates any writing that advocates the use, without the authority of law, of force as a means of accomplishing governmental change within Canada."[31]

To ensure that the foregoing provisions will not inhibit legitimate debate and legal political action, the Code modifies the prohibitions of Section 60. Section 61 states:

Notwithstanding subsection (4) of section 60, no person shall be deemed to have a seditious intention by reason only that he intends, in good faith,
   (a) to show that Her Majesty has been misled or mistaken in her measures;
   (b) to point out errors or defects in
      (i) the government or constitution of Canada or a province,
      (ii) the Parliament of Canada or the legislature of a province
         OR
      (iii) the administration of justice in Canada,
   (c) to procure, by lawful means, the alteration of any matter of government in Canada, or
   (d) to point out, for the purpose of removal, matters that produce or tend to produce feelings of hostility and ill-will between different classes of persons in Canada.[32]

Punishments for seditious offences may be severe. Section 62 stipulates that "[e]very one who . . . (b) publishes a seditious libel . . . is guilty of an indictable offence and is liable to imprisonment for fourteen years."[33]

Although prosecutions for sedition have not been common and prosecutions for seditious libel have been even more rare, the law has been invoked in times of war and other crisis. Until comparatively recently the test applied in determining seditious offences has been the "Stephen" test. It states:

> A seditious intention is an intention to bring into hatred or contempt, or to excite disaffection against the person of, His Majesty, his heirs or successors, or the government and constitution of the United Kingdom, as by law established, or either House of Parliament, or the administration of justice, or to excite His Majesty's subjects to attempt otherwise than by lawful means, the alteration of any matter in Church or State by law established, or to incite any person to commit any crime in disturbance of the peace, or to raise discontent or disaffection amongst His Majesty's subjects, or to promote feelings of ill-will and hostility between different classes of such subjects.[34]

The "Stephen Test" was used in five out of six reported cases in Western Canada during the First World War. It was also applied in *Duval* v. *R*,[35] a Jehovah Witness prosecution in 1938. However, the Quebec's "Burning Hate" case has caused the Stephen definition to be superseded by a far more liberal test. It was held by all justices except the chief justice that, for there to be sedition, not only must the writings complained about raise discontent or disaffection among subjects or provoke ill-will or hostility between different classes, but it must be intended to produce disturbance or resistance to established authority.(*See Case No. 23*)

The newer test, popularly called the Boucher test, is radically different from the test previously used to establish seditious intention. It makes conviction far less likely than previously was the case. This is because of the extreme difficulty of establishing beyond reasonable doubt an intention to incite to rebellion. As D. A. Schmeiser has said, "There is a tremendous gap between proving such an intent and proving an intent to bring the government or administration of justice into hatred or contempt or to create hostility between different classes. The Boucher case overrules most of the previous Canadian cases . . ."[36]

Blasphemous Libel

The law of blasphemous libel is dormant in Canada today. In its original concept it was taken to mean the defaming of God. According to William H. Wickwar, during the 1819-32 period in England, "the essence of blasphemous libel came to consist in its offence 'against the peace of our Lord the King, his crown and dignity,' more than its being 'to the high displeasure of Almighty God, to the great scandal of the Christian religion, and to the evil example of all others,' all of which tendencies were alleged in indictments."[37] In the momentous days when Richard Carlile was fighting his court battles for press freedom in England, the charge was often that of blasphemous libel because, according to Wickwar, "Considering the state of London opinion at that time there can be no doubt that blasphemous libel was the charge most likely to obtain a conviction."[38]

Thomas Dawson points out that, "Even up to the latter part of the nineteenth century it was held by Mr. Justice Stephen . . . that 'a denial of the truth of Christianity in general or in the existence of God, whether the terms of such publication are decent or otherwise,' was a criminal offence."[39] A different view of the law of blasphemy came to prevail after 1883 when Lord Chief Justice Coleridge directed the jury in *R.* v. *Ramsay and Foote* that "if the decencies of controversy are observed, even the fundamentals of religion may be attacked without a person being guilty of blasphemous libel."[40] The Chief Justice adopted the definition found in *Starkie on Libel* that, "The law visits not the honest errors, but the malice of mankind. A wilful intention to pervert, insult, and mislead others, by means of licentious and contumelious abuse applied to sacred objects, or by wilful misrepresentations or wilful sophistry, calculated to mislead the ignorant and unwary, is the criterion and test of guilt."[41]

The Criminal Code of Canada does not define blasphemous libel. Section 260(2) says, "It is a question of fact whether or not any matter that is published is a blasphemous libel."[42] The Code preserves the spirit of the Coleridge *dictum*. Section 260(3) provides that "No person shall be convicted of an offence under this section for expressing in good faith and in decent language, or attempting to establish by argument used in good faith and conveyed in decent language, an opinion upon a religious subject."[43] Section 260(1) lays down that "Everyone who publishes a blasphemous libel is guilty of an indictable offence and is liable to imprisonment for two years."[44]

In 1927 E. J. Murphy wrote an Annotation entitled "Blasphemy" in *Canadian Criminal Cases*.[45] In it he pointed out that the law of blasphemy had slept in obscurity in Canada, and prior to the case which prompted the Annotation only two prosecutions had taken place under it: *R. v. Pelletier* and *R. v. Kinler*. The case, *R. v. Sterry*, was unreported but Murphy commented on it quite extensively. (*See Case No. 24*) No further Canadian blasphemous libel prosecution occurred until *R. v. Rahard*. (*See Case No. 25*)

Chapter VII

Obscenity and Censorship

The law finds few concepts more difficult to deal with than the concept of obscenity. This is because public and private attitudes to the subject reflect so much uncertainty and disagreement. Reactions to the question vary between the widest extremes. For this reason, before an attempt is made to set down and discuss the law of obscenity, it is perhaps helpful to consider the climate and milieu within which the law is enacted and applied.

The Background Attitudes Towards Obscenity

In the realm of moral censorship there are many gradations of opinion between the extremes of deeply-ingrained Comstockery and complete permissiveness. Perhaps the ultimate in Comstockery occurred when some censorious people refused to allow books written by male authors to be placed on bookshelves beside books written by female authors. The term "Comstockery" itself derives form the activities of Anthony Comstock, a reformer spokesman for the New York Society for the Suppression of Vice. In the 1870's he won a dubious glory by helping to create laws which banned books, objects of art, stage plays and subsequently motion pictures. One of the more notable feat of his followers was to contribute in spectacular fashion to the fame of "September Morn," a previously obscure painting which depicted an innocently-naked and nymph-like girl. After an enterprising press agent had hired some children to grimace at the painting and make remarks about it, the predictable reaction of the Comstockians helped to bring popularity and a fortune to the painter.

By contrast, the opposite in permissiveness is suggested ironically by an Art Buchwald article, "The Antipornographers."[1] In it, Malcolm McMoral, author of the first antipornographic novel, *A Kiss on the Cheek*, tells his interviewer, "It's true that the clean novel is considered avant-garde at the moment, but that doesn't mean it's wrong. Someday there will be so many clean books on the market that no one will be shocked any more."

The commonest argument against obscenity and for censorship may perhaps be typified by Pamela Hansford Johnson's *On Iniquity*. It is an account of the ghastly torture and murder of three children on the Midland Moors of England, for which Ian Brady and his mistress, Myra Hindley, were convicted in 1967. One main thesis of the book is that the increase in crimes of sex and violence is largely attributable to obscenity, pornography and sadism in books, films and television. It is a belief that enjoys wide currency.

One thought-provoking line of reasoning, put forth by a writer friend whose writing is neither "dirty" nor prissily afraid of sex, focuses on the "skin" magazines, the *Playboy* imitators that claim so much space on tobacco-store news stands. He observes that the almost exclusive preoccupation of such periodicals is with woman's body, particularly the erogenous areas. He feels that, to the male voyeur who obsessively reads and looks at such publications, woman is made into an "object," the sharer of the sex act and nothing more. "Literature" of this sort helps to implant the conviction that woman is not a person,[2] hardly a human being—only an organ of sex, designed for the gratification of the man who pays his $1.00 for the magazine or who browses at the corner news stand. What happens, according to my friend, is that a *part* of a woman has, for the observer, become the *whole* woman. But this sort of distortion—the confusing of the part with the whole—is the essence of one form of insanity. In extreme form it can mean the sick mind of the madman. The contention is that, through pandering to the prurient interest of the sensualist, that which is obscene can convert a mentally unhealthy but otherwise harmless mind into the mind of the psychopath, a disaster both for the person who becomes thus unbalanced and for the society endangered by his violent acts. According to such a theory pornography and obscenity are the fatal catalysts of the tragic change. The theory is one to which the *Hicklin Test* (to be discussed later), with its applicability to the lowest common denominator of society, would subscribe.

A variant on the theme just considered has been enunciated by Sarel Eimerl. He has said:

These days the worst harm is inflicted by dirty books which give the impression that all women are promiscuous and orgies commonplace. This is absolute nonsense, and I have long suspected that it is propagated by men who are ugly, charmless, and probably virginal, and who are using pornography not only to make money, but also, out of revenge, to degrade other men to their own level of frustration.[3]

A novel objection to obscenity also directs attention to man's attitude towards women. It has been put forward by Hugh MacLennan. Of the growth of published obscenity the Canadian novelist has said:

This strikes me as a significant symptom of a probable change toward authoritarianism. We are now living in an extremely permissive (matrist) society which is manifestly corrupt, intelligent, willing to experiment with anything, luxurious and indifferent to discipline as it used to be understood.

It was like this in the late Middle Ages when the Church was permissive in everything except heresy and the collection of tithes—thus, in a modern state, everything is allowed except treason and non-payment of taxes. When the puritans (who were patrists) attacked the late Medieval Church, they used personal pornography—which is the surest way of degrading women. This is not healthy bawdry; it is absolute hostility and aggression. I therefore believe that the deluge of pornography now flooding the market is a symptom of a trend toward a return to patrist authoritarianism.[4]

The rationale for the permissive approach to obscenity and pornography is to be discerned in the libertarian arguments for freedom generally. Milton's *Areopagitica* and Mill's *Essay On Liberty* are only two of many writings relevant to the problem. The philosophical basis for permissiveness in matters involving obscenity is part and parcel of the liberals' wider argument for the unrestricted clash and interplay of opinion in the free marketplace of ideas. That argument is too well known to require repetition here. It needs only to be added that to the literature of press freedom that the formal and systematic documents of Milton and Mill represent, supporters of the widely tolerant approach have joined their own comments about the anomalies and irrationalities of moral censorship.

To arrive at an attitude towards obscenity and censorship that is personally acceptable it is perhaps instructive to contrast the approach of the Comstockians with that of the "pornographers." The Comstockians say that there is a small part of life which is "bad," unfit to be depicted; this "evil" segment must be cut out of the picture and only the good and wholesome part may be shown. By contrast, the "pornographers" say that such an expurgated version falsifies life, that reality is not reality unless it includes the "basic," carnal facts of life. Apparently to redress the balance, their response has been to focus attention on what the Comstockians have rejected and to ignore the larger and more innocent body of experience which makes up life and which the Comstockians consider to be alone fit to be depicted.[5] Perhaps it is not too sententious to say that each response is untrue to reality, because each fails to consider life as a whole. It seems self-evident that both "decent" and "indecent" must be part of the picture, but each in its proper and natural proportion.

All of which leaves unsettled the debate over obscenity and censorship. Such a debate seems unlikely to be settled as long as there is such a dearth of objective data concerning the effects of obscene or indecent material. However, four studies in this area, while not conclusive, do deserve mention.

One of these was made in Canada in 1952 by the special Senate Committee on Salacious and Indecent Literature.[6] The Committee found that the public shared with the courts concern about literature that (1) might produce lewd thoughts, or (2) might induce overt anti-social conduct, or (3) might generally affect the readers' moral standards and those of society, or (4) might shock or disgust those who might read the material. The testimony which was received showed that the public was also interested in matters not considered in the various Canadian court decisions. Fear was also expressed that objectionable material might have a harmful effect (5) particularly upon the personality and character of young people, and that (6) such matter would give young people a distorted view of life generally and the nature of man and his relations with the opposite sex especially.

Another study of obscenity and pornography was American. It was made by the nineteen-member Commission on Obscenity and Pornography which reported in 1970. Its chairman was William B. Lockhart. By its terms of reference the Commission was required to perform four tasks:

(1) . . . to analyze the laws pertaining to the control of obscenity and pornography; and to evaluate and recommend definitions of obscenity and pornogrpahy;

(2) to ascertain the methods employed in the distribution of obscene and pornographic materials and to explore the volume of traffic in such materials;

(3) to study the effect of obscenity and pornography upon the public, and particularly minors, and its relationship to crime and other antisocial behavior; and

(4) to recommend such legislative, administrative, or other advisable and appropriate action as the Commission deems necessary to regulate effectively the flow of such traffic, without in any way interfering with constitutional rights.[7]

The *Report* was replete with tables of which "Opinions of Sex Educators About Erotic Materials,"[8] "Sex Attitudes and Exposure to Erotica, Age and Church Attendance,"[9] and "Percent Reporting Adolescent Exposure of Photographic Depiction of Coitus"[10] may be taken as representative. Despite the thoroughness of its statistical approach, the labors of the panels "fail[ed] to establish a meaningful causal relationship or even significant correlation between exposure to erotica and immediate or delayed antisocial behavior among adults.''[11]

Of the nineteen commissioners, one resigned before the Commission made its report. Twelve of the reporting members recommended that ''Federal, state and local legislation prohibiting the sale, exhibition and distribution of sexual materials to consenting adults should be repealed.''[12] Five members dissented. Charles H. Keating Jr., the only member appointed to the Commission by President Nixon and one of the commissioners most forthright in his advocacy of censorship, abstained. Two of the dissenters, Rabbi Irving Lehrman and Mrs. Cathryn Spelts, subscribed however to the bulk of the majority report, whereas Professors Otto N. Larsen and Marvin E. Wolfgang (numbered among the twelve supporting the major recommendation) wished to go farther than the majority did in its finding.

Three other recommendations of the Commissioners' majority report were as follows: that juveniles should be protected from pornography;[13] that blatantly sexual public displays should be prohibited and that Congress should impose tougher regulations on sex matter sent unsolicited through the mails;[14] and that a massive sex education program be launched immediately to overcome ''fear and prejudice'' and to give people of all ages a healthier attitude towards sex.[15]

The recommendations of the Lockhart Commission have not been implemented. In predicting that they would not be, Clive Barnes theorized that when Congress decided the traffic in obscenity and pornography to be ''a matter of national concern'' it felt that it had discovered an issue which might be the subject of popular legislation. He calls the Commission ''unusual in that it tells Congress something that Congress did not expect to hear.''[16] The Commission said, in effect, that traffic in obscenity and pornography was not a matter of national concern. Thereupon it would seem that Congress, not finding the issue a popular election issue, lost interest in the subject.

The corresponding British study was that of the Longford Committee on Pornography which reported in 1972.[17] It was under the chairmanship of the Earl of Longford and its membership was made up of fifty distinguished public figures and experts. Its findings were far less liberal than those of the American Lockhart Commission. The British Study Group, as it was sometimes called, made generally anti-obscenity recommendations in the areas of broadcasting, cinemas and theatres, books, magazines and newspapers, advertising, sex education and the legal field.

In January 1973 the Prohibited and Regulated Conduct Project published for the Canadian Law Reform Commission a preliminary study on obscenity.[18] The major part of that publication was a thoughtfully analytical study paper prepared by Richard G. Fox, associate professor, Centre of Criminology and Faculty of Law, University of Toronto. Its considerable value was not to provide empirical data but to isolate and classify the difficult sub-problems that inhere in the complex question of obscenity. By way of a preface the Prohibited and Regulated Project indicated in tentative fashion the direction of its thinking when it said:

> . . . the Project group believes that, where adults are concerned, the possession, sale and distribution of "sexually explicit material" should no longer be penalized.[19]
> The Project believes that the prohibition of obscene matter should be maintained and applied strictly where children are concerned.[20]
> The project believes that the flood of advertising and public display of sexual material should be eliminated so that persons who have no interest in such material and do not want access to it will be protected from the nuisance that it represents.[21]

All four studies just glanced at fail to make definitive judgments, based on quantified data, about the many factors which are ingredients of the larger obscenity question. But they do suggest how difficult are the problems that the question of obscenity poses. Indeed, something of the frustration felt by jurists who have had to wrestle with obscenity cases was suggested by Judge Struble in an Ohio trial in 1948. He said the following:

> Obscenity is not a legal term. It cannot be defined so that it means the same thing to all people, all the time, everywhere. Obscenity is very much a figment of the imagination.[22]

The Basic Canadian Law

Figment of the imagination or not, obscenity has long been regarded as a legal concept. The law has wrestled with that concept with indifferent success for many years. As has been pointed out, today there are few areas which the law deals with in less satisfactory fashion.

Section 159(8) and the Hicklin Test

Until recent times Canada has relied on the common law in its dealings with obscenity. Even in 1892, when section 179 of the Criminal Code was enacted to deal with obscene publications, the Code did not define "obscene," considering that the sense conveyed by the expression itself was sufficient for purposes of the law. Section 179 made it an indictable offence to offer or expose any obscene book or printed matter for public sale. Lacking a definition of obscenity, the judges were left without any uniform standards to apply in administering this part of the Code. In their reliance on common rather than statute law, they quickly came to depend on the *Hicklin Test,* an 1868 definition enunciated by Chief Justice Cockburn of England in the *Queen* v. *Hicklin.*[23] Cockburn's stipulation was that "the test of obscenity is this, whether the tendency of the matter charged as obscenity is to deprave and corrupt those whose minds are open to such immoral influences and into whose hands a publication of this sort may fall."

Ever since it was first formulated, there have been many disagreements with the *Hicklin Test.*[24] One objection is that the test is too subjective, too speculative. It requires the judge to assess the corrupting and depraving effect of the material complained of upon a group of unknown readers. A second stricture is that the test makes the basis of censorship the "lowest common denominator" of the readership. Thus, because adolescent or emotionally unstable persons may get hold of the material complained of, that material is denied to more mature, stable and discriminating people. A third complaint is that the Hicklin criteria, through their failure to deal with the question, permit of the "isolated passage" test for obscenity, as was the case with the early American interpretation of the Hicklin Rule. This test seems to derive from the questionable "I-don't-need-to-eat-the-whole-egg-to-know-that-it-is-rotten" analogy. The "isolated passage" test takes a part of a work out of context and judges it without regard to the literary, artistic or moral purpose of the work and to its overall impact. Certainly the rigid application of the *Hicklin Test* has inhibited freedom of speech and expression and has imposed unnatural restraints on literary creation.

It was to give greater precision to the law and to overcome the objectionable features of the *Hicklin Test* that Justice Minister Davie Fulton introduced in 1959 the Criminal Code amendment which was to become Section 150(8), and which was renumbered Section 159(8) in the 1970 Criminal Code revision. The change was motivated by what Fulton called the "pulp trash" which was appearing on Canadian news-stands in vastly increased quantities following the Second World War. He did not agree with those who believed that, when properly applied, the existing law and the Hicklin criteria were adequate to deal with the problem. Instead he sought a definition which, as he said, would allow Canadian judges to make their decisions with "speed and certainty" by applying simple objective tests in addition to the vague subjective test which had formerly been the only one available. What he hoped to do was to make it possible to distinguish easily between such "pulp trash" and works of genuine literary, artistic or scientific merit.

The result was subsection 8 of Section 150 (now Section 159), which said that:

> For the purposes of this Act, any publication a dominant characteristic of which is the undue exploitation of sex, or of sex, and one or more of the following subjects, namely, crime, horror, cruelty and violence, shall be deemed to be obscene.[25]

The new subsection was to be applied in conjunction with Section 150 (renumbered 159 in 1970), subsection 1(a), and subsection 2(a) which had been placed on the statute books at a much earlier date. Subsection 1(a) reads:

> Every one commits an offence who
> (a) makes, prints, publishes, distributes, circulates, or has in his possession for the purposes of publication, distribution or circulation any obscene written matter, picture, model, phonograph record or other thing whatsoever.[26]

Subsection 2(a) reads:

> Every one commits an offence who knowingly, without lawful justification or excuse,
> (a) sells, exposes to public view or has in his possession for such a purpose any obscene written matter, picture, model, phonograph record or other thing whatsoever.[27]

The change in the law made by the addition of subsection 8 was not greeted with unanimous approval. Many critics found the Fulton amendment just as vague as the *Hicklin Test*. It was pointed out that the phrases "undue exploitation" and "dominant characteristic" are so subjective that moral censorship becomes a highly personal matter. It was contended that the law lends itself to abuse by narrow and bigotted people. Some critics maintained that, although a case could be made for linking sex and violence in the definition, it was a grievous error to make sex so central to that definition.

But the most serious shortcoming of the new law was that it did not make clear whether the Fulton amendment was intended to replace the *Hicklin Test* or merely to supplement it. The evidence of House of Commons debates and of Mr. Fulton's own statements is that it was the second alternative which was proposed. The Justice Minister thought of the new section as a simple, easily-applied formula for dealing with cheap, sex-oriented, meritless news-stand material, while still reserving the *Hicklin Test* for assessing publications that had some redeeming features.

But the legislators did not translate their intention into law. The uncertainty they created was resolved by the *Lady Chatterley's Lover* and subsequent court decisions. The result was contrary to what Justice Minister Fulton had intended. In the Lady Chatterley case (*See Case No. 26*) five justices found the novel not to be obscene, and four held it to be obscene. Professor Charles neatly points up the lack of unanimity of the court:

> How was the novel D. H. Lawrence judged by the court? Of the majority, Cartwright J., Judson J., Martland J., and Abbott J., judged the book by applying section 150(8) [original numbering] exclusively while Mr. Justice Ritchie applied both the *Hicklin* test and the statutory test. Of the minority, Justices Kerwin, Taschereau and Locke applied 150(8) exclusively and Mr. Justice Fauteaux applied both the *Hicklin* test and the statutory definition. Of the two justices who applied the *Hicklin* test, one found the book obscene while the other did not. Of those who applied the statutory definition, four found the book obscene and five did not.[28]

Other judgments found the Fulton amendment to be exhaustive and rejected the *Hicklin* test. One such was the Fanny Hill case, *Regina* v. *C. Coles Co. Ltd.* (*See Case No. 27*) Others which followed the *Lady Chatterley* precedent and strengthened support for the exclusivity of the statutory definition were *Regina* v. *Cameron* (*See Case No. 28*) *Regina* v. *Duthie Books Ltd.* (*See Case No. 29*), *Regina* v. *Salida* (*See Case No. 30*) and *Regina* v. *McLeod and Georgia Straight Publishing Ltd.* (*See Case No. 31*)

Of the competing merits of *Hicklin* and the statutory definition, *Martin's Annual Criminal Code, 1972* said:

> It is possible that the word "undue" can only be interpreted by reference to some test such as that used in *R.* v. *Hicklin*, but the better view seems to be that the test for obscenity as set out in *R.* v. *Hicklin* has now been entirely superseded by s 159(8).[29]

Professor Charles comments:

> Instead of having two tests for use, one of which would be a strict, simple and objective test of fact involving little subjective opinion, we find ourselves with one test, a statutory test, moulded by the

judiciary until it presents a far more liberal test than the common law rule it was intended to supplement. Not a very encouraging example of the effectiveness of the legal process as a method of social control.[30]

Crime Comics Legislation: Section 159, s. 1(b), and s. 7.

Another law relevant to the question of the press and morals (if not of obscenity directly) is that dealing with Crime Comics. The member of parliament associated with this legislation, as he was to be with the 1959 amendment just discussed, was the Hon. Davie Fulton. In this instance he was in opposition when he achieved the considerable feat of moving a private member's bill and seeing it made law. The result, enacted in 1955, was an addition to subsection 1, and a new subsection 7 of Section 150(now Section 159) of the Criminal Code.

Subsection 7 defines a crime comic as ''any magazine, periodical or book which exclusively or substantially comprises matter depicting pictorially (a) the commission of crimes, real or fictitious, or (b) events connected with the commission of crimes, real or fictitious, whether occurring before or after the commission of the crime.''[31]

It seems fair to observe that the Crime Comics legislation has been no more satisfactory than has been the new definition of obscenity. The defects of the Crime Comics legislation are described by D. A. Schmeiser in *Civil Liberties in Canada*.[32]

Section 160

At the same time as the 1959 Fulton amendment was put on the statute books supposedly as an alternative to, but in fact as a replacement for, the *Hicklin Test*, parliament enacted laws which outlined the legal procedure for dealing with charges involving obscenity and Crime Comics. The new legislation was Section 150A of the Criminal Code, renumbered 160 in the 1970 revision. This provided what is known as an *''in rem''* procedure, a procedure brought not against the individual, but against the publication itself. Model for the amendment was the United Kingdom's Obscene Publications Act of 1957.

It seems worthwhile to outline the main provisions of the Canadian legislation.

(a) A judge who is satisfied by information on oath that there are reasonable grounds for believing that any publication, copies of which are kept for sale or distribution in premises within the jurisdiction of the court, is obscene or a crime comic, shall issue a warrant under his hand authorizing seizure of the copies.

(2) Within seven days of the issue of the warrant, the judge shall issue a summons to the occupier of the premises requiring him to appear before the court and show cause why the matter should not be forfeited to Her Majesty.

(3) The owner and the author of the matter seized and alleged to be obscene or a crime comic may appear and be represented in the proceedings in order for the forfeiture of the said matter.

(4) If the court is satisfied that the publication is obscene or a crime comic, it shall make an order declaring the matter forfeited to Her Majesty in the right of the province in which the proceedings take place, for disposal as the Attorney General may direct.

(5) If the court is not satisfied that the publication is obscene or a crime comic, it shall order that the matter be restored to the person from whom it was seized forthwith after the time for final appeal has expired.[33]

One feature of Section 160 for which it has been praised is that its provisions prevent vendors of a book from being found guilty "retroactively" of a crime just because a book or periodical is ruled to be obscene. The vendor may be found guilty of a criminal act only if he persists in selling or offering it for sale after the court warrant against the book or periodical has been issued and unless and until a court order has restored it to the vendor.

One implication of Section 160 that has been criticized rather than praised is that, unless the matter is appealed to higher courts, the verdict of a single judge may determine whether Canadians all across Canada may read a certain book or periodical. A case in point was the Canadian status of *Fanny Hill* which needed a favorable verdict of the Ontario Court of Appeal to restore it to circulation after it had been withdrawn in 1964.[34]

Some Judicial Consequences of the Changed Obscenity Law

In addition to the Criminal Code sections 159(8) and 160, there is other Canadian legislation which has been enacted to deal with obscenity. Because this is perhaps less consequential than the basic law just discussed, it is perhaps better left until later in this chapter after the effects of the 1959 legislative changes have been considered.

When section 159(8) superseded the *Hicklin Test*, the question of "undue exploitation" and (although this did not give rise to so much judicial uncertainty) "dominant tendency" replaced "the tendency to corrupt and deprave" as subjects of judicial opinion. The "isolated passage" test lost its legal validity. A determination of "undue exploitation'' under the Fulton amendment opened up to Canadian jurisprudence such concepts as "shock and disgust," "community standards," "human measuring stick," "evidence of artistic and literary merit," and "motives and intentions" of the writer or artist.

Isolated Passage Test

A story is told about the meddling woman who complained that a male neighbor was offending her sense of decency by undressing near his uncurtained window. A policeman investigated her complaint. "But madam," he said, "from your house you cannot see anyone standing beside that window." "Oh yes you can," she said. "If I put this chair under my bathroom window and stand tiptoe on the chair, I can see him as plain as anything."

This sort of out-of-context viewing is comparable to the "isolated passage" test which was for a long time habitually applied in assessing obscenity. Asking themselves, "Is the publication to be judged as a whole, that is, by its dominant effect, or is it to be judged by reference to isolated passages?" jurists have adopted the second alternative. With minor exceptions[35] it was not until the statutory definition replaced the *Hicklin Test* that the "isolated passage" approach was abandoned in Canada. In the United States the practice was changed by Judge John M. Woolsey in the famous *Ulysses* decision of December 6, 1933. His verdict was affirmed in 1934 by higher court decision, for which Justice Augustus N. Hand wrote the more important parts of the judgment:

> That numerous long passages in *Ulysses* contain matter that is obscene under any fair definition of the word cannot be gainsaid; yet these are relevant to the purpose of depicting the thoughts of the characters and are introduced to give meaning to the whole, rather than to promote lust or to portray filth for its own sake . . . The book as a whole is not pornographic, and, while in not a few spots it is coarse, blasphemous and obscene, it does not, in our opinion, tend to promote lust. The erotic passages are submerged in the book as a whole and have little resultant effect . . .
>
> . . . The question in each case is whether a publication taken as a whole has a libidinous effect. The book before us has such portentous length, is written with such evident truthfulness in its depiction of certain types of humanity, and is so little erotic in its result, that it does not fall within the forbidden class.
>
> It is true that the motive of an author to promote good morals is not the test of whether a book is obscene, and it may also be true that the applicability of the statute does not depend on the persons to whom

the publication is likely to be distributed . . . We believe that the proper test of whether a given book is obscene is its dominant effect. In applying this test, relevancy of the objectionable parts to the theme, the established reputation of the work in the estimation of approved critics, if the book is modern, and the verdict of the past, if it ancient, are persuasive pieces of evidence; for works of art are not likely to sustain a high position with no better warrant for their existence than their obscene content.[36]

Inclusion of the phrase "dominant characteristic" in Section 159(8) of the Criminal Code makes acknowledgment of the Justice Hand interpretation. But the layman, unlike the law professional, has not completely eliminated from his thinking the "isolated passage" approach to the obscenity question. Thus, although the late Honorable George Nowlan was deservedly praised for his refusal to use his office as Minister of Revenue to make him a censor of imported books,[37] he was reputed by the newspapers to have said, "I only have to read a chapter or a few pages to judge whether a book is obscene or not."

Generally speaking, Canadian jurists have, since 1959, come to accept the concept of the "work as a whole" in adjudicating obscenity, even though they have not always been explicit in rejecting the "isolated passage" test. Often their approach to the question has been implicit in the overall manner in which they have formulated their decisions. However, some have made positive pronouncements as part of their *ratio decidendi* or *obiter dicta*. In the *Lady Chatterley's Lover* case, for example, Mr. Justice Judson said:

No reader can find a dominant characteristic on a consideration of isolated passages and isolated words. Under this definition the book now must be taken as a whole. It is not the particular passages and words in a certain context that are before the Court for judgment but the book as a complete work. The question is whether the book as a whole is obscene, not whether certain passages and certain words, part of a larger work, are obscene.[38]

Mr. Justice Ritchie supported Mr. Justice Judson.[39] It is interesting to note that in *Regina* v. *Dominion News Gifts (1962) Ltd.* Mr. Justice Freedman said of the two magazines on trial: "Viewing both magazines as a whole I am unable to say they are obscene" whereas Mr. Justice Monnin said: "Strip the publications of the references to sex and sex matters and there is hardly anything salable left in them." (*See Case No. 32*)

"The book should be viewed as a whole to assess the purpose of the author—whether it was a serious purpose, or a base purpose" was the opinion of Chief Justice Porter in the *Fanny Hill* judgment.[40] "I tested my reaction to them by trying to see each of them whole" said Mr. Justice Laskin in describing how he tried to assess the pictures in the Cameron Art Gallery case.[41] Other cases which took judicial notice of the principle of "considering the work as a whole" were *Regina* v. *Duthie Books Ltd.*[42], *Regina* v. *McLeod and Georgia Straight Publishing Ltd.*[43], and *Regina* v. *O'Reilly and Four Others.* (*See Case No. 33*)

Dominant Characteristic

The element of the new legal definition which militated against the "isolated passage" approach was "dominant characteristic." "Whether undue exploitation of sex has been a dominant characteristic of the matter being adjudged has not," according to W. H. Charles, "troubled the courts greatly."[44]

In reaching his *Lady Chatterley* decision Chief Justice Kerwin considered and rejected the claim that the dominant characteristic was "to show the evils of industrialism in England and the damage it does to the human soul."[45] Mr. Justice Taschereau, however, pointed out that "[t]he law says *a* dominant and not *the* dominant characteristic."[46] Similarly Mr. Justice Fauteux said, "The expression 'a dominant characteristic' does not have a meaning equating to that of the expression 'the dominant characteristic'."[47] Presumably any of the justices might have accepted the contention that a dominant characteristic of *Lady Chatterley's Lover* was to show the evils of industrialism and its damaging effect on the human soul, and still have ruled the book to be obscene if he had found *another* dominant characteristic to be the "undue exploitation of sex." As Mr. Justice Fauteux said, "Thus construed, the subsection still has scope to bar the defence based on the contention that only *the* predominant characteristic of the publication is to be considered."[48] In point of fact, all three justices did find *Lady Chatterley* to be obscene, and did find a dominant characteristic to be the undue exploitation of sex.

Undue Exploitation

The question of what constitutes undue exploitation, as W. H. Charles points out, has proved to be of greater difficulty to the courts than has the question of dominant characteristic.[49] "The phrase 'undue exploitation' is not self-explanatory and does not indicate the standard by which the undueness is to be measured."[50]

Members of the judiciary have offered definitions during the course of Canadian trials and appeal cases. Mr. Justice Taschereau has said, " 'Undue' in the ordinary English language means of course 'unreasonable,' 'unjustifiable.' It conveys the idea that what is said goes beyond what is appropriate or necessary to prove the proposition that one endeavours to demonstrate to the public."[51] Mr. Justice Fauteux resorts to the *Shorter English Dictionary*, where he finds "undue" defined as follows:

> Not appropriate or suitable; improper, unreasonable. Unjustifiable, illegal. Going beyond what is appropriate, warranted or natural; excessive

and "exploitation" as:

> The action of turning to account; the action of utilizing for selfish purposes.[52]

Of the definitions, he says:

> Read together, the first qualifying the second, these words indicate that Parliament recognizes that, within some limits, exploitation of sex in a publication is by no means illegal and never was indeed so considered. Common in literature, moving pictures and other forms of entertainment, and even in commercial publications, exploitation of sex, within or beyond these limits, would entirely be banned by s.s.(8) were it not for the presence of the word "undue" in the provision. The prevention of such a result is truly the intended purpose and purport of the word. That this may well be its true significance is suggested by its otherwise unbounded vagueness and consequential ineffectiveness to indicate *per se* with any degree of the certainty required in criminal matters, the limits beyond which exploitation of sex in a publication is prohibited. On this view "undue" is synonymous to "illegal," one of the dictionary meanings ascribed thereto, and one then must and only has to refer to the other provisions of s. 150 [now s. 159], which exhaustively states the substantive law of obscenity, to ascertain the limits beyond which exploitation of sex in a publication becomes illegal.[53]

Mr. Justice Judson, whose *Lady Chatterley's Lover* decision was opposite to that of Justices Taschereau and Fauteux, agreed that "[t]he use of the word 'undue' recognizes that some exploitation of the theme is a common occurrence,"[54] but added, "What I think is aimed at is excessive emphasis on the theme for a base purpose. But I do not think that there is undue exploitation if there is no more emphasis on the theme than is required in the serious treatment of a novel with honesty and uprightness. That the work under attack is a serious work of fiction is to me beyond question. It has none of the characteristics that are so often described in judgments dealing with obscenity—dirt for dirt's sake, the leer of the sensualist, depravity in the minds of an author with an obsession for dirt, pornography, an appeal to a prurient interest, etc.''[55]

In *Regina* v. *Dominion News & Gifts (1962) Ltd.* Mr. Justice Schultz said of an article which he characterized as "using dirt for dirt's sake" that "[i]t would be difficult to find a more obvious instance of undue exploitation of sex.''[56]

In *Regina* v. *C. Coles Co. Ltd.* Mr. Justice Roach associated a definition of "sex" with definitions of "undue" and "exploitation" when he said:

> Sex means simply the division of the human species into male and female. It includes the physical differences between male and female relative to the reproductive faculties of each and the phenomena consequent upon that division.
>
> *Exploitation* of sex simply means the utilization of sex as an element in the composition of the written matter.
>
> *Undue* means not agreeable to a standard, excessive, immoderate, inordinate.[57]

In the same case Chief Justice Porter (Justices Gibson and MacKay concurring) asserted, "The test of 'undueness' is objective and requires consideration of a number of factors.''[58] What these factors might be will be discussed later in this chapter.

Delivering the judgment of the Court, Mr. Justice Bull, in *Regina* v. *Duthie Books Ltd.*, related exploitation to baseness when he said:

> To my mind it is equally "base" to treat sex in a vulgar, repulsive and ugly manner for the purpose of encouraging people to think of it and treat it as something less than beautiful and normal, and to sweep it from one's consciousness and under the rug. I am convinced that an exploiting purpose to bestialize and vilify sex is as base as to use it as an aphrodisiac or aid to pruriency.''[59]

Other Canadian judgments have also made baseness a criterion of undue exploitation.

There has been some disposition to equate the "undueness" of exploitation which is a criterion of the obscenity definition with the financial gain which may be made by selling obscene material. But in *Regina* v. *Prairie Schooner News Ltd. and Powers* (*See Case No. 34*),

Manitoba Appeal Court Justice Freedman characterized as erroneous "the learned trial Judge's view . . . that the phrase 'undue exploitation of sex' meant exploitation in the economic sense, that is to say exploitation for profit."[60] Mr. Justice Dickson, now a Supreme Court of Canada justice, observed:

> In the early part of his judgment the Judge adopted the definition of "exploitation" contained in the *American College Dictionary*, "utilization for profit, selfish utilization" and concluded that which is forbidden is the use of sex for the excessive and selfish purpose of profit. He held that the appellants were guilty of making profits out of sex, and in the result found them guilty. The Judge's finding in this respect was, with respect, in error . . . There is nothing in the authorities to support the interpretation placed on the phrase 'undue exploitation' by the Judge.[61]

"Shock and disgust" versus "corrupt and deprave."

When the statutory definition of obscenity replaced the *Hicklin Test*, it shifted the emphasis from the "tendency to corrupt and deprave" to the potential of the offensive material to "shock and disgust." Whether a work or action shocks or disgusts has been taken as one of the determinants of "undue exploitation" as a "dominant characteristic."

It seems useful, at this point, to try to reconstruct, albeit a little speculatively, what reasonably seems to have been the thinking of some of the legislators when they enacted the Fulton amendment. This may be done in terms of "corrupt and deprave" and "shock and disgust." We may theorize that the formulators and supporters of the new subsection (8) felt that the existing test was too lenient when it judged the plethora of "pulp trash" by its tendency to corrupt and deprave. Now, under the new law, just so long as it shocked and disgusted (shocked whom they did not say), it would be adjudged obscene. It didn't need to tend to corrupt and deprave. More meritorious material—*Ulysses, Lady Chatterley's Lover* and the like—could still shock and disgust without being declared obscene. It was only when that more worthwhile material had a tendency to corrupt and deprave that it exceeded allowable limits. Unexpectedly, of course, Canadian courts have made "undue exploitation" as a "dominant tendency" with its implication of "shock and disgust" the test of *both* types of material being assessed. Perhaps even more unexpectedly, as W. H. Charles has explained,[62] what was intended to be a test more severe than the *Hicklin* rule has been converted, by judicial decision, into a more lenient test. (How this has occurred is indicated later in this chapter in the consideration of "Human Measuring Stick," "Community Standards," "Evidence of Merit" and "Motive and Intention.")

Several legal decisions subsequent to 1959 have taken account of whether material alleged to be obscene is shocking and disgusting. Mr. Justice Taschereau observed of *Lady Chatterley's Lover* that, "Nobody would seriously think that the novel could be shown on television or that any respectable publisher would make available to the public in a newspaper or a magazine the complete story of 'Lady Chatterley's Lover' without shocking the feelings of normal citizens."[63] Justice Fauteux found the meaning of "obscenity" to be expanded to include a publication a dominant characteristic of which is exploitation of sex "if . . . such an exploitation is shocking and disgusting, though not necessarily shown to have the tendency to corrupt or deprave."[64] Mr. Justice Judson gave it as his opinion that "the enactment of s. 150(8) had the effect of expanding the meaning of the word 'obscene' . . . and thus of protecting the public against the shocking and disgusting in addition to the depraving and corrupting aspects of obscenity."[65] In *Regina* v. *McLeod and Georgia Straight Publishing Ltd.*, County Court Justice Darling spoke of obscenity as having "more to do with the capacity to disgust or offend rather than any potential to 'deprave or corrupt'."[66]

It is interesting to note that some witnesses before the 1952 Senate Committee on Salacious and Indecent Literature[67] both maintained that they were shocked and disgusted by much of the literature under review and also that such matter would corrupt and deprave those who would read it. Yet the point has sometimes been made that something cannot shock and disgust *and also* corrupt and deprave. This was the viewpoint expressed in *R.* v. *Beaver.*[68] As Mr. Justice MacLaren said, "There can be no doubt that the language complained of is so foul and disgusting that it would be repulsive to most persons reading it, and is so gross that there would be no danger of its corrupting their morals."[69] The reasoning is that the two ideas are mutually exclusive because it is the attractive and not the replusive that seduces and causes addiction. A somewhat similar anomaly was suggested by the humorous contretemps which occurred when members of the Alberta legislature and their wives viewed the film *Tom Jones* in order to assess its obscenity. Their verdict was that it did corrupt and deprave. The verdict prompted a critic to make the tongue-in-cheek demand that the government resign on the grounds that they had viewed a film that, by their own admission, was corrupting, and that they had become a corrupt government.

The Human Measuring Stick

In any consideration of obscenity, the factors of "corrupting and depraving," "shocking and disgusting" and "undue exploitation" suggest subsidiary questions: Who is to be shocked and disgusted? Who is to be corrupted and depraved? Who is to be exploited unduly? Is the test to be individual and personal? Is it to be applied with reference to a community and if so what community? What allowance is to be made for the motives and intentions of the author? What weight is to be attached to the opinions of literary experts?

A question that must be asked about the matter being tested is this: Is the tendency to deprave and corrupt or to shock and disgust to be judged by reference to an average or reasonable adult or by reference to a child or abnormal adult?

In the United States in 1913 Judge Learned Hand "pronounced a famous criticism of the rule which judged literature by its effect on the young, the salacious and the weak, but he felt constrained to follow it."[70]

The monumental *Ulysses* decision[71] delivered by Judge John M. Woolsey on December 6, 1933, offers more helpful guidance, not only in the United States, but in other countries as well. To assess the effect of the book, Judge Woolsey read it once in its entirety and read the passages complained of many times. What he tried to do was determine the reaction *Ulysses* would produce in the "reasonable man," the "person with average sexual instincts," the man described as *l'homme moyen sensuel* by the French. To avoid making "his reagent too subservient" to his "own idiosyncrasies" he enlisted the aid of what he called "literary assessors." What he did was check his impressions with two of his friends who satisfied the standard of taste and judgment he had outlined. Without telling them his opinion, he provided each independently with a legal definition of "obscenity" and asked each to read the book and to say whether he thought *Ulysses* to be obscene according to that definition. Judge Woolsey reported that, "Both agreed with my opinion that reading *Ulysses* in entirety . . . did not tend to excite sexual impulses but that its net effect on them was only that of a somewhat tragic and powerful commentary on the inner lives of men and women."[72]

An obliquely related consideration was suggested in the "trial" of *Lady Chatterley's Lover* in England in 1960. Even the circular nature of the "tendency-to-corrupt-those-likely-to-be-corrupted" aspect of the *Hicklin Test* seemed to provide no argument for the censorship of the book if the evidence given by Miss Sarah Beryl Jones, Classics Mistress at Keighley's Grammar School, was to be accepted. She said that most schoolgirls knew the meanings of the four-letter words when they were 10, that most girls younger than 17 found *Lady Chatterley's Lover* boring, but that the book had an educational value to girls older than 17.[73] Which brings to mind the apocryphal quip of the man who was indignantly asked how he would like it if his fifteen year old daughter read *Lady Chatterley's Lover.* His answer: "I wouldn't mind. But I'd hate to have my gamekeeper read it."

Some Canadian decisions have made an attempt to distinguish between the reactions of the mature-normal and the immature-abnormal. In *R.* v. *Stroll*[74] it was held that there was no obscenity in displaying in shop windows ties on which colored silhouettes of women were imprinted even though female breasts were revealed. Judge Proulx, of the Montreal Court of Sessions, who said, "If these ties are suggestive, then it would be necessary to put brassieres on cows and diapers on dogs,"[75] ruled that "the law was made to protect the modesty of normal persons, not to bridle the imagination of hot-blooded, vicious or overly scrupulous persons."[76] In *R.* v. *National News Co.*, (1953), C. C. C. 26, the Ontario Court of Appeal passed judgment on four novels and seven picture magazines. Although the Court did find the material obscene, it tried to assess its effect on a normal segment of the community. The mentally unbalanced and lunatic fringe were thereby excluded from consideration. However the effect of the material on young people was still made a yardstick of judgment.

The Community Standards Test

It would be a mistake to try to decide what constitutes obscenity without reference to the milieu in which the obscenity or supposed obscenity is committed. The tastes, feelings and state of mind of the community do have a bearing on whether writing should be tolerated or suppressed. A book which would horrify a Victorian society that insisted on speaking of the "dark" and "white" meat of a chicken because it considered the words "leg" and "breast" improper might not cause the slightest stir in an England used to the Hogarthian realism of the eighteenth century. Judges need to consider how permissive is the society whose laws they try to administer. This suggests that there should be a community standards test for obscenity. Judge Learned Hand fostered this approach, and gave a definition of obscenity at the same time, when he based the test on "the present critical point and the compromise between candor and shame at which the community has arrived here and now."[77]

How this applies has been well described by Professor Charles,[78] particularly with regard to the *Lady Chatterley's Lover* case. He makes a pointed analysis of the legal issues involved and concludes that it was this case which has been responsible for making the community standards test a part of Canadian jurisprudence since 1962. Mr. Justice Fauteux took account of the concept because he felt the Fulton amendment had expanded the *Hicklin rule.* Matter could now be obscene even though it did not necessarily have a tendency to corrupt and deprave, if the dominant characteristic of the publication was an exploitation which was undue. And the test of undueness was whether the exploitation was shocking and disgusting, *"having regard to the existing standard of decency in the community."* (italics mine)[79] Mr. Justice Judson also made the "standards of acceptance prevailing in the community" the test of the "undueness" as stipulated in Section 159(8). He pointed out that this test had been accepted in Australia and New Zealand after Fullagar, J., in *R.* v. *Close* (1948) V.L.R. 455 at p. 465 had enunciated it:

> There does exist in any community at all times—however the standard may vary from time to time—a general instinctive sense of what is decent and what is indecent, of what is clean and what is dirty, and, when the distinction has to be drawn, I do not know . . . that today there is any better tribunal than a jury to draw it . . . I am very far from attempting to lay down a model direction, but a Judge might perhaps, in the case of a novel, say something like this: "It would not be true to say that any publication dealing with sexual relations is obscene. The relations of the sexes are, of course, legitimate matters for discussion everywhere . . . There are certain standards of decency which prevail in the community, and you are really called upon to try this case because you are regarded as representing, and capable of justly applying, those standards. What is obscene is something which offends against those standards.[80]

Mr. Justice Ritchie also found that the Fulton amendment expanded the meaning of the word "obscene" and also regarded the *Hicklin Test* as leaving "out of account publications which are obscene in the sense of being offensive and shocking to the community standards of decency unless they can also be said to have a tendency to deprave and corrupt."[81] However, he also said:

> I do not think that this Court is bound by, nor would I follow, those authorities which have tended to construe the Hicklin definition as meaning that literature available to the community is to be limited by the standard of what is considered to be suitable reading material for adolescents, but I do think that in discharging his duty under s. 150A [now s. 160] if a Judge is satisfied that the publication before him is likely to have a lowering effect on the moral fibre of adolescent boys and girls or of any other significant segment of the community he would be justified in declaring such a publication to be 'obscene' . . .[82]

He considered that the burden of determining what was offensive to community standards rested with the judge,[83] and was firm in asserting that what was to be deemed obscene "must be offensive to community standards or be likely to deprave or corrupt a recognizable segment of the public."[84]

In 1962, the year the *Lady Chatterley's Lover* case was decided, when the Manitoba Appeal Court confirmed the lower court decision that *Escapade* and *Dude* were obscene,[85] Mr. Justice Samuel Freedman, dissenting, professed to judge the magazine by the standards of the community. He warned that the judges must be wary of erecting their personal tastes or prejudices into legal principles. He considered that the number of readers a publication had was a relevant factor in determining community acceptance even though it was not an absolutely definitive test. Community standards were to be determined neither by those with the lowest taste or interest nor exclusively by the rigid, austere, conservative and puritan segment of society. Rather, according to Mr. Justice Freedman, something approaching the general average of community thinking and feeling needed to be determined. Difficult as they are to apply, objective standards are preferable to subjective assessments, based on the personal tastes and predilections of individual judges. And for Mr. Justice Freedman, community standards should be contemporary, taking into account present day attitudes to sex. Moreover, in his opinion, those standards must also be local, which means they have to be Canadian.[86] The importance of Mr. Justice Freedman's opinion was affirmed when the Supreme Court of Canada reversed the Manitoba Appeal Court decision. The seven Supreme Court justices unanimously approved and adopted the reasons he gave for his dissenting judgment.[87] Other cases in which the Court subscribed to the Freedman *ratio decidendi* on community standards were *Regina* v. *Duthie Books Ltd.*,[88] and *Regina* v. *O'Reilly and Four Others.*[89]

In the case of *R.* v. *Cameron*[90] the Ontario Court of Appeal rejected the appeal of Miss Dorothy Cameron from her conviction on charges of exposing to public view obscene pictures. The finding of the Court was that "[t]he standards of the community by which obscenity is to be tested are contemporary and Canadian and are the middle path of interest and tolerance in the community, not standards set by those with an interest in art and for the style and method of the artist."[91]

The *Regina* v. *Great West News Ltd. et al*[92] brought an opinion on the relation of expert evidence to the determination of community standards. Mr. Justice Dickson gave it as his opinion "that the courts have not found it necessary to call upon expert testimony to describe the standards of the community. Such evidence is, of course, admissible but that is not the same thing as saying it is essential."[93]

Regina v. *McLeod and Georgia Straight Publishing Ltd.*[94] elicited further *dicta* on the subject. Mr. Justice Darling said: "Society seems to have moved from a 'paternalistic' to a 'permissive' one, certainly in the area of sex mores . . . but this does not mean to say that the community has moved to the degree of maturity in my opinion necessary to enable the law to abandon all obscenity strictures of any kind."[95]

Regina v. *O'Reilly and Four Others*[96] drew from York County Court Justice Lyon the ruling that in determining the limits of community acceptability or tolerance the "manner and circumstances of the exposure are relevant . . . and thus what may be tolerated as acceptable in a legitimate theatre may not be tolerated when another medium, for example, television, is utilized."[97]

Giving the findings of the whole Court, Ontario Appeal Court Justice McGillivray ruled the film showing of *Columbus of Sex* by McMaster University students was obscene. (*See Case No. 35*). He rejected the defence contention that special allowance should be made for the fact that the audience came from the university community, saying "no exception is to be made for the university community even if it is viewed as having standards differing from those of the Canadian community about it."[98]

The admissibility of community survey techniques in determining community standards was usefully discussed by Mr. Justice Dickson in *R.* v. *Prairie Schooner News Ltd. and Powers.*[99] He said:

> Essential to admissibility is the requirement that the witness testifying be possessed of expert knowledge. Essential also is the selection of the proper "universe," i.e. that segment of the population whose characteristics are relevant to the question being studied. In the case at bar, the "community" whose records are being considered is all of Canada. The universe from which the "sample," i.e. the individuals to be polled, is to be selected must be representative of Canada and not be drawn from a single city. If, and only if, the sample is correctly selected can it be said that the opinions found to exist in the sample are representative of the entire universe.[100]

Of the survey results that had been offered in the lower court, Mr. Justice Dickson said:

> It cannot seriously be contended that the miniscule and parochial sample selected . . . constitutes a prototype of national tolerance to the particular publications, the subject of the present charges. If the survey was intended simply as a non-scientific amalgam of the views

of a small number of unidentified people it falls foul of the rule against hearsay. In my view the survey was wholly inconclusive, of no probative value, and the Judge was correct in declining to permit it to be admitted as evidence.[101]

In *R. v. Times Square Cinema Ltd.*, (*See Case No. 36*) an opinion survey was found to be no more acceptable. At the lower court trial the defence had sought to introduce expert testimony as to the community standard of tolerance and acceptance based on two opinion survey polls. In rejecting the polls, Mr. Justice Jessup asserted,

In my view, when an opinion survey or poll is put forward simply as the foundation of an expert's opinion as to community standards, then questions which would be vital on the question of admissibility, if the survey were put forward as evidence *per se*, become matters going simply to the weight of the expert's opinion because they affect the premises of such opinion. Such questions include whether public opinion polling is, in fact, a science, whether approved statistical methods were used, whether adequate social research techniques and interviews were employed and whether the questions asked were scientifically evocative of a fair sample of opinion. A further matter going to the weight of the expert's opinion is the breadth of the community reflected in the survey. I think clearly the opinion of an expert as to community standards of tolerance must be as to the standard of the whole community of Canada and an opinion with respect to the standard in only a segment of such national community is irrelevant and perhaps inadmissible.[102]

The Evidence of Literary, Scientific and Other Merit

A consideration parallel to that just discussed is suggested by the question "To what extent, if at all, is evidence admissible about the literary, artistic, scientific or other merit of the publication?" Judge Woolsey thought it proper to solicit the opinions of two friends when he was assessing the worth of *Ulysses*, but in this case it was the amateur of good sense who served as his "literary assessor." No literary and certainly no scientific experts were called upon. Indeed it had been the practice until very recent times, particularly in British law and particularly under the *Hicklin Test*, to debar the "expert" from obscenity trials. One of the first departures from this practice occurred in the English trial of *Lady Chatterley's Lover* already referred to.[103] A few of many witnesses for the defence were Graham Hough and Mrs. Joan Bennett, Cambridge lecturers in English, and Helen Gardner, reader in Renaissance English literature at Oxford, as well as Rebecca West, the

Bishop of Woolwich, Professor Vivian Pinto, Francis Williams, E. M. Forster, Norman St. John Stevas, Stephen Potter and C. Day Lewis.

A Canadian example in line with the changed trend occurred in the *Peyton Place* hearing in 1958. Dr. A. M. Beattie as a professor of English, Professor Frank Underhill as an eminent historian, and Campbell McDonald as a working journalist, gave expert testimony on the merit of the book. It seems clear that all three witnesses would have been happier to make their stands on behalf of a worthier candidate but they felt that to reject *Peyton Place* because of its literary and related weaknesses would have made it more likely that much better creations would be similarly denied entry at a later time. It should be remembered the the *Peyton Place* case was heard by the tariff board rather than by a court of law, but the hearing may have had a certain precedent value in that several subsequent legal cases adopted the practice of hearing expert evidence.

That evidence of merit is a legitimate concern of the courts is implied by Section 159(3) of the Criminal Code. That subsection states:

> No person shall be convicted of an offence under this section if he establishes that the public good was served by the acts that are alleged to constitute the offence and that the acts alleged did not extend beyond what served the public good.[104]

Section 159(3) is to be applied in conjunction with Section 159(4) which says:

> For the purposes of this section it is a question of law whether an act serves the public good, but it is a question of fact whether the acts did or did not extend beyond what served the public good.[105]

The lower court proceedings which led up to the Supreme Court hearing that produced the landmark decision in the *Lady Chatterley's Lover* case heard oral evidence from three literary experts. These were Hugh MacLennan, Morley Callaghan and Harry T. Moore, who testified on the literary and artistic merit of *Lady Chatterley's Lover* and D. H. Lawrence's place in English literature. Written evaluations by American literary critics were also considered. This expert opinion was reviewed when the Supreme Court gave its judgment. Of the four justices giving the minority verdict against the book, Chief Justice Kerwin found that the onus of making the final decision about obscenity must lie with the tribunal rather than with the experts.[106] Mr. Justice Taschereau said "too much weight has been attached to the expert evidence adduced"[107] and "art can co-exist with obscenity and does not exclude it."[108] Mr. Justice Fauteux held that "evidence of experts . . .

has been excluded under *Hicklin* jurisprudence''[109] and ''[w]hatever be the outstanding position held by Lawrence as a writer, this book offers no evidence that an expert in literature necessarily qualifies, for that reason as a *custos mores*.''[110] Mr. Justice Locke made no reference to the issue. Of the five justices giving the majority opinion for the book, Mr. Justice Ritchie found expert evidence to be admissible under the *Hicklin Rule* and Criminal Code, section 150(8) [now section 159(8)]. Mr. Justice Judson said, ''One cannot ascertain a dominant characteristic of a book without an examination of its literary or artistic merit and this . . . renders admissible the evidence of the author and others on this point.''[111] Justices Cartwright, Abbott and Martland concurred with Mr. Justice Judson.

Robertson Davies and Arnold Edinborough were the literary experts who gave lower court evidence in the *Fanny Hill* case. In reviewing that lower court verdict, Ontario Court of Appeal Chief Justice Porter said, ''It is our duty, after carefully examining the book itself, to determine what weight should be put upon any expert evidence that may be tendered.''[112] But Mr. Justice Roach said, ''although the element of 'undueness' in the proscription imposed by s. 150(8) makes the evidence of experts in the field of literature relevant as to the literary and historical merits of the publication in question, the essential purpose of the statute is to protect public morals and such experts are not, usually, experts on questions of morality and accordingly they should not be asked nor permitted to give opinion evidence as to the moral qualities of a book.''[113]

In the Dorothy Cameron case[114] five expert witnesses gave evidence for the defence. Conflicting opinions about their acceptability were expressed by Mr. Justice Aylesworth and Mr. Justice Laskin. Mr. Justice Aylesworth felt that ''where there is a clear and unequivocal offence against community standards, artistic merit will not obliterate the obscenity that is thereby established.''[115] He also held that ''[t]he argument that the pictures conferred a benefit on art students by depicting with artistic merit the human form, and on the public by educating them in the appreciation of art failed because to accomplish these ends the exposure of obscene drawings was unnecessary.''[116] By contrast, Mr. Justice Laskin held that:

> Expert evidence is admissible on the issue of ''undueness'' although even when such evidence is uncontradicted it must be weighed by the Court. The determination of contemporary community standards, viewed in national terms, must come from experience of art since a standard connotes something more than a personal reflex. Accordingly, expert evidence to assist the Court is indispensable and the Court ought not to be left by the Crown to rely on the pictures

themselves to make its appraisal of the drawings in the light of community standards.

While the Magistrate was entitled to discount the expert evidence for the defence, he was not entitled, when artistic merit had been clearly shown, to rely on an entirely subjective appraisal and so find that the Crown had proved its case beyond a reasonable doubt. He was not entitled to supply the evidence that should have come from the Crown. Although the existence of artistic merit in the work does not necessarily preclude a finding of undue exploitation of sex as a dominant characteristic, it will be a rare instance in which the dominance can be so suppressed by a sexual theme as to make the exploitation of sex a dominant characteristic which is undue.[117]

In the County Court hearing which led to the order for forfeiture of *Last Exit to Brooklyn,* five experts gave evidence. The British Columbia Court of Appeal rejected the appeal from the lower courts order.[118] Delivering the judgment of the Court, Mr. Justice Bull said "that any literary or artistic merit there may be therein, and any sincere and valid purpose of the author disclosed thereby, are clearly submerged by the undue and decided over-emphasis of the objectionable characteristics."[119]

In *Regina* v. *Great West News Ltd. et al*[120] Mr. Justice Dickson, giving a judgment in which Manitoba Chief Justice Smith concurred, said "In some of the cases a book or work of art may be predominantly characterized by an appeal to sexual interests but also embody literary or sociological or other values. Expert evidence to assist the court is, in such circumstances both admissible and desirable."[121]

In *Regina* v. *Goldberg and Reitman*[122] the experts whose evidence was considered were Pierre Berton, Joan Fox, an experienced film critic; the curator of the Canadian Film Archives in Ottawa; a member of the Ontario Board of Obscenity;[123] a curator from the Art Gallery of Ontario; and three professors from McMaster University. At the Wentworth County Court trial, they testified that the film "on trial" had artistic merit. But when it was assessed by the Ontario Court of Appeal their evidence did not prevail and the appeal from the lower court obscenity conviction was dismissed.

Motives and Intentions

It is often hard to dissociate literary, artistic and other merit from the motives and intentions of the creative artist. Therefore, if community standards and evidence of merit are to be factors in the determination of obscenity, so too should be motives and intentions. In the past, as long as the *Hicklin Test* dominated obscenity decisions, they have not been. Even until fairly recent times the practice has been to disregard the purpose for which the book was written or the work of art created. This approach has accorded with the presumption that a person intends the natural consequences of his acts.[124] In the Artemus Jones libel appeal decision, Lord Chancellor Loreburn was denying the relevance of motives, no matter how blameless, when he said of the *Sunday Chronicle* reporter, "His intention . . . is inferred from what he did."[125] In the past, censors and judges considering obscenity have usually done the same. In some instances the jurists have made a nominal acknowledgment of the fact that motive may be relevant without allowing such motive to determine their verdicts.

More recently they have taken account of the intention of the writer, artist or performer. In the United States, in the *Ulysses* decision already cited, for example, Judge Woolsey left no doubt about his stand. At one point he spoke of "another aspect of the book which I have further to consider, namely, Joyce's sincerity and his honest effort to show how the minds of his characters operate."[126] His verdict was: "I do not anywhere detect the leer of the sensualist"[127] and "Joyce sought to make a serious experiment in a new, if not wholly, literary genre."[128]

In Canada a willingness to consider motives and intentions seems to have come about with the supplanting of the *Hicklin Test* by section 159(8) of the Criminal Code. On the face of it, a consideration of the purpose of the creator of "obscenity" would seem to run counter to section 159(5) of the Code, which says: "For the purposes of this section the motives of the accused are irrelevant."[129] Some recent Canadian judicial opinions would seem to disregard this enactment, except that in these cases it is *usually* the seller, the distributor or the exhibitor rather than the "creator" who is accused. That "intention" was to be made a criterion of obscenity rulings was perhaps implied in the phrase "undue exploitation" of the Fulton definition. The expression was introduced to take account of "the traffickers in pulp trash" whose overriding motive was to sell sex either alone or in conjunction with crime, horror, cruelty or violence for crass commercial profit. Presumably financial profit was not to be regarded as a legally acceptable motive, whereas serious literary or artistic or scientific purpose was considered justification under the law for the matter being assessed, although, as indicated by Justices Freedman and Dickson in the *Prairie Schooner* case[130] "undue exploitation" was not to be defined in terms of economic gain.

Other Obscenity Laws

Having considered the implications of the basic obscenity law, we may now turn our attention to other Canadian legislation dealing with obscenity.

Tariff Item 99201-1

The use of the courts to determine obscenity applies not only to matter dealt with by the Criminal Code but also to material handled by Tariff Item 99201-1 of Schedule C of the Customs Tariff.[131] This item prohibits the importation into Canada of "books, printed paper, drawings, paintings, prints, photographs or representations of a treasonable or seditious, or of an immoral or indecent character."[132] Before 1958 it was the duty of the Minister of National Revenue, acting on the advice of senior members of his department, to judge whether certain importable books and periodicals were obscene. A list of banned books was then prepared, on the basis of which such publications might be denied entry at the border.

For many years such publications as Faulkner's *Sanctuary*, Joyce's *Ulysses* and Radclyffe Hall's *Well of Loneliness* were thus excluded. After Blair Fraser had begun preparation of a *Maclean's* article entitled "Our Hush, Hush Censorship,"[133] the prohibition against *Ulysses* was quietly lifted. But the system itself was not to be changed until after the 1958 appeal by Dell Publishers against the ruling which had excluded *Peyton Place*, a novel by Grace Metalious. The appeal was heard by the Tariff Board. Expert testimony favoring admission of the book was given by Professor Frank Underhill, Dr. A. M. Beattie, and Mr. Campbell McDonald. A witness opposing the book was the Rev. James R. Mutchmor. The Board voted two to one to admit *Peyton Place*. At the time the decision was given, no appeal from a tariff board ruling was possible, except where a question of law was involved, in which case the Exchequer Court of Canada would be called in to adjudicate the special legal issues raised. Shortly after the *Peyton Place* hearing, however, an amendment of the Act took away from the Tariff Board the power to hear appeals, and gave the jurisdiction to County or District Court judges outside Quebec, and to Superior Court judges in the province of Quebec. The change was welcomed by the Tariff Board, which had not enjoyed having to perform a difficult task for which it felt it had no special competence.

It is to be noted that just because a book or periodical is allowed by Customs to enter Canada, this does not mean that it is immune from subsequent prosecution under Sections 159 or 160 of the Criminal Code. This fact was tested in *Regina* v. *Prairie Schooner News Ltd. and Powers*.[134] Contending, in the lower court, that 227 paperback books and 29 magazines, charged as obscene were not obscene, the defence maintained "that even if the publications are obscene they should still be acquitted because they operated under a *bona fide* mistake of fact that the publications were not obscene. This defence is based on the circumstance that the magazines and books, all originals in the United States, had been allowed entry into Canada by the Canadian Customs Department."[135] Mr. Justice Freedman disposed of the question by ruling, "To say that non-prohibition of these publications by the Customs Department has the effect here claimed would be to deprive the court of its proper function . . . The simple truth is that the determination of obscenity is essentially a matter of opinion . . . If, somewhere along the way, someone (no matter how highly placed, and whether in the Customs Department or elsewhere) expressed an opinion that a publication was not obscene, it would remain just that, an opinion and no more."[136] This judgment made it unnecessary for the Manitoba jurist to settle another matter only glanced at: "Whether the phrase 'of an immoral or indecent character' in Item 99201-1 of Sched. C of the *Customs Tariff* is the equivalent of the term 'obscene' in the *Criminal Code* is debatable."[137]

The Post Office Act

Section 164 of the Criminal Code provides that "Every one commits an offence who makes use of the mails for the purpose of transmitting or delivering anything that is obscene, indecent, immoral or scurrilous . . ."[138] [although there are certain exemptions from the prohibition as mentioned in subsection (4) of section 162]. Section 7 of the Post Office Act[139] provides a means of censorship against such offensive material, and this includes obscene as well as blasphemous or seditious matter. Under the terms of the Act, the Postmaster General may prohibit delivery of mail directed to or mailed by persons whom he, on reasonable grounds, believes to be committing an offence by means of the mails. The only right of appeal against such a prohibition is to a board of review, composed of three persons nominated by the Postmaster General. This board must include a member of the legal profession. Sole power of the board is to make recommendations to the Postmaster General, who is not required to accept its advice. He may decide to rescind his original order or allow it to stand, after which no further appeal is permitted. It is also within his discretion to revoke his prohibitory order after he is satisfied that the person affected will not again use the mails for a wrongful purpose. The Postmaster General may require an undertaking to that effect from the person against whom the order has been made.

Obscenity In The Movies

A form of the mass media, if not of journalism, which seems particularly "obscenity prone" is the movies. Censorship of motion pictures comes under provincial law. All provinces except Prince Edward Island have acts to regulate the operation of theaters and the showing of films. These are:

(British Columbia) *Motion Pictures Act*[140]
(Alberta) *Amusements Act*[141]
(Saskatchewan) *The Theatres and Cinematographs Act*[142]
(Manitoba) *The Amusements Act*[143]
(Ontario) *Theatres Act*[144]
(Quebec) *Cinema Act*[145]
(New Brunswick) *Theatres, Cinematographs and Amusements Act*[146]
(Nova Scotia) *Theatres and Amusements Act*[147]
(Newfoundland) *The Censoring of Moving Pictures Act*[148]

The foregoing statutes deal with such matters as the building where films may be shown and the licensing of projectionists, but they also concern themselves with the censorship of films. The Alberta, Ontario, New Brunswick, Nova Scotia and Newfoundland acts provide a censor or board of censors to approve, prohibit or regulate the exhibition of films within their respective provinces. The Manitoba act provides that the Lieutenant Governor in Council may appoint a film classification board composed of not more than fifteen persons,[149] and that, if deemed desirable the Lieutenant Governor in Council may co-operate with the governments of other provinces in Canada in appointing a joint film classification board, composed of not more than fifteen persons.[150] It is to be noted that in 1973 a film classification board classification was insufficient to protect the film, *Last Tango In Paris*, from prosecution for obscenity under the regular obscenity laws, and it took acquittal on the obscenity charges rather than a favorable classification to provide permission for the film showing in Manitoba. In British Columbia the officer who performs these functions is known as the "film classification director," and appeals from his decisions may be made to an appeal board.[151] In Saskatchewan the director appointed to administer the Act is the chairman of the Saskatchewan Film Classification Board.[152] In Quebec regulation of films was performed by the Board of Cinema Censors until the 1966-67 session changed the name of the body to "Cinema Supervisory Board," and the name of the Act from "Moving Pictures Act" to "Cinema Act."[153] To censor films shown in that province, Prince Edward Island borrows the services of the New Brunswick censor.

Not only are the censorship agents empowered to approve or disapprove motion picutres *in toto*, but in the British Columbia,

Saskatchewan, Ontario statutes it is specified that they may also "remove by cutting or otherwise" parts of films they do not approve of. Other matters of a related nature that are dealt with in a consistently similar fashion include: stamps or certificates of approval for film showings; the issuance of licences; penalties in the form of fines and imprisonment for violations of the respective statutes. Provision for the censorship of motion picture advertising is included in the British Columbia, Alberta, Saskatchewan, Manitoba, Ontario and Quebec laws.

Some provinces use a system of film classification. Section 9(2) of the British Columbia act classifies films as follows:

(a) *General,* being suitable for all persons;
(b) *Adult,* being unsuitable for or of no interest to persons under the age of eighteen years;
(c) *Restricted,* being suitable only for persons of the age of eighteen or over.[154]

Section 9(3) says: "Unless authorized by the director, or unless the person is accompanied by his parents or other responsible adult person, no person under the age of eighteen shall attend or be permitted to attend a motion-picture theatre at which a film classified as 'restricted' is exhibited or displayed."[155]

By section 29.19(i) of the provincial act, the Alberta Lieutenant-Governor in Council may make regulations "prescribing the classification of films as family pictures or pictures for universal exhibition or any other system of division."[156] By section 8(2)(c) of its act, Saskatchewan classifies films as general, adult and restricted adult.[157] Section 3(2) of the Ontario Theatres Act says that the Board of Censors "has power . . . (e) to classify any film as adult entertainment, and (f) to classify any film as restricted entertainment."[158] By implication any other accepted films not so classified are "general" films. Section 21(4) of the Ontario Act stipulates that "No person apparently under eighteen years of age shall be permitted to purchase a ticket of admission or be granted admission to or permitted to remain in a theatre where a film classified as restricted entertainment is about to be or is being exhibited."[159]

By an amendment enacted in 1967, Section 10 of the Cinema Act of Quebec provides that the Cinema Supervisory Board

shall authorize the showing of a film by means of a visa indicating as follows the class of spectators for which it is granted:
(a) "Film for all": spectators of all ages

(b) "Film for adolescents and adults": spectators at least fourteen years of age

(c) "Film for adults only": spectators at least eighteen years of age.[160]

The Board may also issue a special visa indicating a particular class of spectators to whom (also when and where) a film may be shown.[161]

What is not acceptable for public viewing is left to the discretion of the censors in British Columbia, Alberta, Ontario, New Brunswick and Nova Scotia. Section 4 of the Newfoundland act speaks of films considered "injurious to the morals of the public.[162] Section 10 of the Quebec Cinema Act, an amendment placed on the statute books in 1967, permitted a film to be shown if, in the opinion of the Cinema Supervisory Board, "its showing is not prejudicial to public order and good morals."[163]

Section 23(2) of the Manitoba Act provides that the film classification board shall "(a) classify any film or slide which in its opinion is unsuitable for viewing by children or by a family by reason of sex, nudity, violence, foul language or other reason, in such a manner that the film or slide shall be restricted to viewing only by persons eighteen years of age or over."[164] Section 24(1) says: "Any peace officer or inspector on the instruction of the board may order the removal from all public places of any advertisement relating to any film or slide if the advertisement is of an immoral, obscene, or indecent nature, or depicts any murder, robbery, or criminal assult, or the killing of any person."[165]

Section 15(1) of the Saskatchewan statute says that,

No person may insert in a newspaper or periodical any advertisement regarding a film that

(a) gives details of a criminal action or depicts criminals as admirable or heroic characters;

(b) is immoral or obscene or suggests lewdness or indecency;

(c) offers evil suggestions to the minds of young people or children;

(d) is for any other reason injurious to public morals or opposed to the public welfare.[166]

Under the old Quebec Motion Pictures Act, children under the age of 16 were, with certain very limited exceptions, not admitted to picture shows, but by an amendment enacted in 1967 (which also changed the name of the act from Motion Pictures Act to Cinema Act) this strict prohibition was lifted and children were allowed to attend according to the categories of films previously indicated.

Most acts provide for regulations by which the lieutenant-governor-in-council may make specific stipulations whereby the Act is enforced.

Miscellaneous Legislation

There are many laws relating to obscenity which have a general rather than a specifically journalistic application. In this connection, the part of the Criminal Code entitled "Offences Tending To Corrupt Morals," (which includes Section 159 and Section 160 previously discussed as well as Sections 161 to 167) provides a useful reference. Section 159(2)(c) and (2)(d) should be of special interest to the advertising departments of newspapers.

Section 159(2)(c) says:

> Every one commits an offence who knowingly, without lawful justification or excuse, . . . offers to sell, advertises, publishes an advertisement of, or has for sale or disposal any means, instructions, medicine, drug or article intended or represented as a method of causing abortion or miscarriage.[167]

Section 159(2)(d) says:

> Every one commits an offence who knowingly, without lawful justification or excuse, . . . advertises or publishes an advertisement of any means, instructions, medicine, drug or article intended or represented as a method for restoring sexual virility or curing venereal disease or diseases of the generative organs.[168]

These two subsections are rarely invoked. In 1961, after the accused company had mailed to Winnipeg householders circulars advertising its prophylactic and condom products, Keystone Enterprises Ltd. was tried summarily under section 150(2)(c) [now 159(2)(c)][169] The defence that it was the intention of the accused to advertise an article to be used for safeguarding health was rejected, and the defendant was convicted and fined $25.00. But in giving judgment, Magistrate Rice noted, "There is only one reported case on the subject, decided some 60 years ago, but it had to do with medicine and not the product advertised by the accused."[170]

Obscenity per se and Logophobia

If a concept may be borrowed from the area of libel, it may be said that the obscenity thus far dealt with is obscenity *per quod.* In our examination of legal decisions, and in our consideration of such questions as "community standards," "human measuring stick" and "motives and intentions" the idea has been implicit that accompanying circumstances are the determinant of what is obscene.

By contrast, a narrower viewpoint is that a specific act or piece of writing or display may be denominated "obscene" by reason of some intrinsic quality of that act or piece of writing or display. Such obscenity might be called obscenity *per se.*

Those who subscribe to the belief that obscenity is inherent—and these may be a decreasing number of people—are the farthest removed in their thinking from those who consider that obscenity is a figment of the imagination. Those who are of the obscenity *per se* school subscribe to the "isolated passage" test of obscenity. They are the people who believe that nakedness is obscene.[171] And they are usually afflicted with logophobia.

"Logophobia" means fear of words. Much censorship derives from logophobia. Thus, for the censorious, it is not the act but the naming of the act which is shocking. Such persons are less disturbed by the news that a woman is living in sin than they would be by the speaking or writing of the four letter verb which denotes the basic action of living in sin. Critics claim that such an attitude is akin to the taboos of primitive tribes.[172]

A parallel is to be seen in the preference for the euphemism to the blunt expression. An example from the social welfare field will illustrate. Thus in past days there were people, just as there are today, who suffered hardship because they were poor. Altruists helped them by giving them money, food or clothing. In doing so the benefactors were said to be displaying charity, one of the trinity of the virtues, faith, hope and charity, so that the benevolence became known as "charity." For a time the term was an honorable one, but presently it took on a derogatory connotation. The beneficiaries resented the word as something to be ashamed of. So a new word, free from such connotations, was sought. Language-makers reasoned that the act of benevolence was performed to relieve hardship and suffering. So "relief" became the euphemism for what had formerly been "charity". But after an interval pejoration set in again, and the word "relief" lost respectability in its turn. So now "social welfare" has become the substitute expression. And it may be that "social welfare" will wear out eventually also.

It is possible that the shock words of sex and scatology have undergone a similar process, dating back to mediaeval times when priests could, in an unembarrassed way, use all the four-letter words in describing bodily functions in letters of instruction and admonition which they addressed to the convent nuns for whose moral welfare they had a responsibility.

One might even theorize, with at least a small claim to plausibility, that the "obscenity" of some words and the "non-obscenity" of others relate in part to their sounds. Some words describing sex and excretion use guttural, dental, labial and hissingly sibillant sounds—and are unacceptable. Some words are liquid, unstaccato, and soothingly sibillant sounds—and are acceptable. The difference in sound if not in acceptability is illustrated by the contrast between the last verse of Masefield's *Cargoes* and the first two verses. The serenity and tranquility of

Quinquireme of Ninevah from distant Ophir,
Rowing home to haven in sunny Palestine,
With a cargo of ivory,
And apes and peacocks,
Sandalwood, cedarwood, and sweet white wine.

OR

Stately Spanish galleon coming from the Isthmus,
Dipping through the Tropics by the palm-green shores,
With a cargo of diamonds,
Emeralds, amethysts,
Topazes, and cinnamon, and gold moidores.

is strikingly different from the abrupt ugliness of

Dirty British coaster with a salt-caked smoke stack,
Butting through the Channel in the mad March days,
With a cargo of Tyne coal,
Road-rails, pig-lead,
Firewood, iron-ware, and cheap tin trays.[173]

It might not be completely fanciful to suggest that mere oral and aural differences account for the fact that of two words which mean the same thing one is considered, in polite society, to be proper, and one is considered improper. "Copulate" is acceptable; "fuck," unacceptable. "Coition," "fornicate," "vagina," "clitoris," "penis," "testicles," "urinate" and "defecate" are sanctioned where their use is necessary. "Cunt," "cock," "balls," "piss" and "shit" are taboo words.

It might be claimed that the oral-aural taboos being discussed are more a matter of aesthetics than of obscenity. And aesthetics would seem to be a factor in determining not only sex taboos but scatology taboos as well. Use of the word "dirty" to describe "obscene" writing makes the point.

Another theory is that the distinction between "obscenity" and "non-obscenity" is a social one. The so-called "lower" classes may be immune from logophobia. The fact that there is an increasing use of the once-forbidden words may mean that class distinctions are breaking down. Increasing linguistic freedom may be in part a triumph for the "natural man" Lawrence extolled in *Lady Chatterley's Lover.*

It has reasonably been argued that logophobia should not exist. It has reasonably been argued that there is no obscenity in words but rather in the hatred and cruelty behind the words. This was the thesis of Arnold Edinborough and Robertson Davies when giving expert evidence in the *Fanny Hill* case.[174] When, as reported to the author, a number of young people "liberated" a Winnipeg church by running down the aisles during a service and shouting four letter words, the obscenity surely lay in the cruelty and hostility of the invaders rather than in their words.[175] Edward Sagarin condemns the use of the word "scum" as meaning "semen" because of the attitude the word conveys.

> And this is scum! That is what our language calls these most precious drops without which humanity could not continue. This is more than simple irony. It is bitter tragedy. This is more than a confession of man's contempt for sex, his view of sexuality as an abominable and generally dirty practice. It is a confession of his contempt for life—particularly and specifically his own, the human life.[176]

By contrast, opponents of the obscenity *per se* school of thought find no obscenity in calling a man a "son of a bitch," while smiling and poking him playfully in the ribs—thereby conveying the idea that the person so addressed is a "gay dog." Even if Prime Minister Trudeau did say to his House of Commons opponents "Fuck off!" there would be no obscenity if he said it in such a way as to convey the idea of "fuddle duddle," "fiddle faddle" or "pish tush." There is probably more humor than obscenity in the pseudo-philologist's derivation of the word "fuck" as an abbreviation of "file under carnal knowledge." It was innocent amusement that caused English and Canadian Second World War soldiers to use the neologisms, "snafu," "tarfu," "fafu," and "fubar." They did so knowing "snafu" was an abbreviation of "situation normal, all fucked up," "tarfu" an abbreviation of "things are really fucked up," "fafu" an abbreviation of "fucking awful fuck up," and "fubar," an abbreviation of "fucked up beyond all recognition."

An innocence of a different kind was displayed by Robert Browning when he tried his hand at etymology. As Noel Perrin tells it:

> . . . the editors of the *Oxford English Dictionary*, . . . interested to find a contemporary use of "twat" wrote to Browning to ask in what sense he was using it. Browning is said to have written back that he used it to mean a piece of headgear for nuns, comparable to the cowls for monks he put in the same line. The editors are then supposed to have asked if he recalled where he had learned the word. Browning replied that he knew exactly. He had read widely in seventeenth century literature in his youth, and in a broadside poem called "Vanity of Vanities," published in 1659, he had found these lines, referring to an ambitious cleric:
>
> They talk't of his having a Cardinall's Hat;
> They'd send him as soon as an Old Nun's Twat.
>
> If you are sufficiently delicate and sheltered, it is possible to take the last word as meaning something like a wimple, and Browning did. A fugitive and cloistered virtue can get into difficulties that even Milton didn't think of.[177]

Morality and Law

Those whose approach is liberal and permissive contend that such factitious elements of so-called obscenity as have just been discussed should not govern our handling of what is claimed to be pornographic or indecent. They believe also that many of the measures taken to deal with obscenity may have ridiculous consequences. Past moral censorship of the movies provides an example: Soon after the Hays office was set up, a film contained a sequence in which a man and a woman entered the woman's bedroom and spent a few innocuous minutes together, after which the man left. But the Hays code said that no scene might depict a man and woman, unaccompanied and not man and wife, together in a lady's bedroom—and this couple was unmarried and unaccompanied. So the bedroom scene was deleted. What the audience saw was a man and a woman open a bedroom door and enter the room beyond it. They saw the door close, looked at the outside of the door, saw the door open, presumably after a time lapse, and then saw the man emerge alone. Wherefrom the audience concluded that the "worst" had happened.

A final consideration reiterates a thesis strongly believed by many serious students of the obscenity question. It is their conviction that, in an individual personal context at least, it is a mistake to make obscenity the subject of criminal law. What Canadians do in private circumstances is a moral question and not a legal question at all. Because Canadian society is a pluralistic society, what one segment of that society adopts as its *moral* law must not be imposed on the rest of the nation by means of *criminal* law. With one exception obscenity may be treated as sin but must not be treated as crime: it is only when what is termed ''obscene'' causes overt behavior dangerous to the welfare of society or of other individuals that the intervention of the law is justified. To anyone familiar with Prime Minister Trudeau's announcement that he intended to take the government out of the bedrooms of the nation and with the philosophy underlying the Criminal Code amendments concerning homosexuality and gross indecency,[178] the *rationale* for divorcing immoral behavior in obscenity matters from the law is well known.

Chapter VIII

Copyright

If the law of obscenity is uncertain and unsatisfactory, so too is the law which deals with copyright. In the case of obscenity a critical source of difficulty is the problem of bringing a legal concept into harmony with the heterogeneous social mores of the community and of the nation. In the case of copyright, technology is the ingredient in the situation which has caused confusion in and ineffectiveness of the law. And in the case of copyright also, international law complicates the situation for the Canadian journalist, author, musician and artist.

Definitions

In his authoritative book, *The Canadian Law of Copyright and Industrial Designs*, Dr. Harold G. Fox quotes two definitions of copyright.[1] One is: "the right to multiply copies of a published work, or the right to make the work public and still retain the beneficial interest therein."[2] The second is: "the exclusive right of multiplying copies of an original work or composition, and consequently preventing others from so doing."[3] Another useful working definition of copyright is "the right, secured by law, to authors of literary, musical and artistic works to prevent any reproduction of their works without their consent."[4] The definition contained in the Canadian Copyright Act is half a page long and is more detailed.[5]

The right inherent in copyright is seen to be of a dual kind: it involves the exclusive right to publish and the exclusive right to multiply copies of a work. Thus, whereas a reader who buys a novel may otherwise do what he wants with *his* copy he may not republish that book nor may he make copies of it, those rights being vested in the publisher who made the contract with the novelist and paid money to him for his copyright. What the reader buys is a *physical* property. What the copyright holder retains is said to be *incorporeal* property.[6]

Historical Background of Canada's Present Copyright Law

Canada's present copyright law is the result of several developments. It has been marked by a change from common to statute law. It has been influenced by early practices and legislation in England. It has been affected by Canada's place and role in the British Empire, particularly before the Canadian Copyright Act of 1921. And it has been conditioned and shaped by international law, so that it is virtually impossible to extensively consider Canadian domestic copyright without reference to international agreements in the copyright field. For these reasons it seems useful to lead up to a consideration of current Canadian copyright by sketching in the historical background of the subject.

The reader interested in a more detailed discussion might profitably consult Harold G. Fox's *The Canadian Law of Copyright and Industrial Designs*,[7] *The Protection of Literary Property*[8] by Philip Wittenberg, and *Copyright, Modern Law and Practice*,[9] by P. F. Carter-Ruck, E. P. Skone James and F. E. Skone James. Fox points out that, under Roman law, the right of an author to ownership of his productions, at least if they were literary as opposed to artistic, was unknown.[10] During the Middle Ages, before the invention of printing from moveable type, copying was generally permitted provided the copier did not claim authorship.[11] Some years after the introduction of printing into England in 1476, restrictive legislation was passed, more to protect the domestic printing industry and to serve as a censorship device than to safeguard the rights of authors in their works.[12] Henry VIII's 1529 statute instituted royal control of printing through the granting of both privilege and patent[13] but "these printing privileges were not granted in any way as a recognition or protection of the author's right but only as a commercial monopoly of printing."[14] The genesis of the printer's or bookseller's copyright derived from the monopolies granted to the Stationers' Company in the late sixteenth century and thereafter.[15] Until its abolition in 1641 the Star Chamber Court was the agency by which the Crown exercised authority over the press.[16] In 1649 the first statute regulating printing required the licensing of books and provided for fines against those who pirated books registered with the Stationers' Company, but the company was denuded of much of its power in 1653 and 1655.[17] Licensing Acts of 1662, 1685 and 1692 added little to the protection of authors.[18] In the 1709-1710 session of parliament England's first Copyright Act was enacted.[19] Although the new law set a limit on the duration of copyright, London booksellers, registered with the Stationers' Company, tried to maintain that they held copyright to certain books in perpetuity under the common law.[20] Although there was some question as to whether copyright existed at common law prior to the 1709 legislation, various legal judgments and judicial opinions supported the idea that common law copyright had so existed.[21] But that the 1709 Act superseded the common law right was established by *Donaldson* v. *Beckett*, (1774), 4 Burr. 2408, 2 Bro P. C. 129.[22] That Act was replaced by the Literary Copyright Act of 1842, which in turn was replaced by the Copyright Act, 1911.[23]

The Imperial Copyright Act of 1842 had legal effect in the British colonies and therefore in the provinces that were to become Canada.[24] This despite the fact that Lower Canada had passed its own copyright act in 1832[25] and the united province of Canada had enacted legislation in 1841.[26] After the British North America Act created the new Dominion of Canada in 1867, the federal government passed copyright acts in 1868 and in 1872, although the latter was disallowed by the Imperial authorities on the ground that it conflicted with Imperial legislation.[27] A copyright act of 1875 was embodied in the Revised Statutes of Canada 1886, and preserved with amendments in the Revision of 1906.[28] A new Canadian Copyright Act, 1921 came into force on January 1, 1924.[29] It had the effect of repealing all the enactments relating to copyright that had been passed by the Imperial Parliament so far as they applied to Canada.[30]

This latter development was part and parcel of the growing autonomy of the Dominion. If copyright had been a purely domestic matter, it would have been easy enough to be governed by consideration of autonomy alone, and to pass copyright laws without reference to any other country. But a publisher in one country may publish for readers, viewers or listeners of that country the books, plays, pictures, films or music created by the authors, playwrights, painters, film makers or musicians of another country. And this applies not only to countries of the British commonwealth, but to other countries as well. The fact that literary, musical, dramatic and artistic creation crosses international boundaries complicates the copyright question. If the whole world followed one uniform copyright practice the situation would be comparatively simple. But it does not.

The fact is that, while living in their own country, nationals are not subject to the laws of another country. Thus Country A may pass a copyright law. Citizen b of Country B flouts that law by plagiarizing or pirating a book written by Citizen a of Country A. Citizen a has no redress. Citizen b is not punished. Later, Countries A and B remedy the situation by signing a copyright treaty which provides mutual protection for the citizens of both countries. But this doesn't do author a or author b any good if citizen c of Country C, which has no copyright treaty with Countries A and B, decides to plagiarize and pirate the creations of authors a and b. What is needed to assure authors of invariable copyright protection is a copyright convention to which all countries subscribe. The trouble is that it is most difficult to secure a consensus among all countries. What in fact has happened is that some countries have signed one convention, some countries have signed another convention, while the remaining countries have signed no convention. This means that authors, artists and musicians have protection within the countries of their own convention, but they still run into trouble from the signatories of the rival conventions or from non-convention countries. Of course, where countries subscribe to more than one convention, the authors, musicians and artists in that country enjoy a wider protection.

Typical of the grievances which authors have against the copyright practice of an earlier day have been the experiences of such prominent writers as Charles Dickens. American publishers pirated many of his works, publishing him with impunity in the United States and paying him nothing. What is sometimes forgotten is that Dickens was not the only person made unhappy by the practice. Many American authors complained that if the publishers had not concentrated on Dickens and other foreign writers, native authors would have had a better chance to be published in their own country.

It was to remove this kind of injustice that agreements between countries were signed and copyright conventions evolved. The United Kingdom's International Copyright Act of 1844 did not protect foreign authors sufficiently to allow Great Britain to be represented at the International Copyright Convention, but that situation was remedied by the International Copyright Act of 1886.[31] Great Britain joined the conferring powers which drew up the Berne Convention of 1886, establishing an International Copyright Union.[32] The Convention was amended at Paris in 1896 and revised at Berlin in 1908, at Rome in 1928, and at Brussels in 1948.[33] Ten countries were members of the Union when it was first formed but its numbers have grown to more than fifty.[34] When Great Britain joined the Union in 1887 it did so also on behalf of its colonies and possessions, and these included Canada. The Additional Act of Paris in 1896 also had effect in Canada, but it was not until the Canadian Copyright Act of 1921 came into force in 1924 that the Rome Revision of 1908 applied to Canada. This delay was in spite of Great Britain's earlier adherence. Canada also adheres to the Rome Revision, but so far has not taken steps to put the Berlin Revision into force.[35]

A second convention, the Universal Copyright Convention, was formulated at Geneva in 1952.[36] It was U.N.E.S.C.O. sponsored. There were ninety signatories, including Canada, but when the Convention came into effect September 16, 1955, Canada was not a member. As of March, 1956 those countries which subscribed to the Convention were Andorra, Cambodia, Chile, Costa Rica, France, the German Federal Republic, Haiti, the Holy See, Israel, Japan, Laos, Luxembourg, Monaco, Pakistan, the Philippines, Spain, Switzerland,

and the United States. A notable absentee from both Conventions was Russia, but May 27, 1973 it began to adhere to the Universal Copyright Convention.[37]

Philip Wittenberg has contrasted the Berne and Geneva Conventions:

> Unlike Berne, the Universal Copyright Convention is not self-enacting legislation. The protection given by it is what is called 'national' protection, that is, citizens of each state of the Union enjoy in the other states the rights accorded by that state to its citizens. Since the rights must be determined by domestic legislation, each member country is required to have an effective copyright system. There is no definition or enumeration of works protected, such as has been contained in the Berne Convention. All such details are left to the several countries.[38]

The third major copyright convention is the Buenos Aires Convention, which is one of the Pan-American Copyright Conventions. *The Protection of Literary Property,* which was published in 1968, listed its members as follows: Argentine, Bolivia, Brazil, Chile, Colombia, Costa Rica, Dominican Republic, Ecuador, Guatemala, Haiti, Honduras, Mexico, Nicaragua, Panama, Paraguay, Peru, the United States and Uruguay.[39]

Notwithstanding the advantages gained through adherence to the Berne or International Copyright Convention after 1924, Canadian writers and similar creative artists were for a long time dissatisfied with the amount of protection their works were given. The cause of their bitterness was their relationship to American publishers. In the days when the poetry of Edna Jacques enjoyed a popularity comparable to that of Edgar Guest, an American organization made a large sum of money through the sale of one of the Canadian poet's poems for which they paid her no royalties. When Joseph McCarthy was at the height of his witch-hunting activities, an obscure American record company pirated and sold a recording of the CBC play, "The Investigator," without acknowledgment and without payment being made. More recently American publishers have reaped the profits on text books written by Canadians, printed and distributed only in small numbers by Canadians before the American publisher took over production and sale of the book without consulting author or Canadian publisher.

Cause of these and many other injustices was the fact that the United States did not subscribe to the Berne Copyright Convention, that Canada did not subscribe to the Geneva Convention, and that the 1924 Copyright agreement between Canada and the United States contained clauses which most Canadian writers considered inimical to Canadian literary interests.

The 1924 agreement gave the United States the full protection of the Canadian Copyright Act without the performance of any special formalities. Canadian citizens were entitled to United States copyright benefits.[40] However, the condition of this enjoyment was that the published work should be wholly manufactured in the United States.[41]

Some relief from this restriction was possible to Canadians through a special provision of the U. S. Act. This permitted a temporary, or *ad interim*, copyright to be secured in the United States for a foreign work in the English language, if application was made by the foreign copyright holder within six months of publication. The temporary protection had two limitations. It lasted for only four months when the agreement was first made, although the period was extended to five years in 1949.[42] Regulations permitted the import into the United States of not more than 1500 copies of the work during the *ad interim* period of protection.[43]

Dissatisfaction over copyright in Canada led to the appointment of the Ilsley Royal Commission which reported in 1958 after a three-and-a-half year study. Fifteen recommendations were made on matters which ranged from the "broadcasters' right," recordings, musical works, and photographs to books and ratification of the Universal Copyright Convention.

Effective August 10, 1962, Canada became a member of that Universal Copyright Convention.[44] This membership gives protection to Canadian works in the other countries that have ratified the convention.[45] Canada still retains the protection provided in more than fifty countries by the Berne Convention.

The most welcome gain achieved by the 1962 action was the removal of the handicap for Canadian authors who wish to sell their works in the United States. Hugh MacLennan, Thomas Raddall, Pierre Berton and other Canadian authors popular abroad may print and publish their works in Canada and then collect royalties on those works. The fact that since ratification of the Geneva Convention the Queen's Printer has exported at least 1,500,000 copies of the RCAF books on 5BX and 10BX exercises to the U. S. Air Force illustrates the kind of gain made.[46]

One feature of the situation still leaves the Canadian publishers and printers unhappy. An American author who wished to publish first in Canada to obtain the protection provided by both the Berne and Geneva Conventions risks the loss of U.S. domestic copyright. He is hampered by the condition that, under the terms of the "manufacturing clause," no more than 1,500 copies of his work may be imported into the United States without forfeiting protection in his own country. The result is that American authors are unlikely to seek out Canadian printers and publishers. Canadian printers and publishers are thus deprived of the right to tender on equal terms with American companies for American works.

In addition to its application to the works of the United States and domiciliaries, the foregoing restriction applies to the following two categories of works as described by Philip Wittenberg:

> 2. Works which could have qualified protection under our [American] law by virtue of the UCC, but which have not qualified for the exemption from the requirements of the manufacturing clause because of failure to use the notice of copyright provided for in the Convention.
> 3. Works by authors who are citizens of countries with which the United States has established copyright relations, but who are not citizens of a country party to the UCC and who do not first publish the work in a country party to the Convention.[47]

Copyright Today As It Affects Canadians

As has already been indicated, copyright in Canada is governed by the Copyright Act of 1921, as subsequently amended, and by Canada's adherence to the International Copyright Convention (Berne Convention) and the Universal Copyright Convention (Geneva Convention.) Dr. Fox makes the point that, "The Conventions identify the countries the citizens of which enjoy copyright protection, but it is the text of the Copyright Act that definitively provides the protection. International law does not have priority; it is the domestic law that is supreme.[48]

Term of Copyright

Duration of copyright for the International Copyright Convention countries is the lifetime of the author and a period of fifty years after his death. Section 5 of the Canadian Copyright Act makes the same stipulation with respect to Canada's domestic copyright. Under the Universal Copyright Convention, the term of copyright is a much more complicated matter. It is dealt with in Article IV. That article states:

> 1. The duration of protection of a work shall be governed . . . by the law of the Contracting State in which protection is claimed.
> 2. The term of protection for works protected under this Convention

shall not be less than the life of the author and 25 years after his death.

However, any Contracting State which, on the effective date of this Convention in that State has limited this term for certain classes of works to a period computed from the first publication of the work, shall be entitled to maintain these exceptions and to extend them to other classes of works. For all these classes the term of protection shall not be less than 25 years from the date of first publication.

Any Contracting State which, upon the effective date of this Convention in that State, does not compute the term of protection on the basis of the life of the author, shall be entitled to compute the term of protection from the date of the first publication of the work or from its registration prior to publication, as the case may be, provided the term of protection shall not be less than 25 years from the date of first publication or from its registration prior to publication, as the case may be.

If the legislation of a Contracting State grants two or more successive terms of protection, the duration of the first term shall not be less than one of the minimum periods specified above.[49]

For the Canadian author writing in English, his most important non-Berne treaty market is undoubtedly the United States. In that country books may be copyrighted for twenty eight years after publication or registration, with the option of renewing for an additional twenty eight years. This is the copyright which Canadian writers may enjoy in the United States by complying with UCC and United States copyright conditions.

Section 8(1) of the Canadian Copyright Act specifies that in the case of joint authorship the fifty years of posthumous copyright shall date from the death of the last author to die.[50] Section 9 provides that copyright in a photograph shall subsist for fifty years from the making of the original negative. Copyright is to be vested in the owner of the negative at the time that negative was made.[51] Comparable conditions govern copyright in records, perforated rolls and other contrivances by means of which sounds may be mechanically produced. In this case first ownership of the plate from which the contrivance derives determines where copyright ownership lies. This is laid down in Section 10.[52] Section 11 describes conditions under which copyright belongs to the crown.[53]

Article IV3 of the Universal Copyright Convention provides "that the term of protection in these Contracting States which protect photographic works, or works of applied art in so far as they are protected as artistic works, shall not be less than 10 years for each of said classes of works.''[54]

Registration of Copyright

It is only with reference to the Universal Copyright Convention that the Canadian author needs to take steps to ensure copyright. Within the context of the International (Berne) Convention and of the Canadian Copyright Act there appears to be little the author need do to ensure copyright for his own work. In Canada the author does not have to apply for copyright. That is, copyright is automatic. In Canada, the Canadian author has the exclusive right of multiplying for sale copies of an original work or composition in literature and art. As Dr. Fox points out, citing *King Features Syndicate Inc.* v. *Kleeman Ltd.*, [1941] 2 All E.R. 403 at 407 *per* Lord Maugham, ''It is useful to remember that the Copyright Act 1921, requires no registration and confers a right in an unpublished as well as a published work.''[55]

The Berne Convention outlines the same condition. After Article 4(1) has referred to the rights of the nationals of the countries of the Union, Article 4(2) states:

The enjoyment and the exercise of these rights shall not be subject to the performance of any formality; such enjoyment and such exercise are independent of the existence of protection in the country of origin of the work. Consequently, apart from the express stipulations of the present Convention, the extent of protection, as well as the means of redress secured to the author to safeguard his rights, shall be governed exclusively by the laws of the country where protection is claimed.[56]

The Universal Copyright Convention makes greater demands on the author or other creative person. Certain formalities do have to be complied with. Article III 1 of the Convention requires that copies of the work for which copyright is claimed within the countries of the Union shall bear the symbol © accompanied by the name of the copyright proprietor and the year of publication ''placed in such manner and location as to give reasonable notice of claim of copyright.''[57] Article III 4 says: ''In each Contracting State there shall be legal means of protecting without formalities the unpublished works of nationals of other Contracting States.''[58]

It is to be noted, however, in connection with United States copyright, that:

Although copyright is secured by publication with statutory notice there are certain formalities that must be complied with as a prerequisite to the right to sue for the enforcement of copyright. These include registration and deposit, which are covered by Sections 11, 13 and 14 of the [American] Copyright Law.

Section 11 merely provides that a person entitled to copyright may obtain registration by complying with the provisions of the law, including the deposit of copies, and that upon such compliance the Register of Copyright shall issue a certificate.

Section 13 provides that after copyright has been secured by publication there shall be promptly deposited in the Office of the Register of Copyrights two complete copies of the best edition thereof then published, or if the work has been published in a foreign country and is by an author who is a citizen or subject of a foreign state or nation, one complete copy of the best edition then published in such foreign country.[59]

As the same author says:

. . . Each contracting state has the right to impose conditions prerequisite to judicial relief, provided that such conditions are equally applicable to nationals of the state in which protection is claimed.

In addition, a concession was made to the United States in that any contracting state was allowed to regard as its own nationals domiciled therein. This permits us to require of foreigners domiciled in the United States the same formalities as are imposed on our own citizens.[60]

In the Canadian domestic field, even setting aside the requirements of the UCC and of the United States Copyright Act, the question of copyright is not such an academic matter as the remarks made earlier about not performing special formalities would suggest. For one thing, "to *hold* copyright" is not always quite the same as "to *prove* copyright." For this reason it is sometimes useful to take steps which will protect against plagiarism by publication of an author's work without permission. Thus an author may register his work in order to establish priority of authorship. Registration is merely a certificate of ownership. Its value is to provide proof of authorship and copyright. Section 37 to 40 of the Copyright Act deal with registration of copyright, and Section 41 sets forth the fees to be paid for that registration.[61] Section 52 provides for the deposit of two copies of the copyrighted book with the librarian of parliament.[62]

It has been suggested that a measure of value which an author might take is to mail his own manuscript to himself by registered mail. By preserving his registered parcel unopened he can thereby create worth-while evidence should authorship of the work ever be disputed.

It is also of value to write "Copyright Reserved" or some such phrase on manuscripts when the author wants to make it clear that by putting his work into typescript he is not surrendering copyright. This device would appear to be worthwhile with respect to limited publication. Philip Wittenberg deals with the concept lucidly when he says:

> The author, in the very act of creating, creates in himself a right of property in the work produced. Out of his labor comes a property from which he has the right to exclude others . . .
>
> The property exists not in the paper or other physical embodiment, but in the expression. The making of copies will not in and of itself divest the author of his right. It is only when he distributes the copies to the public that his right is lost. There may be restricted publication which does not indicate an intention to dedicate the work to the public. So, for instance, if a teacher distributes notes to a class, but with the understanding that the students will not make or give copies thereof and that the notes will be used solely for the purposes of the classroom, that is is not a dedication to the public generally . . .
>
> The publication, to be effective as a dedication, must be a general publication. A limited publication which communicates the contents of a manuscript to a definite group and for a limited purpose, and without the right of diffusion, reproduction, distribution, or sale, is considered a "limited publication," which does not result in loss of the author's common-law right to his manuscript.[63]

Of course, involved copyright questions arise when authors sign contracts with publishers. "First Serial Rights Only" and "North American Rights Only" are phrases which suggest that authors do not sell all rights in their compositions, and that author-publisher contracts are not uniform. Says Dr. Fox:

> It will be seen . . . that, while the usual form of contract is one in which the publisher agrees to bear the entire cost of publication, paying to the author either a royalty on each copy sold or a percentage of the profits resulting therefrom there may be variations of such contracts in that the author may bear the entire expense of printing and publishing, merely employing the publisher. In other cases the publisher may purchase the work from the author, publish at his own expense and reap the entire profit, while in other cases the publication may be a joint adventure between the author and publisher. Works may, therefore, be published in consideration of royalties or on a profit-sharing basis, or on commission, or for a single

payment. The publisher may reserve an option on future work of the author and on rights such as dramatic, film or foreign rights not comprised in the original grant.[64]

Clearly where copyright is under consideration, each contract must be considered separately.

Reciprocal Rights

The key to satisfactory copyright arrangements on an international basis is the granting of reciprocal rights. The wider the reciprocal rights granted the wider the area of copyright coverage.

The International Copyright (Berne) Convention provides for reciprocal rights in Articles 4, 5 and 6. Article 4 states:

> Authors who are subjects or citizens of any of the countries of the Union shall enjoy in countries other than the country of origin of the works, whether unpublished or first published in a country of the Union, the rights which the respective laws do now or may hereafter grant to natives as well as the rights specially granted by the special Convention.[65]

Article 5 provides:

> Authors being subjects or citizens of one of the countries of the Union who first publish their works in another country of the Union shall have in the latter country the same rights as native authors.[66]

Article 6 stipulates:

> Authors not being subjects or citizens of one of the countries of the Union, who first publish their works in one of those countries, shall enjoy in that country the same rights as native authors, and in the other countries of the Union the rights granted by the present Convention.[67]

The Universal Copyright Convention confers a comparable reciprocity by Article II of the Convention:

> 1. Published works of nationals of any Contracting State and works first published in that State shall enjoy in each other Contracting State the same protection as the other State accords to works of its nationals first published in its own territory.
> 2. Unpublished works of nationals of each Contracting State shall

enjoy in each other Contracting State the same protection as that other State accords to unpublished works of its own nationals.

3. For the purpose of this Convention any Contracting State, may, by domestic legislation, assimilate to its own nationals any person domiciled in that State.[68]

The Canadian Copyright Act contains provisions to implement the reciprocal arrangements of the International Copyright Convention. Section 4 of the Copyright Act enacts that:

(1) Subject to the provisions of this Act, copyright shall subsist in Canada for the term hereinafter mentioned, in every original literary, dramatic, musical and artistic work, if the author was at the date of the making of the work a British subject, a citizen or subject of a foreign country that has adhered to the Convention and the British protocol thereto set out in the Second Schedule, or resident within Her Majesty's Dominions; and if, in the case of a published work, the work was first published within Her Majesty's Dominions or in such foreign country; but in no other works, except so far as the protection conferred by this Act is extended as hereinafter provided to foreign Countries to which this Act does not extend.

(2) Where the Minister certifies by notice, published in the *Canada Gazette*, that any country that has not adhered to the Convention and the Additional Protocol thereto, set out in the Second Schedule, grants or has undertaken to grant, either by treaty, convention, agreement or law, to citizens of Canada the benefit of copyright on substantially the same basis as to its own citizens or copyright protection substantially equal to that conferred by this Act, such country shall, for the purpose of the rights conferred by this Act, be treated as if it were a country to which this Act extends; and the Minister may give such a certificate as aforesaid, notwithstanding that the remedies for enforcing the rights, or the restrictions on the importation of copies of works, under the law of such country, differ from those in this Act.[69]

A few examples will illustrate how reciprocity of copyright operates. A Canadian author may write a book in which copyright would inhere in British Commonwealth countries and in other Berne Convention countries such as Germany until fifty years after his death. By fulfilling the condition of imprinting the symbol © as well as the name of the copyright owner and year of publication on each copy of his book he can gain copyright of twenty eight years and the option to renew for a further twenty eight years in the United States. It should be remembered, however, that the conditions of registration and deposit as described above should be complied with.

By publishing his book in Canada, an American author can secure the protection of the Berne Convention for the period of his lifetime and an additional fifty years in the countries of the International Copyright Union. Or a citizen of Argentina might first publish his book in Canada and gain in Canada the copyright privileges of the Canadian Copyright Act and in the other Berne Convention countries the rights granted by that Convention. Or the Andorran author of an unpublished book would enjoy in the United States the protection an American national enjoys, since both Andorra and the United States subscribe to the Universal Copyright Convention.

Originality and Copyrightability

For a work to be copyrightable it must be original. As used here the word "original" is not to be taken as meaning "never-to-have-existed-before." It need not involve an idea that has never been previously thought of. The essence of originality is not novelty. Indeed, ideas are not copyrightable and the courts have not protected property in ideas unless those ideas can be reduced to a concrete form, as when a patent for an industrial design is involved.[70] It is the expression of thought in which the work is clothed of which originality is required.[71] In effect this means that to possess copyright as author's work must not be copied from another nor must the work have been in the public domain.[72] Elaborating on the concept of originality, Dr. Fox has said:

> In order to be entitled to copyright a work must be original in the sense that the author has created it by his own skill, labour and judgment. It will be seen, therefore, that the owner of copyright has no monopoly in the subject matter. Others are at liberty to produce the same result provided they do so independently and though they are not the first in the field their work is none the less original in the sense in which that word is used in the Copyright Act.[73]

It is only in their form or expression that themes, plots of novels or plays, and subjects of essays or articles can be protected.

A case illustrative of the problems of copyrightability just touched on was *Deeks* v. *Wells. (See Case No. 37)*

Titles of Works

As Dr. Harold Fox explains in fuller detail in *The Canadian Law of*

Copyright and Industrial Designs,[74] titles of books or other works are, generally speaking, not copyrightable. An exception is made only where the name or title of such works is of such a length as to constitute a literary composition of the author. Otherwise, an author of a book with a certain title may successfully launch an action to prevent a second author from using the same or similar title only on the grounds that the second author is "passing off" his work as the first author's work, and not on the grounds of copyright infringement. One might well surmise that such a suit might have been appropriate in 1795-6 when Louis Roy launched a newspaper with the same title as Edward Edwards' *Montreal Gazette*. In addition, "[t]he new paper was made almost identical in format, apparently in an attempt to confuse the reader and capture opposition patronage."[75]

Newspaper Copyright

In the public mind at least the copyright considerations of the newspaper journalist are less well-known than copyright for the short story writer, novelist or poet. The central fact that should be understood is that news as such is not copyrightable, but that the form of the news report and the language with which that news is clothed do enjoy copyright.[76] Except for serial stories and tales, articles from one newspaper may be freely reproduced by other papers unless such borrowing has been expressly forbidden, but the source of that article must be indicated. These conditions are laid down in Article 9 of the Revised Schedule of the second Berne Convention, which also provides that the legal consequences of the breach of this obligation shall be determined by the laws of the country where protection is claimed.[77] The portion of Article 9 which excepts serial stories and tales from the privilege reads:

> Serial stories, tales, and all other works, whether literary, scientific, or artistic, whatever their object, published in the newspapers or periodicals of one of the countries of the Union may not be reproduced in the other countries without the consent of the authors.[78]

The different nature of news is spelled out in the same article: "The protection of the present Convention shall not apply to news of the day or to miscellaneous information which is simply of the nature of items of news."[79]

That the borrowing which Article 9 otherwise permits is sometimes forbidden is indicated by the following typical newspaper notice:

The fact that newspaper editors and reporters deal in news, a commodity which is in the public domain, probably accounts for the long tradition of free exchange of news-items in Canadian journalism. Witness the first issue of Canada's first newspaper, *The Halifax Gazette*, which was made up mainly of European news stories. Or witness the newspapers of William Lyon Mackenzie's day, when Reform journals were filled with borrowings from other Reform journals, and tory papers were filled with borrowings from other tory papers. Today The Canadian Press is able to operate because there is a co-operative pooling of stories. Editorials as well as news items are borrowed and not by C. P. members alone. Such practices are considered to be quite proper, although, as has been pointed out, only when acknowledgment is made and only when the owner of copyright does not prohibit the borrowing.

Far from resenting the borrowing of editorials, most newspapers feel flattered to have their ideas repeated by their colleagues. They do not expect payment by the debtor newspaper. Indeed, a daily (e.g. *The Ottawa Journal* in those years when it is so) will boast that it is the "most quoted newspaper in Canada." To document its boast, the proud claimant will refer not only to the *Hansard* record but to the evidence of borrowing provided by the national clipping service to which it subscribes. To the *Times-Journal* of what was Ft. William and to the *News-Chronicle* of what was Port Arthur, such papers must be especially grateful because, in the past at least, the Lakehead organs seem to have printed more borrowed than original editorials.

The long tradition of free and easy newspaper borrowing should not lead the journalist to believe that he can reprint anything his colleagues have published. As has been noted, the language of a newspaper article *is* copyrightable. (This implies, of course, that the passage for which originality is claimed must be substantial enough and long enough that the so-called borrowing is not the result of an accidental similarity of phrasing.) The protection seems only fair. It would not be just, for example, that Robert J. C. Stead should have had to give up all his rights to his poem "Kitchener" just because he wrote it first for member newspapers in the Western Press Association which carried the memorial verses a day or two after the British war hero's death in 1916. Today the notation that such-and-such an item is exclusive to the

Ottawa Journal and the *Guardian* of Manchester, or that an item is "Copyright, the Toronto *Star*" is a reminder that an editor is not free to pick up everything he sees. It should be remembered that Canadian newspapers were able to carry the "Ask Henry" column only because they paid the Toronto *Telegram* syndicate for the privilege of doing so. *The Ottawa Citizen* has run the Sydney Harris column regularly only because it has paid money to the syndicate which handles the column.

Our earlier discussion about news not being copyrightable should be contrasted with the fact that where confidential news or information is involved, it is possible to protect it not by legal proceedings claiming infringement of copyright but by legal action which has as its basis an implied contract or obligation not to disclose.[81] As Dr. Fox points out:

> [I]n the several *Exchange Telegraph Co.* cases it was held that a company carrying on the business of supplying information relative to the price of stocks and shares, the results of race meetings and cricket news, had a right of property in such news and information and was entitled to an injunction, restraining a third party from surreptitiously obtaining or copying any such news collected by it and from publishing, transmitting or communicating any such news if obtained from a subscriber in breach of confidence or contract.[82]

Another case outside the realm of copyright, but dissimilar to the Exchange Telegraph cases, involved the protection of news as a "quasi-property" against unfair competition. This was *International News Service* v. *Associated Press*.[83] In it the International News Service was alleged to have taken news from the Associated Press and given it to its own clients. Mr. Justice Pitney described the nature of the offence claimed:

> Complainant's service, as well as defendant's, is a daily service to daily newspapers; most of the foreign news reaches this country at the Atlantic seaboard, principally at the City of New York, and because of this, and of time differentials due to the earth's rotation, the distribution of news matter throughout the country is principally from east to west; and, since in speed the telegraph and telephone easily outstrip the rotation of the earth, it is a simple matter for defendant to take complainant's news from bulletins or early editions of complainant's members in the eastern cities and at the mere cost of telegraphic transmission cause it to be published in western papers issued at least as early as those served by complainant. Besides this, and irrespective of time differentials, irregularities in telegraphic transmission on different lines, and the normal consumption of time

in printing and distributing the newspaper, results in permitting pirated news to be placed in the hands of defendant's readers sometimes simultaneously with the service of competing Associated Press papers, occasionally even earlier.[84]

In finding in favor of the Associated Press, Mr. Justice Pitney characterized the actions of International News Service in the following terms:

Stripped of all disguises, the process amounts to an unauthorized interference with the normal operation of complainant's legitimate business precisely at the point where the profit is to be reaped, in order to divert a material portion of the profit from those who have earned it to those who have not: with special advantage to defendant in the competition because of the fact that it is not burdened with any part of the expense of gathering the news. The transaction speaks for itself, and a court of equity ought not to hesitate long in characterizing it as unfair competition in business.[85]

The learned justice said further to the decision favorable to the complainant:

It is to be observed that the view we adopt does not result in giving to complainant the right to monopolize either the gathering or distribution of the news, or, without complying with the copyright act, to prevent the reproduction of its news articles; but only postpones participation by complainant's competitor in the process of distribution and reproduction of news that it has not gathered, and only to the extent necessary to prevent that competitor from reaping the fruits of complainant's efforts and expenditure, to the partial exclusion of complainant, and in violation of the principle that underlies the maxim *sic utere tuo*, etc.[86]

Mr. Justice Pitney also condemned the International News Service's behavior in the following words:

Regarding news matter as the mere material from which these two competing parties are endeavoring to make money, and treating it, therefore, as *quasi* property for the purpose of their business because they are both selling it as such, defendant's conduct differs from the ordinary case of unfair competition in trade principally in this that, instead of selling its own goods as those of complainant, it substitutes misappropriation in the place of misrepresentation and sells complainant's goods as its own.[87]

Of special interest to the working journalist is the situation which arises when a reporter or columnist (such as Eric Nicol, Garry Lautens or Maggie Grant) wishes to collect some of his past writings and issue them as a book. When he first wrote the piece he gave rights in them to the newspaper or news service (e.g. Southam News Services) which employs him. This means that if he wishes to issue those collected selections as a book he must get permission from his paper or news service. But this does not mean that the paper or news service can issue a collection of his writings without his consent. The practical effect of this situation is that there must be a mutual agreement between journalist and employer before such a book may be published.

This provision is taken care of by Section 12(3) of the Copyright Act which states:

> Where the author was in the employment of some other person under a contract of service or apprenticeship and the work was made in the course of his employment by that person, the person by whom the author was employed shall, in the absence of any agreement to the contrary, be the first owner of copyright; but where the work is an article or other contribution to a newspaper, magazine, or similar periodical, there shall, in the absence of any agreement to the contrary, be deemed to be reserved to the author a right to restrain the publication of the work, otherwise than as part of a newspaper, magazine or similar periodical.[88]

Newspaper summaries of public lectures do not infringe the copyright in those lectures. Indeed, even full reports are permitted "unless," in the words of Section (2)(e) of the Copyright Act, "the report is prohibited by a conspicuous written or printed notice affixed before and maintained during the lecture at or about the main entrance of the building in which the lecture is given, and, except whilst the building is being used for public worship, in a position near the lecturer.[89]

It should perhaps be added that if a lecture is delivered to only a small select audience rather than to the general public, its publication may be restrained on the grounds that such publication would be a breach of confidence.

However, it should be noted, according to Section 18 of the Copyright Act, that, "Notwithstanding anything in this Act, it shall not be an infringement of copyright in an address of a political nature delivered at a public meeting to publish a report thereof in a newspaper."[90]

Droit Moral

An author, even after he has surrendered copyright in his work, has the right to prevent distortion of that work. In continental jurisprudence this is known as *droit moral*. As laid down in Section 12(7) of the Copyright Act the provision reads: "Independently of the author's copyright, and even after the assignment, either wholly or partially, of the said copyright, the author shall have the right to claim authorship of the work, as well as the right to restrain any distortion, mutilation or other modification of the said work which would be prejudicial to his honour or reputation."[91] The wording here is practically identical with that of Article 6 bis (1) of the Rome Revision of the International Copyright Convention. Dr. Fox makes the point that when such mutilation occurs an author has the right to sue for damage to his reputation, but the basis of the action he might launch would be in the area of libel rather than in the area of copyright.[92]

Immoral Works

The question sometimes arises as to whether a work of an immoral nature is copyrightable. One important case with a bearing on the matter was *Pasickniak* v. *Dojacek*. (*See Case No. 38*)

Dr. Fox has commented on this and related decisions to sum up the present law on the question:

> Copyright is not denied in a work that is immoral or otherwise objectionable, but . . . the courts will not lend the plaintiff any assistance in the maintenance of his rights in such a case. Where the work is merely coarse and nasty, relief will not necessarily be refused, but where the work is found to be so obscene or immoral that the publication of it would be an offence against the law, the plaintiff cannot recover damages because he could not lawfully have sold the work.
>
> Generally speaking, it may be said that if a work is obscene or immoral, indecent, blasphemous or irreligious to an extent amounting to blasphemy, scandalous, fraudulent, tending to deceive the public, or seditious or libellous, the court will not intervene to protect such a work from infringement.[93]

Catalogues, Directories and Other Compilations

A copyright in a catalogue, directory or other compilation differs from a copyright in a novel, a history, a philosophical treatise or other more "creative" work. An author who creates a novel, history or philosophical treatise and obtains copyright for his work, may restrain publication by a second author of a book that closely approximates the first author's work. In such a case it may be assumed that plagiarism has occurred.

In contrast, two authors, working independently, might each compile a directory of the same city. Because the "raw material" is identical in each case it is more than likely that each man's product will be virtually identical to the other man's product. But this fact does not imply that one man has copied from the other. Neither will be empowered to restrain publication by the other. The copyright each man enjoys has been earned by the original *labor* he has expended. There will be nothing to prevent a third entrepreneur from making a third and similar directory and selling it in competition with the others. What he must not do is simply *copy* one of the existing directories. If he does so he may be sued for infringement of copyright.

It will be readily seen that where a "cut and dried" work such as a directory is involved, it may be hard to tell whether the similarities of two publications is the result of identity of subject or of plagiarism. To detect such plagiarism and to entrap the plagiarist some compilers insert deliberate errors in their work. If the errors reappear in the rival's work, this is taken as evidence that literary theft has occurred.[94]

Radio, Television, Films and Mechanical Contrivances

Radio, television, films and mechanical contrivances have raised copyright problems at least as difficult as those raised by the print media. The basic rights conferred on the copyright holder, be he author or anyone to whom the author has assigned that copyright, is specified as a *sole* right. Section (1)(d) assigns that right "in the case of a literary, dramatic, or musical work, to make any record, perforated roll, cinematographic film, or other contrivance by means of which the work may be mechanically performed or delivered."[95] As has been mentioned earlier, the term of copyright in records and perforated rolls is fifty years from the making of the original plate from which the contrivance was directly or indirectly derived. The person who was the owner of such original plate at the time when such plate was made is deemed to be the author of the contrivance.[96] Section 3(1)(e) says that the "copyright . . . includes the sole right in the case of any literary, dramatic, musical or artistic work, to reproduce, adapt and publicly present such work by cinematograph, if the author has given such work an original character; but if such original character is absent the cinematographic production shall be protected as a photograph.''[97] As has been previously indicated, the term of copyright for photographs is fifty years from the making of the original negative from which the photograph was directly or indirectly derived. The owner of such a negative at the time when such negative was made is deemed to be author of the photograph so derived.[98] Section 3(1)(f) assigns sole right ''in case of any literary, dramatic, musical or artistic work, to communicate such work by radio communication.''[99]

The Canadian Copyright Act does not mention television, but apparently it is taken account of by such phrases as ''or otherwise'' when section 2(g) defines ''dramatic work'' as including ''any piece for recitation, choreographic work or entertainment in dumb show, the scenic arrangement or acting form of which is fixed in writing *or otherwise* [italics mine] . . .''[100]

As provided by the Copyright Act, composers of musical works and the authors of the lyrics are paid royalties for the public performance of their works, whether live or mechanical.[101] Such payments are made for radio and television programs, including commercials, which are policed to determine monies due.[102]

The process that produces a motion picture film is not identical with the process by which telecasting produces images on the television screen. The difference was described by Mr. Justice Cameron in *Canadian Admiral Corporation* v. *Rediffusion Inc. et al:*[103]

In an ordinary camera, light from the scene to be photographed is focused by means of a lens on a sensitive emulsified surface of a film or plate. A change is produced in the emulsion which can be developed by the proper chemicals into a reproduction of the scene in negative form; and by reprinting from the negative a postive picture is produced. Cinematographic films are produced in much the same way. The result in each case is a negative and photograph, or a series of negatives and photographs in material form having a more or less permanent endurance.

The function of a television camera is quite different, namely, to convert a picture—which is light—into an electric signal which can be transmitted or radiated as electromagnetic waves (Herzian waves) through the ether.

Dr. Fox states that ''there cannot be copyright in a mere oral broadcast nor can there be copyright in the telecasting of a public event such as a football match.''[104]

It perhaps needs to be stressed that the remarks made earlier in a more general context about the copyrightability of language, about the uncopyrightability of news, and about the question of originality apply with equal force with reference to radio, television, film and mechanical contrivances. A fuller discussion of the copyright problems in these areas might easily take our study beyond the ambit of this book. The reader interested in exploring further the intricacy of copyright in the electronic media field might look at an American case of recent vintage. This was *Fortnightly Corporation* v. *United Artists Television Inc.*,[105] a case which grew out of the cable transmission of films, without payment of additional royalties, to viewers beyond the viewing areas of originating stations. It is probably because of the kind of problems which this case explored that the American Copyright Act has been called the "Model T Copyright Law.[106]

Fair Dealing and the Effects of Reprography

In similar vein, the Canadian Copyright Law has been called "a horse and buggy act."[107] That the description is apt arises from the fact that not only is television not mentioned in the Canadian Copyright Act but also that modern reprography is operating to subvert the fair dealing provisions of the Act to the considerable detriment of the copyright holder.

Provision for fair dealing is contained in Section 17 of the Copyright Act. Section 17(2) says in part:

> The following acts do not constitute an infringement of copyright:
> (a) any fair dealing with any work for the purposes of private study, research, criticism, review, or newspaper summary . . .[108]

This proviso accompanies recognition of the right to quote short passages without permission and to paraphrase longer passages that do not constitute a substantial portion of that work as a whole. Thus a person might quote a line or two from a poem or a few paragraphs from a book either in a literary criticism or as a part of a piece of independent creative writing. The real criterion of fair use is that there should not be an act of stealing sufficiently serious to result in damage to the author.

Until recent times the mechanical difficulty of copying material for the modest use just described deterred abuse of fair dealing provisions. But the invention of the photocopier and other instruments of reprography has dramatically changed the situation. Formerly when hand-copying was the chief method at hand or when mimeo and ditto duplicators were the most sophisticated devices available it was uneconomical to make single copies of extensive length. The latter process required a master, a stencil the special preparation of which was time-consuming and expensive. By contrast, because the photocopier requires no master (indeed, the original is the "master") it is cheap and easy to make copies by Xerox and related methods.[109]

Many uses of the photocopying process are legitimate and very useful. Companies can send their clients copies of their accounts. Receipts can be issued. Photographs of wanted persons can be sent across the nation. Cheques, price lists, prospectuses, medical information and so on can be reproduced and distributed rapidly. In this way, thousands of dollars and thousands of expensive man-hours of labor may be saved.

Roy C. Sharp has assessed other results of this technology, however. He has written:

> Copy machine installations have increased from a few thousands in the early 1950s to many hundreds of thousands in the mid-1960s; the number of copies made by these machines has expanded from a few million in the early 1950s to over 10 billion in 1965 and will, it is estimated, have increased to over 25 billion for 1970. A study of photocopying practices in the United Kingdom reports that the 409 libraries surveyed made 1,118,143 photocopies of articles and journals, and 55,674 photocopies of extracts of books in the year under review. Photocopying is even more extensively practised in North American than in the United Kingdom . . . [I]n the United States it [was] estimated that 3 billion pages of published material were copied in 1969, of which almost 1.8 billion pages were copyrighted material. By extrapolation, it can be conservatively estimated that by 1971 some 2.2 billion pages of copyrighted material will be copied annually. Of this, 1.7 billion pages will be from journals and periodicals, 400 million pages will be from books, and 100 million pages from other copyrighted material.[110]

Elsewhere Mr. Sharp has pointed out that there are no comparable studies on copying in Canada but that the situation is not too dissimilar. He gives as an example a publicly funded school board making several hundred copies of a substantial part of copyrighted books without permission of the copyright holder.[111]

Chris Braithwaite has called attention to the following examples:

> The University of Toronto library provides copies to students for 5 cents a book page, turning out about 33,000 copies a month on five machines.
> The Toronto Public Library copies 1.5 million pages a year for patrons of its reference collection at rates about 15 cents to $1.50 a page.
> The Education Centre Library answers about 20 requests a day for

research materials. They come from students, teachers, psychologists, guidance counsellors and administrators. Unless the original is requested, the material is copied from books or directly from microfilmed periodicals.

The centre's documentation department makes particularly imaginative use of its Xerox machine. Seven magazines named Content are published there and distributed to the Board of Education staff. Each consists of copies of the table of contents of the scholarly journals in a particular field. Staff members can obtain copies of the articles that interest them by circling the titles.

The department indexes about 300 journals in Content, and copies roughly 20,000 articles a year.[112]

An excerpt from a Canadian Authors Association brief to the Economic Council of Canada (which in 1970 was studying Canadian copyright law) adds further detail to the picture of the Canadian situation:

Copyright is being eroded daily in Canadian and American educational institutions from kindergarten to postgraduate university course. The massive amount of mimeographing and photocopying in schools and libraries is staggering. Part of the reason for this is the complex school budget, which allows little for book purchase, but "any amount" for stationery, including photocopying paper. The paper is paid for, but never the author.

Some educational institutions have used their tax-provided funds to establish commercial presses which advertise photocopying services. In defiance of copyright the University of Michigan notoriously photocopies entire books for sale.

Such abuse of the author's material is in breach of the law, and as taxpayers authors are compelled to support the robbery. Indeed, we know of instances of photocopying without a single sale by publisher, and not a cent of royalty to the author. The publishers' sample copies are used, or a copy sent on approval, even a gift copy from author to teacher.

Part of the invasion of copyright is due to ignorance on the part of teachers, librarians, and professors. Some fantastic and false excuses are promulgated, such as "any amount of an author's work may be copied so long as you do not put the author's name on it!" A single example is that of a professor of English at a Toronto university asking the stenographers' pool to mimeograph 500 copies (for free distribution) of 27 poems by a Canadian poet.[113]

Special photocopying problems are raised by large corporations involved in industrial and technical research. Such corporations have their own industrial libraries which will copy technical articles for departments within the corporation. What often happens is that a department may request and receive from the library one copy of the article, after which the department may use its own photocopier to run off thirty or forty additional copies, one for each member of the staff.[114]

An advance on "on-the-spot" reprography is long distance machine copying. Facsimile transmission has been achieved by the use of telephone lines and microwave systems. How this further complicates the copyright situation will be considered presently.

What has been called adjuncts to machine copying are the microphotographic processes known as microfilm and microfiche. Microfilm is photographic reproduction reduced in size. Microfiche is similar in being photographic copy, but here the size reduction is vastly greater. As "The Law of Copyright: Reprography and Computer" says:

Sixty to seventy slides, each containing a copy of an eight by eleven inch page, may be placed on one four by five microfiche card. Both of these media are tremendous space savers; for example, in microfiche form, the Encyclopedia Britannica could easily be stored in a shoe box.[115]

The seemingly limitless duplication of copyrighted material which technology has made possible and which has just been indicated appears to have been made only through a clear violation of the Copyright Act. Under the fair dealing provision, a student may Xerox a single copy of a substantial part of a work for his own private study and research. But, according to Roy C. Sharp, he may not make copies for others. Nor may libraries legally make copies and distribute them to students and researchers.[116]

Those who go beyond the limited privileges allowed by the fair dealing proviso of the Copyright Act have been condemned. Herman Wouk, author of the *Caine Mutiny*, has said, "Copying without compensation is piracy."[117]

An opposite viewpoint is held by many librarians who feel they have a moral obligation to serve the public by disseminating knowledge, through the use of photocopiers if necessary. As Chris Braithwaite points out, "Most librarians are convinced . . . that the provision of a single copy of a copyright work is both moral and legal."[118]

It seems clear that the conflicting viewpoints represent a serious dilemma: how is the free interchange of knowledge to be encouraged without robbing the author and publisher of the just returns for their labors? How are the interests of author and publisher to be protected without inhibiting the spread of learning for the public good?

One solution to that dilemma that has been suggested involves the payment of royalties on photocopies. The system proposed would depend on identifying books by a nine-digit Standard Book Number. Photocopiers would be licensed and equipped to make a taped record of the number of every book copied. The tapes would be sent periodically to a clearing center where royalties would be levied on machine users and sent to the owners of copyright.[119]

The proposal seems a promising one—or at least if would be if it weren't for the fact that facsimile transmission of copyrighted material may bypass the registering devices that can be installed in a static photocopier. Miniaturized storage and facsimile transmission combined with indexing and access by computer suggest problems of copyright[120] which have not yet been fully explored and with which the present law of copyright is not adequate to deal.

Chapter IX

The Problem of Privacy

The areas of the law thus far discussed are, despite their shortcomings, reasonably complete. They are recognized legal concepts. On the other hand, the right of privacy,[1] which is an aspect of the individual's liberty which ought to be of concern to the journalist, does not enjoy the same sort of recognition in Canada or in the United Kingdom. Anthony A. Thompson has pointed out that "the concept of privacy, as such, is unknown and unprotected by English law."[2] In Canada there is no recognized *common* law right to privacy.[3] In both countries some law in other areas does confer a limited right which is akin to the right of privacy and this will be discussed presently. But in England the gains for the principle of what has been called the right to be let alone are indirect ones. In Canada, with three exceptions which will be considered below, the same fact is true.

The American Privacy Law

Such is not the case in the United States. In that country there is a privacy law. It seems useful to consider its nature so that, using it as a basis for comparison, it will be possible to more clearly delineate the Canadian legal situation in this area.

Alan Westin[4] has traced with some care the genesis of the privacy right from the earliest days of the American republic. He says:

> [T]he notion put forward by legal commentators from Brandeis down to the present—that privacy was somehow a "modern" legal right which began to take form only in the late nineteenth century—is simply bad history and bad law.[5]

Nevertheless, for the purposes of this short chapter, it is probably sufficient to take as starting point a landmark article which appeared December 15, 1890 in Volume IV, Number 5 of the *Harvard Law Review*. The seminal study was entitled "The Right to Privacy" and was written by Samuel D. Warren and Louis D. Brandeis.[6] What motivated it was what the authors apprehended to be an increase in intrusive gossip within the pages of the mass circulation newspapers of the day.[7] In tracing the development of the idea of privacy, Warren and Brandeis considered the existing laws to guard the individual from battery in its various forms, to afford him freedom from actual restraint and to protect his property. They extended the principles underlying such concepts to include the processes and products of the mind. They cited the English decision in *Albert* v. *Strange*.[8] That case had its beginning when Queen Victoria and the Prince Consort made etchings for their own pleasure and that of their friends and intimates. Mr. William Strange, a printer and publisher, obtained plates of some of those etchings, advertised their public display and offered for sale a catalogue of his projected exhibition. Prince Albert filed suit to recover the etchings and to have all previously printed copies of the catalogues destroyed. Warren and Brandeis emphasized the fact that, in finding in favor of the plaintiff, the court not only prohibited the reproduction of the etchings but also the publishing of a description of them. They construed the decision as recognition of a more liberal doctrine than that of the mere protection of property. Their reasoning took them to the viewpoint "that the protection afforded to thoughts, sentiments and emotions expressed through the medium of writing or of the arts, so far as it consists in preventing publication, is merely an instance of the enforcement of the more general right of the individual to be let alone."[9] They asserted that the "principle which protects personal writings and all other personal productions, not against theft and physical appropriation, but against publication in any form, is in reality not the principle of private property, but that of an inviolate personality."[10]

Having arrived inductively at their thesis, the authors then proceeded to reinforce and elaborate on it, drawing their examples this time not from property-related cases, but from cases the *ratio decidendi* of which are grounded on an illegal breach of an implied contract or of a trust or confidence. Taking into account the fact that techniques of photography had so improved as to make it possible for photographers to take pictures surreptitiously, whereas previously tedious sittings had been required, the eminent jurists maintained that a narrow interpretation of doctrines involving contract, trust or confidence is insufficient to cover many contemporary situations and that once again it was necessary to invoke a doctrine of inviolate personality. They used similar reasoning and arrived at a similar conclusion after a discussion of the law of trade secrets.

Not only did Warren and Brandeis assert the existence of the law of privacy. They also described and delimited what they conceived the law to be. They did so in a series of six propositions:

1. The right to privacy does not prohibit any publication of matter which is of public or general interest.[11]

2. The right to privacy does not prohibit the communication of any matter, though in its nature private, when the publication is made under circumstances which render it immune from attack according to the law of slander and libel.[12]

3. The law would probably not grant any redress for the invasion of privacy by oral publication in the absence of any special damage.[13]

4. The right to privacy ceases upon the publication of the facts by the individual, or with his consent.[14]

5. The truth of the matter published does not afford a defense.[15]

6. The absence of 'malice' in the publisher does not afford a defense.[16]

The two jurists recommended that remedies for an invasion of privacy should be an action for damages in all cases, and, in a very limited class of cases, an injunction to prohibit and prevent the continuation of the offence. More tentatively, they felt that though it was "desirable that the privacy of the individual should receive the added protection of the criminal law, . . . the protection of society must come mainly through the recognition of the rights of the individual."[17]

In the years since the 1890 article, the right of privacy as conceived by Warren and Brandeis has been expanded in American law. In 1903 New York state passed the nation's first privacy statute. It prohibited the unauthorized use of a person's name or picture for advertising or trade purposes. Virginia, Utah and Oklahoma are other states which have enacted privacy legislation,[18] as has the District of Columbia.[19] Donald G. Pember lists the following as the states in which the law of privacy has been recognized: Alabama, Alaska, Arizona, Arkansas, California, Connecticut, Delaware, Florida, Georgia, Illinois, Indiana, Iowa, Kansas, Kentucky, Louisiana, Maryland, Michigan, Mississippi, Missouri, Montana, New Hampshire, New Jersey, New York, North Carolina, Ohio, Oklahoma, Oregon, Pennsylvania, South Carolina, South Dakota, Utah, Virginia, and West Virginia.[20] The District of Columbia falls into the same category.[21] The only states in which the concept has been rejected are Nebraska, Rhode Island, Texas and Wisconsin.[22] In the remaining states, either no reported cases to test the privacy concept have been found, or reported cases have neither recognized privacy nor rejected it, or cases in which the right to privacy seemed to be an issue have been decided on other grounds.[23]

A footnote in Donald R. Pember's *Privacy and the Press* conveys an idea of the extent of American privacy litigation. He says:

About 600 cases provided the basis for this study. [i.e. the study of which his book consists] Of this total, between 350 and 450 can be regarded as true invasion of privacy suits, depending on how an invasion of privacy is defined. The remainder were actions based on copyright violations, unfair competition, libel and other adjacent legal areas. Using the base figure of 350 privacy suits reported during the past 82 years, 149 of these were litigated in New York. Following New York, California reported 20 suits, Georgia and Kentucky each reported 15, and Pennsylvania reported 14. Again, of the 350 total, 216 involved the mass media, broadly defined to include such media as handbills and labels on consumer products. During the first forty years of the law's growth there were only 53 suits reported. Of this number, New York recorded 32.[24]

The field covered by American privacy law is suggested by Dean William Prosser, whom Gillmor and Barron have called the *doyen* of American tort scholars.[25] He has classified the right to privacy as embracing four separate wrongs:

1. Intrusions into an individual's seclusion, solitude or private affairs;
2. Public disclosure of embarrassing facts about an individual;
3. Publicity which places an individual in a false light in the public eye;
4. Appropriation, for the defendant's advantage of the plaintiff's name or likeness.[26]

It must not be implied that any absolute judicial agreement exists concerning the weight to be attached to the privacy law or to the countervailing interests represented by that law and the first amendment provision to guarantee press freedom. Just how diverse are the opinions which relate to the right of privacy as a legal concept in the United States may be gathered from a reading of pages 471 to 501 of Donald M. Gillmor and Jerome A. Barron's *Mass Communication Law.*

The English Privacy Law, or Lack of It

As has been pointed out, English privacy law is very deficient, particularly by contrast with American privacy law. Speaking of Britain, Anthony A. Thompson has written: "Only one law designed for the protection of personal privacy as such has ever been passed in this country—eavesdropping . . . The law was repealed as obsolete in 1964."[27] H. Phillip Levy has described how Lord Mancroft's bill in 1961 failed to pass because of the difficulty of defining privacy in such a way as to establish an acceptable balance between the freedom of the press and the rights of the individual. He has noted that two private members' bills introduced into the British parliament in 1967 were equally unsuccessful.[28] The concept of privacy still remains unknown and unprotected in English law. There have been rare occasions when the law has awarded *de facto* remedies for invasion of privacy, but such remedies have come about almost as accidental by-products of laws designed for quite another purpose: the protection of property, the prevention of trespass, the maintenance of copyright, for example. The outcome of *Albert* v. *Strange*, discussed earlier, is illustrative of this sort of oblique concession to the idea of privacy.

What the law fails to do in this area is, to some degree, compensated for by the British Press Council. This body does not have the legal powers of a court. It cannot punish, award damages or order injunctions. All it can do is censure, exercise moral suasion, and, thereby, perhaps, prevent the continuation or the repetition of the offence. One class of complaints the Council has dealt with has been categorized as "Intrusion and Invasion of Privacy." These have been subdivided into: Intrusion on Bereavement; Private Grief; Private Life of Persons In The Public Eye; Photographs; Complaints Arising Out of Court Proceedings; Invasion of Private Residence; and Hounding. In his book, *The Press Council*,[29] H. Phillip Levy has listed 37 complaints dealt with between 1953 and 1967. Fifteen of these complaints were upheld.

The Privacy Law of Canada

As is true of so many other aspects of its national life, privacy law in Canada occupies a place somewhere between that of the United Kingdom and the United States. Canada is closer to the Mother Country in that both nations are deficient in common law in the privacy field. But the fact that British Columbia, Manitoba and Saskatchewan recently enacted statute law has moved the Canadian position a small way towards the American position. An account of this provincial legislation will be provided later in this chapter.

It is to be noted that the new federal Protection of Privacy Act[30] is a misnomer inasmuch as its narrow preoccupation is with the legalities and illegalities of electronic surveillance and because it leaves untouched the other wide areas in which invasion of privacy may occur.

Apart from the limited protection that this Act gives, and outside of the provinces of British Columbia, Manitoba and Saskatchewan, the only recourse the victim has by which he can combat threats to his privacy is to the common law of torts or to related provisions of the criminal law. Perhaps the most pertinent tort is the tort of trespass.

Harry Street has described it in terms applicable to the Canadian as it is to the English situation:

> This [tort] enables the occupier to sue someone who enters his land or searches his goods without the authority of law and without the occupier's permission. The occupier can be compensated for the damage inflicted on him, and might get an injunction restraining any further unlawful entry. By a recent decision of the House of Lords the damages are restricted to the harm suffered—that award could include aggravated damages for injured feelings—whereas other parts of the Commonwealth have understandably refused to follow the House of Lords and can still award exemplary damages which go beyond compensation and seek to punish the defendant or make an example of him. An action for trespass is restricted to those in possession. A hotel guest does not possess his room; nor does a hospital patient. The householder cannot sue in trespass to goods when his telephone is tapped; the telephone utility, not the householder, possesses the wires. If the cameraman spies on a household from the roadway, the occupier could sue because he is presumed ordinarily to possess that half of the roadway adjoining his building, but his wife could not sue if the house were not also in her name. These are serious limitations on the availability of trespass in the context of privacy.[31]

Another tort which may be relevant is the tort of nuisance. It may be invoked in the case of harassment by telephone calls of the occupant of his home, for example. Harry Street indicates the scope of this tort when he says:

> The man who constructs a system of mirrors in his garden to see what happens on the doctor's couch in the consulting room next door may also be suable. Again the reporter who pesters the bereaved mother is immune if the mother does not possess the house either solely or at least jointly with her husband.[32]

A third tort, that of defamation has already been discussed extensively. The difficulty of relating privacy to the law of libel is that true and therefore non-defamatory statements which invade privacy are not actionable even though the public interest is not served by those statements. Moreover, because it is impossible to libel the dead, a journalist might write untruths about a dead person in such a way as to, in effect, invade the privacy of surviving relatives, provided those relatives are not themselves defamed. Two other areas of the civil law which confer benefits somewhat akin to what a privacy law would provide are those which permit suits for breach of contract and injunctions to prevent breaches of confidence.

Criminal law does little to safeguard individual privacy. Of some relevance are Criminal Code Sections 38 to 42.[33] These sections are grouped under the heading, "The Defence of Property." Marginal descriptions indicate the content of this part of the Code: Defence of movable property; Assault by trespasser; Defence with claim of right; Defence of dwelling: Defence of house or real property; Assault in case of lawful entry: Trespasser provoking assault. Section 173 of the Criminal Code deals with "Trespassing at night."[34]

A statutory provision somewhat related to the tort of nuisance is section 381 of the Criminal Code, which deals with the crime of intimidation.[35]

A Canadian case in which existing law was applied in the interests of personal privacy was *Robbins* v. *Canadian Broadcasting Corp. (Quebec). (See Case No. 39)* Another case, this time not settled in favor of the plaintiff, added nothing to the common-law in support of the right of privacy, but it did explore the relationship to the privacy concept. *(See Case No. 40)*

It seems probable that regional Press Councils will one day be called upon in Canada, just as the single national Press Council in the United Kingdom is called on, in an attempt to restrain invasions of privacy. There is not, as yet, however, a body of Canadian decisions to match the British decisions previously referred to. This is because Press Councils did not make their appearances until very recently, and then only in certain parts of the country. It was not until 1972 that those in Ontario and Alberta became operative. The Ontario Council has eight member newspapers with 55 percent of the province's daily circulation. The Alberta Council has five dailies as members. Windsor, Ontario, has a community council. The Quebec Council was formed in June, 1973.

As has been indicated earlier, the only three provinces with statutory provision for the right of privacy are British Columbia,[36] Manitoba[37] and Saskatchewan.[38] The three statutes are quite similar, with those of Manitoba and Saskatchewan having the greater resemblance to each other. All three make it a tort actionable without proof of damage, for a person, wilfully and without claim of right to violate the privacy of another.[39] All three place in the prohibited category of offences surveillance and eavesdropping whether or not accompanied by trespass.[40] The Manitoba and Saskatchewan Acts instance, as auditory or visual surveillance devices, eavesdropping, watching, spying, besetting or following.[41] All three statutes make actionable the unauthorized use of a name or portrait of another for advertising property or services.[42] The Manitoba and Saskatchewan legislation makes it an offence to listen to or record conversations passed by means of telephones or telecommunications "otherwise than as a lawful party thereto"[43] or to use without consent letters, diaries or other personal documents of a person.[44]

All the legislation contains qualifications and exceptions to their main provisions. These are intended to take account of such considerations as consent to invasion of privacy, the exercise of legal privilege, public interest, and performance of their duty by peace officers and similar officials.

The Manitoba and Saskatchewan Acts set out the remedies available in an action for violation of privacy. These are listed as damages, an injunction, an order to the defendant to account to the plaintiff for profits resulting from the violation, an order to the defendant to deliver to the plaintiff all articles or documents acquired by the defendant as a result of the violation, and other relief necessary under the circumstances.[45] Both the British Columbia and Saskatchewan Acts stipulate that action for violation of privacy must be begun within two years from the discovery of the alleged violation and that the right of action is extinguished by the death of the person whose privacy is alleged to be violated.[46]

Present and Future Considerations

The reader is probably aware by now that this chapter has ōmitted discussion of one wide area of privacy invasion. "Computer data banks," "wire tapping," "bugging," and "electronic surveillance" are terms which suggest the extent to which technology can be used to make an Orwellian intrusion into a person's hitherto secret existence. The revelations of the Watergate scandal demonstrate the levels at which such devices may be employed. Such offences as these technical means make possible do not relate in any way that is peculiar to the practice of journalism. It is for this reason that the subject has not been considered in this book. But readers who are interested in further investigation into this theme might consult books and articles referred to in the endnotes to this chapter. The immediacy of the problem is indicated by the fact that the federal parliament should have passed the Protection of Privacy Act in 1974.

As it is with so many other aspects of press law, it would seem that the critical question central to the privacy issue is how can the rights of the individual be balanced against society's need to know. It is a question which, in terms of specific news situations, can be very real. And it is a question which can arise in news stories of major importance or in news stories of a minor, routine nature.

Sheila Ascroft has written:

> For our modern society, already threatened by electronic and computer invasions, both the social and legal recognition of a right to privacy becomes imperative. Provincial laws and press councils are a beginning but not enough. There is too much reliance on the competency and responsibility of the journalist in this matter. His guidelines are vague and idealistic, and he too is only human.
>
> A right to privacy would not only protect the individual but also provide a definite guideline for the journalist. It need not sacrifice the right to information within the public's interest but merely the information which is of private interest.[47]

It is conceivable that in the future statute law will provide surer guidance in the privacy area. As this chapter was being written, La Ligue des Droits de L'Homme of Montreal "called for an all-embracing law protecting individual privacy with a permanent commission to administer the legislation."[48] The suggestion of this civil liberties group might be acted upon, or the other Canadian provinces might follow the example of British Columbia, Manitoba and Saskatchewan to bring about a privacy law in a more piece-meal fashion. It will be interesting to see whether either of these developments occurs.

Chapter X

Government Secrecy and The Press

Professor Hugh Lawford has written:

> [T]he enactment of legislation to protect privacy will provide an opportunity for enacting the more important rules to protect freedom of information. [Former] Justice Minister Turner has promised a Canadian Freedom of Information Act, but there are few signs that his department regards the legislation as urgent. Canadians should urge him to raise its priority. No legislation should be enacted to protect privacy without legislation to protect freedom of information.[1]

If an impression left by the last chapter was that the law does not properly safeguard the privacy of the private person, the converse suggestion this chapter makes is that existing law and practice do too much to safeguard the privacy of the public official and the public institution. Private should be private and public should be public. Many critics of the existing state of affairs contend that there is too much secrecy in Canada. It is felt that neither the private citizen nor the journalist has sufficient access to the information which the government is too prone to classify.

Secrecy In Other Countries

The United States

In Canada the situation contrasts unfavorably with that in the United States, Sweden and even Great Britain. The American emphasis on security which prevailed during the Second World War carried over into the post-War period but the situation had been greatly improved by the mid-1960's. In 1953 the agencies empowered to classify information was reduced by Executive Order; the ''restricted'' classification was abolished. In 1961 the United States established a system by which classified documents were put into one of four declassification groups. As a result most classified documents now fall into a group which ''demotes'' them automatically every three years until they reach the lowest category of secrecy. This has meant that any material in this group is completely declassified at the end of twelve years. Professor Donald C. Rowat describes the other declassification groups in the following terms:

> The second group steps down from one degree of secrecy to another only after twelve years; the third group are extremely sensitive documents, to be downgraded on an individual basis; and the fourth group contains information over which the United States has no jurisdiction.[2]

The determination and inquisitiveness of the press as well as the traditional openness of the American government have made the United States much more liberal and open than Canada in giving access to official documents. Individual departments and agencies may make their own rules about disclosing such material. In practice they classify for much shorter periods than does the Public Archives, which has a fifty-year rule to govern materials placed on deposit. A thirty-year rule is applied by the United States State Department, for example, but the period is reduced by ten years when anyone demonstrates a legitimate need for the information.[3] Even this freedom does not go far enough to satisfy every critic. Thus, in 1961, in a famous letter to his secretaries, President Kennedy said that ''any official should have a clear and precise case involving the national interest before seeking to withhold from publication documents or papers fifteen or more years old.''[4]

According to Professor Lawford:

> An even more important development in the American system was the enactment in 1966 of the Freedom of Information Act. This new law gives an American citizen the right to obtain information from an agency and gives him the power of enforcing that right by court action. The key policy of the Act is that disclosure is made the general rule rather than the exception. All individuals are given equal rights of access to government information. The burden is placed upon Government to justify withholding a document rather than upon the citizen to justify obtaining the document. And the cases in which documents are not to be available to the public are stated specifically and narrowly.[5]

Indicative of the openness of the American system is the fact that the United States Supreme Court permitted publication of the top-secret Pentagon study of the Vietnam war on the grounds of protecting the public's right to be informed.[6]

Despite a fairly general approval of the regulations which govern the American classification system, there is a certain body of opinion that holds that that system is less liberal than it appears to be. The defect, so say some critics, is that officials, almost always over-cautious, are too prone to overclassify. William S. Moorhead indicates the nature and magnitude of that over-classification when he writes:

William G. Florence, a retired Air Force security classification official, estimated that the Defense Department had at least twenty million classified documents, and that in his judgment more than 99 per cent of them did not warrant security classification protection . . . [Former] U. N. Ambassador and Supreme Court Justice Arthur J. Goldberg, testified that in his judgment and experience, "75 per cent of these documents should never have been classified in the first place; another 15 per cent quickly outlived the need for secrecy; and only about 10 per cent genuinely required restricted access over any significant period of time."

A Defense Department witness . . . estimated . . . that Defense had about one million cubic feet of classified documents. When translated into linear feet at two thousand pages per linear foot, the classified holdings would make eighteen stacks of classified document pages, *each as high as the Washington Monument!* A State Department witness estimated that his department had about 150 million documents in files and that about 35 million of them were classified. Dr. James B. Rhoads, Archivist of the United States, testified that the National Archives is responsible for the staggering total of *some 470 million pages of classified documents.*[7]

Sweden

Of the Swedish system, Professor Rowat has observed that, "whereas in most countries all documents are secret unless a specific authority is given for their release, in Sweden they are all public unless legal provision has been made for them to be withheld."[8] The limits on such rights of access are stipulated in the Constitution and are defined clearly in a special statute. These include such matters as state security, diplomatic negotiations or police investigations. Some defenders of Canadian practice in the government secrecy field would argue that there is less difference between the Swedish and Canadian experience than proponents of the Swedish approach claim: they say this is so because the exceptions permitted in Sweden allow for widely applied secrecy measures.

Great Britain

Great Britain has long been regarded as being in the tradition of countries that support government secrecy. Its approach does not seem to match the openness of the United States and Sweden. But in one respect at least it is more liberal than Canada. Its legislation confers the right to use or to copy documents in the archives, a privilege which the Canadian Public Archives fails to confer. The British Public Records Act expressly sets forth that documents shall be accessible to the public after thirty years. The Act requires an official to provide reasonable facilities to enable the public to inspect and secure copies of public records. Access to documents less than thirty years old may also be arranged under certain circumstances.[9]

A legislative measure which is regarded as inimical to openness of government and which differentiates the climate of official secrecy in Great Britain and the United States is the Official Secrets Act. In this area Canada resembles the United Kingdom inasmuch as Canada too has an Official Secrets Act.[10]

Secrecy in Canada

In 1971 Hugh Lawford wrote:

> Probably because of the existing bias of so much of our law toward freedom of speech, we have never enacted detailed legislation to provide for a right of access to information—even to information under government control . . .
>
> Unlike a number of other governments, the Canadian Government has never spelled out fully the terms on which its documents can be used. Canada has never enacted a clear law respecting clearance of documents and access to unpublished documents. Although Canada has established a national archives collection and has staffed the Public Archives with scholarly and helpful officials, the rules governing access to the archives have been left vague and apparently arbitrary. Although the Public Archives Act provides for the transfer of records from the custody of various government departments in the archives and for the acquisition of other documents by the Dominion Archivist, the act fails to make any provision governing conditions of access to the documents. Unlike the legislation in Great Britain, the Canadian Act fails to confer any right to use or to copy any documents in the archives.
>
> In fact, although the Public Act seems to contemplate that Orders-in-Council will be passed respecting the custody of certain doc-

uments, no Order-in-Council appears to have been made under the act. If there are such Orders-in-Council, they have not been published as required under the Regulations Act. Since it is common knowledge that many government files have been transferred to the Archives, one must guess at the authority by which the transfer was made. And more important, Canadians must guess about which documents have been transferred and what conditions have been attached concerning access to the documents transferred.

If there is no law giving Canadians the right to inspect government documents in archives collections, there is very little law or even policy on access to current material still in the possession of government departments or agencies. Some documents are treated as ''public documents'' and made freely available for inspection. However, these documents tend to be a fairly limited group of formal papers, such as appeals to administrative tribunals. Once one moves beyond this limited group, almost all departments and agencies regard their files as closed to persons who are not public servants. Occasionally, a trusted scholar is permitted to see a particular set of files, normally on the condition that no material from the files is to be quoted without official approval. It is even difficult to discover who is responsible for granting permission to see government documents. Until fairly recently, a common assumption was that access to Canadian government papers was subject to a 'fifty-year rule.' That is, any document fifty or more years old was regarded as open to the public. Yet it is difficult to find any legal authority for the fifty-year rule or for the shortening of the period to thirty-five [*sic!*] years announced recently by the Prime Minister. Certainly there are files older than fifty years which the Government refuses to make available to the public.

A Canadian finds it impossible to know what law governs access to government files. He has no assurance that a department even has the personnel to undertake clearance of its files. Indeed, the procedure for declassification and release of government files (if there is one) has never been publicized. Although Professor Donald C. Rowat of Carleton University has reported that there is a Treasury Board minute which requires that a department must secure permission from the Dominion Archivist if it wishes to withhold documents longer than thirty-five years [*sic!*], Treasury Board minutes, unlike Orders-in-Council, are not published in the Canada Gazette and distributed to depository libraries. Perhaps it is typical of our Federal Government's attitude to information that the rule governing access to government documents is itself inaccessible.[11]

When Professor Lawford incorrectly referred to the shortening of the declassification period to *thirty-five* years, he was of course adverting to the announcement made in the House of Commons by Prime Minister Trudeau May 1, 1969, specifying, "Release To Archives Of Records In Existence For Thirty Years."[12] The Prime Minister stipulated that, "Certain records will be exempted from public access, particularly those the release of which might adversely affect Canada's external relations, violate the right of privacy of individuals, or adversely affect the national security."[13] Subsequently Mr. Trudeau described in fuller detail, by House of Commons announcement, the exceptions to the rule requiring release of documents. On June 7, 1973 the Cabinet approved Cabinet Directive No. 46, which spelled out procedures under such headings as "Transfer of Records to the Public Archives," "Access to Public Records in the Public Archives," and "Access to Public Records retained in a Department."

It is unlikely that such measures would meet all of Professor Lawford's objections to official practice in the government secrecy field. Certainly not every scholar is happy with his access to archival material. Professor James Eayrs is numbered among the ranks of discontented researchers. When he tried to breach governmental security, the undersecretary of state for external affairs wrote to him:

> Your desire is to be given personal access to classified files—a privilege (not a right)—in contravention of established government policy and the regulations for the protection of such information. I would venture to write that scholars for centuries have written history with authority and truthfulness without having access to secret files.[14]

Eayrs' blunt reaction was, "Buzz off, buster."[15]

One argument that has been made for maintaining secrecy is that government files contain information of value to competitors and rivals. It is possible that personal records could be the source of blackmail in some instances. But it is more than likely that other material is not all that sensitive. A second argument is that a threat of imminent revelation induces an undesirable self-consciousness in diplomats and government officials and inhibits their performance in the public service.

The counter argument is that the prospect of immediate scrutiny by historians or journalists will impel the statesman, politician or civil servant to perform with honesty and without subterfuge. Moreover, to severely restrict access by Canadian historians to Canadian documents can often mean that other countries' versions of an international event will prevail. On this point James Eayrs has quoted Lord Acton on access: "To keep one's archives barred against the historians is tantamount to leaving one's history to one's enemies.''[16] To which Eayrs adds succinctly, "And to the U. S. state department."[17]

It is not only the historians and journalists who have been inhibited in their pursuits by the restrictions on government access just discussed. The Federal Court Act passed in 1970 seems to hold a threat of a different kind to governmental openness. Leslie Katz, teaching fellow of Osgoode Law School, York University, has described the nature of the threat:

> The provisions [of the Federal Court Act] allow the Government to prevent litigants from offering as evidence in court, or from examining, any document where the Government declares that disclosure would be injurious to international relations, national security or federal-provincial relations or would disclose a confidence of the federal Cabinet. If any of these four justifications for non-disclosure is offered, the court is foreclosed from even examining the document in question and the Government's objection is to be treated as conclusive.
>
> Contrary to what might have been expected, these provisions extend beyond the new Federal Court and apply to all other federal and provincial courts.[18]

The full impact of the Federal Court Act probably still remains to be seen.

Another factor that may increase government secrecy in the near future is the computer, according to Professor Lawford. At present the inefficiencies of the governmental information system have helped to disclose to the public what might otherwise have remained unknown. Today many copies of documents have to be made so that they can be circulated to those civil servants and government officials who have to see and read them. They are handled by a certain number of clerical personnel. Inevitably it quite often happens that at least one copy falls into the hands of a journalist or a member of the public who turns it over to the press. In that way the document is given wide dissemination, and the right of the citizen to know is served. But if conventional methods are replaced by a fully developed computer system such fortuitous "leaks" will be eliminated. Television screens will permit information to be passed among authorized officials without unauthorized persons intervening. Only the original of the document need be in a permanent form. Extra copies will be unnecessary. The names of viewers of such televised documents may be recorded electronically so that unauthorized disclosure may be traced and punished. As Professor Lawford says, "The computer permits the creation of a system in which access to government information can be rigidly controlled and usage of government information can be strictly monitored.''[19]

Undoubtedly the computer seems likely to add to the problems of government secrecy which the Canadian journalist faces.

The foregoing discussion may have left the misleading impression that it is only at the national government level that the journalist is concerned with the question of access to news. It is more likely that the average reporter will confront the question of secrecy at a less senior level. Quite often it is the municipal act of the province in which he is reporting (in Saskatchewan the Village Act of Saskatchewan for example) that will serve as the framework for what he may report. And what he may report is implied in terms applicable to every citizen. The journalist would be well advised to consult the appropriate act of his province to learn the groundrules concerning the openness of council meetings and similar matters.

Postscript

The Changing Media Law

Although many of the facets of media law have been discussed in some detail in the preceding chapters, no exploration of the subject can be complete and final. Oliver Wendell Holmes's observation that jurists spend their lives shovelling smoke suggests that legal "facts" ought to be expressed as probabilities rather than certainties. When the journalist asks, "If I report this, or write that or broadcast that other thing, what will happen to me?" the best answer is not, "This will happen" but rather "This will probably happen."

And even the probabilities change. It is possible that Canadian contempt citations for scandalizing the court may follow the English lead and fall into disuse. The judgment rendered in *Slim* v. *Daily Telegraph Ltd.*,[1] though a British decision, may influence Canadian jurisprudence to allow a wider latitude of interpretation of fair comment as a defence in libel actions arising out of political controversy. Amendments to Canadian copyright law are long overdue and may be enacted in the not-too-distant future. Judgments of the American Supreme Court in 1973 seem to have markedly reduced the almost complete permissiveness which Charles Rembar claimed existed as a result of the trials of *Lady Chatterley, Tropic of Cancer* and *Fanny Hill* in the United States;[2] the climate of acceptability in Canada may similarly change. Also, legislation may create a law of privacy applicable to all Canadians.

The journalist should be alert to such changes. After he has become imbued with such basic media law as has been discussed in previous chapters, he should keep his knowledge up-to-date by studying contemporary mass media legal decisions, by familiarizing himself with current legislation and by reading articles describing and analyzing the newest developments of the law of the press

It is by such means that he will increase his competence and add to his value as a journalist.

Endnotes

Chapter I

Introduction

1. The operation of Canadian broadcasting under the regulation of the Canadian Radio-Television Commission is exceptional. The *rationale* for its existence is to be found in the nature of airways as a limited public commodity.

2. The main sources for the historical material in this section are: Thomas Dawson, *The Law of the Press* (London: P. S. King and Son, 1927); William H. Wickwar, *The Struggle For The Freedom Of The Press, 1819-1832* (London: George Allen & Unwin, 1972); and John King, *The Law of Defamation in Canada: Slander and Libel in Canada* (Toronto: The Carswell Company, 1907).

3. It wasn't until the end of the 1819-32 struggle that the revolt of the juries began and the tide of popular feeling turned. See Wickwar, p. 197. At p. 204 Wickwar said: "The revolt of the juries paved the way, however, for a Freedom of the Press that was based on the reluctance of the juries to indict for seditious libel, rather than on any fundamental change in the Law of the Constitution."

4. P. G. Osborn, *A Concise Law Dictionary* (London: Sweet and Maxwell, 1964), p. 97

5. Glanville Williams, *Learning the Law* (London: Stevens and Sons, 1969), p. 6. At p. 5, Williams points out "that the same act may be both a crime and a civil wrong. For instance, suppose that at the railway station I entrust my bag to someone who offers to carry it for reward, and he runs off with it. He has committed the crime of theft and two civil wrongs—the tort of conversion and a breach of his contract with me to carry the bag safely."

6. *Id.*, at p. 7.

7. *Op. cit. supra*, n. 4, at p. 315.

8. *Op. cit. supra*, n. 5, at p. 72.

Chapter II

Contempt of Court

1. J. C. McRuer, "Criminal Contempt of Court Procedure: A Protection To The Rights Of The Individual," *Canadian Bar Review*, v. 30, 1952, p. 225.

2. *Ibid.*

3. Sir John C. Fox, *The History of Contempt of Court 1* (1927), cited in Donald M. Gillmor and Jerome A. Barron, *Mass Communication Law Cases and Comment* (St. Paul: West Publishing Co., 1969), p. 420.

4. Ronald G. Atkey, "The Law of the Press in Canada (1)," *Gazette: International Journal for Mass Communication Studies*, v. 15, no. 2, 1969, p. 115.

5. P. G. Osborn, *A Concise Law Dictionary* (London: Sweet & Maxwell, 1964), p. 86.

6. D. A. Schmeiser, *Civil Liberties in Canada* (London: Oxford, 1964), p. 223.

7. *Roach* v. *Garvan*, [1742] 2 Atk. 469, 471 Chancery.

8. Thomas Dawson, *The Law Of The Press* (London: P. S. King and Son, 1927), p. 94.

9. L. A. Powe Jr., "*The Georgia Straight* and Freedom of Expression in Canada," *Canadian Bar Review*, v. 48, 1970, p. 433.

10. *Op. cit. supra*, n. 4 at p. 115. The citation he gives is *In Re Campbell and Cowper*, [1934] 3 W.W.R. 593 (Alta.) The newspaper's three contemptuous articles had commented on the action for seduction of Vivian MacMillan and her father against Alberta Premier J. E. Brownlee.

11. *Op. cit. supra*, n. 6 at p. 226.

12. *Ambard* v. *A. G. Trinidad and Tobago*, [1963] A.C. 322, 335.

13. *Op. cit. supra*, n. 4 at p. 116.

14. *Ibid.*

15. *Op. cit. supra*, n. 9.

16. *Id.*, at p. 434.

17. *Id.*, at p. 436.

18. J. J. Robinette, *Libel, Defamation, Contempt of Court and the Right of the People to be Informed* (Newspaper-legal seminar held in the Royal York Hotel, Toronto, March 27, 1962), p. 11.

19. Wilfred Kesterton, "Journalism," in John T. Saywell (editor) *Canadian Annual Review for 1962* (Toronto: University of Toronto Press, 1963), p. 352. Members of the radical Doukhobor group had aroused public resentment because of their defiance of civil authority, because of their nude parades, and because of their practice of burning their homes and other buildings. Before sentence was passed on the Nelson accused, Dennis Williams, managing editor of the *Trail Times*, wrote an editorial calling for severer penalties than he expected to be levied against the Sons of Freedom defendants. For his contempt of the court Williams was fined $300.

20. Criminal Code. R.S.C. 1970, c. C-34, s. 9(2).

21. *Id.*, s. 9(1).

22. *Id.*, s. 9(3).

23. *Id.*, s. 8.

24. *Op. cit. supra*, n. 4 at p. 118.

25. *Op. cit. supra*, n. 18 at p. 17.

26. *Id.*, at p. 18.

27. *Op. cit. supra*, n. 8 at p. 105.

28. Wilfred Kesterton, "Journalism," in John T. Saywell (editor), *Canadian Annual Review for 1961* (Toronto: University of Toronto Press, 1962), p. 344.

29. Wilfred Kesterton, "Mass Media," in John T. Saywell (editor), *Canadian Annual Review for 1965* (Toronto: University of Toronto Press, 1966), p. 489.

30. *Radio Chum 1050 Ltd. et al.* v. *Board of Education for City of Toronto*, (1964), 44 D.L.R. (2d) 671 (Ont. C.A.). The appeal was from a Board of

Education decision to exclude the mass media's electronic equipment and tape recorders from the board's meetings.

31. Criminal Code, R.S.C. 1970, c. C-34, s. 467. When first put on the statute books the Criminal Code amendment was numbered section 452A. But in 1970 there were a consolidation and renumbering of the Statutes of Canada. This meant that, starting with Section 98A of the 1953-54 Code, numbers were different from what they had been. Unless there is special reason to do otherwise, reference hereafter will be to the 1970 Statute and the new numbers.

32. *Id.*, s. 470.

33. Wilfred Kesterton, "Journalism," in John T. Saywell (editor), *Canadian Annual Review for 1962* (Toronto: University of Toronto Press, 1963), p. 352. The *Tribune* carried a news story quoting police testimony which included a statement made by Clarence Russell Richardson, charged with capital murder but subsequently convicted on a reduced charge of manslaughter. Magistrate Dubienski fined the Southam Company $250 and costs for the offence.

34. Wilfred Kesterton, "Mass Media," in John T. Saywell (editor), *Canadian Annual Review for 1966* (Toronto: University of Toronto Press, 1967), p. 432. Radio station CJOB was fined fifty dollars and costs after it pleaded guilty to publishing statements by one of the accused in the preliminary hearing of five persons charged in a $383,000 gold robbery.

35. Criminal Code, R.S.C. 1970, c. C-34, s. 162(1)(a).

36. *Id.*, s. 162(4)(c).

37. *Id.*, s. 162(1)(b).

38. *Id.*, s. 441.

39. Juvenile Delinquents Act, R.S.C. 1970, c. J-3, s. 9(1).

40. *Op. cit. supra*, n. 18, at p. 13. Robinette well described the situation and related it to the Truscott case:

Assume for a moment that the child is over fourteen, and is, for example, charged with murder, and then the Juvenile Court judge says, "I am not going to try it, it is to be tried in the ordinary criminal courts." What is your position then?

Well, the position is a very curious one. When the case is transferred to the ordinary criminal courts you start off with a preliminary inquiry before the magistrate. Now the magistrate has a discretion at all times to hold any preliminary inquiry privately, but if he holds it publicly, and ninety-nine per cent of them do, there is absolutely no restriction in the statute on the newspaper reporting everything that occurs at the preliminary inquiry except the tendering of an admission or confession. Peculiarly enough, the *Code* does cover the situation at the trial, because there is a section in the *Code* which provides that in the case of the trial of children under sixteen, where the accused is or appears to be under the age of sixteen years, his trial shall take place without publicity, whether he is charged alone or jointly with another person.

So a silly situation has arisen. You may recall the child charged with murder at Goderich two or three years ago, I think it was the Truscott case . . . Now in the Truscott case, the matter came up first in the Juvenile Court. The newspapers couldn't mention any names or even a charge against him. The

Juvenile trial court judge said, that having regard to feeling in the community and the seriousness of the charge, it should go to the ordinary criminal courts.

It then went before a magistrate, who did not hold the preliminary hearing *in camera*, and the newspapers published everything that occurred at the preliminary hearing, including the names, as they were quite entitled to do. Then the boy was committed for trial, and at the trial at Goderich the newspapers were not permitted under the Code to publish any of the details of the evidence.

Of course, that is absurd, there is a gap in it.

41. Criminal Code, R.S.C. 1970, c. C-34, s. 442.

Chapter III

Free Press-Fair Trial

1. *Schenck* v. *U.S.*, 249 U.S. 47, *per Holmes J.* at p. 52 (1918).

2. D. A. Schmeiser, *Civil Liberties in Canada* (London: Oxford, 1964), pp. 228-230.

3. *Craig* v. *Harney*, 331 U.S. 367 (1947).

4. *Id.*, at p. 376.

5. *Op. cit. supra*, n. 2, at p. 230.

6. Alfred Friendly and Ronald L. Goldfarb, *Crime and Publicity* (New York: Vintage Books, 1968), p. 315.

7. *Sheppard* v. *Maxwell*, 384 U.S. 333, 16 L.Ed.2d 600, 88 S.Ct. 1507 (1966).

8. Donald M. Gillmor and Jerome A. Barron, *Mass Communication Law: Cases and Comment* (St. Paul: West Publishing Co., 1969), p. 352.

9. *Ibid.*

10. Its members, under the chairmanship of Paul C. Reardon, were Grant Cooper, Edward J. Devitt, Robert McC. Figg Jr., Abe Fortas (1964-1965), Ross L. Malone, Wade H. McCree Jr., Bernard S. Meyer, Robert G. Storey, Lawrence E. Walsh, and Daniel P. Ward.

11. Advisory Committee on Fair Trial and Free Press, *Standards Relating To Fair Trial and Free Press* (New York: American Bar Association, 1968), pp. 13-14.

12. "Press On Trial," *The Economist*, October 29, 1966, p. 473.

13. Harold Felsher and Michael Rosen, *The Press In The Jury Box* (New York: Macmillan, 1966) p. 198.

14. The Hon. J. C. McRuer, *Royal Commission Inquiry Into Civil Rights, Report Number One, Volume 2* (Toronto: Queen's Printer, Ontario, 1968), pp. 765-766.

15. *Op. cit. supra*, n. 13, at p. 200.

16. *Id.*, at 202.

17. *Op. cit. supra*, n. 14, at pp. 763-764.

18. *Id.*, at p. 764.

19. *Id.*, at pp. 764-765.

Chapter IV

The Revealing of Sources

1. Frank Flaherty, "Journalistic Privilege In Canada," unpublished paper prepared for The Canadian Press, 1962.

2. D. A. Schmeiser, *Civil Liberties In Canada* (London: Oxford 1964), p. 100.

3. *Id.*, at p. 95 *et seq.*

4. Donald M. Gillmor and Jerome A. Barron, *Mass Communication Law: Cases and Comment* (St. Paul: West Publishing Co., 1969) p. 237.

5. This disregards the occasions when an informant tells the reporter something merely as background without wishing that the information be published. But in that case, if the reporter respects the informant's desire that neither information nor source be divulged, the problem of revealing a source to a court will not arise.

6. *Op. cit. supra*, n. 4, at p. 237.

7. The state of New York enacted a shield law after the Gillmor and Barron book was published.

8. *Op. cit. supra*, n. 4, at p. 237.

9. *Garland* v. *Torre*, 259 F.2d 545 (2d Cir. 1958).

10. *Ibid.*

11. In *Re Taylor*, 412 Pa. 32, 193 A.2d 181 (1963).

12. (Unsigned article) "A Voice From Watts," *Newsweek*, June 20, 1966.

13. (Unsigned article) "Jailed over story in defunct paper," *Globe and Mail*, October 10, 1972.

14. (Unsigned article) "Newsmen v. the Courts," *Time*, January 1, 1973.

15. *Ibid.*

16. *Time*, November 27, 1972.

17. *Op. cit. supra*, n. 14. Since this part of the text was written an article by Robert A. Wright in the *New York Times* of June 28, 1974 spoke of Farr as having served a virtually open-ended sentence. He was said to have spent 46 days in county jail. Although Wright pointed out that a verdict favorable to Farr ruled "that he could not be sent back to jail indefinitely with the intention that the incarceration would coerce him into revealing his sources" the article indicated that he was still scheduled for court appearances at which he could conceivably be sentenced to imprisonment for failure to disclose.

18. *Montreal Gazette*, March 15, 1969.

19. *Something Else*, CBC Public Affairs Program, March 20, 1969.

20. *The Way It Is*, CBC Public Affairs Program, April 27, 1969.

21. (Editorial), *The Gobe and Mail*, March 20, 1969.

22. *Ibid.*

23. *Ibid.*

24. *Op. cit. supra*, n. 20.

25. *Op. cit. supra*, n. 19.

26. *Ibid.*

27. *Ibid.*

28. *Op. cit. supra*, n. 19 and 21 for example.

29. *Op. cit. supra*, n. 20 for example.

30. *Supra*, p. 33. John Smith claimed that "giving assurances that information divulged confidentially will be so treated is as much part of his function as it is a lawyer's." Even if he had possessed the lawyer's "immunity" Smith would not have been entitled to withhold evidence later, because Pierre Catellier, the pretended "terrorist" whose anonymity he had tried to protect, took the witness stand after a senior CBC official had disclosed the interviewee's identity.

31. *Op. cit. supra*, n. 19.

32. *Ibid.*

33. *Op. cit. supra*, n. 21.

34. *Op. cit. supra*, n. 19.

35. *Op. cit. supra*, n. 20.

36. *Op. cit. supra*, n. 19.

37. *Op. cit. supra*, n. 20.

38. *Ibid.*

39. *Ibid.*

40. *Ibid.*

41. *Ibid.*

42. *Ibid.*

43. *Ibid.*

44. *Ibid.*

45. *Ibid.*

46. Evidence of Canadian journalists' sensitivity to the occupational hazards implicit in Canadian disclosure laws is to be found in the Montreal-based intra-media magazine, *Content*. In the April/May 1974 issue there was a sample act entitled "An Act To Protect The Public's Access To The News."

47. *Op. cit. supra*, n. 19.

Chapter V

Civil Defamation

1. R. L. McEwen and P. S. C. Lewis, *Gatley on Libel and Slander* (London: Sweet & Maxwell, 1967), p. 14.

2. *Id.*, at 44.

3. Alexander Stark, "Dangerous Words," paper delivered to Canadian Managing Editors' Conference, Niagara Falls, Ontario, January 28, 1950.

4. *Ibid.*

5. *Scott* v. *Sampson*, (1882), 8 Q.B.D. 503.

6. For the distinction between libel and slander see also *Op. cit. supra*, n. 1, at pp. 78 and 79.

7. *Youssoupoff* v. *Metro-Goldwyn-Mayer*, (1934), 50 T.L.R. 581, C.A.; 78 S.J. 617.

8. *Per* Lord Loreburn L.C., in *Hulton* v. *Jones*, [1910] A.C. 20 at 23 and 24.

9. *Id.*, at p. 20.

10. Quoted in: Joseph Dean, *Hatred, Ridicule or Contempt* (New York, Macmillan, 1954), pp. 130-131.

11. R. F. V. Heuston, *Salmond on Torts* (London: Sweet & Maxwell, 1969), p. 182.

12. *Id.*, at p. 247. This stipulation refers to slander only.

13. *Op. cit. supra*, n. 1, p. 51.

14. Harry Street, *Freedom, The Individual and the Law*(Hammondsworth: Penguin, 1967), p. 157.

15. An example of an exception was *Platt* v. *Time International of Canada Ltd.*, [1964] 44 D.L.R.(2d) 17.

16. Ronald G. Atkey, "The Law of the Press in Canada (2)," *Gazette: International Journal for Mass Communication Studies*, v. 15, no. 3, 1969, p. 192.

17. This principle also applies under Quebec civil law. When in 1970 Fernand Ouellet was required to pay $300 to the daughters of Henri Bourassa, it was not because his book on Julie Papineau was adjudged to harm a dead person but because injury to the dead person can create damages to the memory of the living.

18. *Op. cit. supra*, n. 1, at p. 11.

19. The Libel and Slander Act, R.S.O. 1970, c. 243, s. 1(1)(b).

20. The Defamation Act, R.S.M. 1970, c. D20, s. 19(c).

21. e.g., *Op. cit. supra*, n. 19, s. 2.

22. Defamation Act, R.S.N.S. 1967, c. 72, s. 2.

23. *Op. cit. supra*, n. 19, s. 1(1)(a).

24. *Id.*, s. 8(3).

25. *Op. cit. supra*, n. 11, at p. 204.

26. *Op. cit. supra*, n. 1, at p. 571.

27. *Ibid.*

28. Section 10(3) of the Alberta Act, for example, says, "Nothing in this section applies to the publication of seditious, blasphemous or indecent matter." [The Defamation Act, R.S.A. 1955, c. 87, s. 10(3)].

29. J. J. Robinette, *Libel, Defamation, Contempt of Court and the Right of the People to be Informed*, (Newspaper-legal seminar, Toronto, March 27, 1962), p. 3.

30. *Ibid.*

31. *Op. cit. supra*, n. 1, at p. 462.

32. *Op. cit. supra*, n. 19, p. 23.

33. *Op. cit. supra*, n. 29, at p. 4.

34. *Op. cit. supra*, no. 1, at p. 147.

35. *Ibid.* Gatley gives as reference *Per* Lush J. in *Shapiro* v. *La Morta*, (1923), 40 T.L.R. at p. 41.

36. *Ibid.* Gatley gives as reference *Per* Atkin L.J. in *Shapiro* v. *La Morta*, (1923), 40 T.L.R. at p. 203.

37. *Ibid.* Gatley gives as reference *Per* McCardie J. in *British R.T. Co.* v. *C.R.C.*, [1922] 2 K.B. at p. 269.

38. *Op. cit. supra*, n. 11, at p. 208.

39. *Op. cit. supra*, n. 19, s. 4(1).

40. It might be noted that this law is not inconsistent with Mr. Robinette's

dicta about the "Many Years Ago" example, cited earlier. His comments refer to a report that is itself defamatory (or alleged to be defamatory). The "contemporaneously" or thirty days rule covers a report of statements made by someone alse, which statements are defamatory.

41. *Op. cit. supra*, n.11, at p. 214.

42. *Op. cit. supra*, n. 19, s. 3(1).

43. *Id.*, s. 3(2).

44. *Id.*, s. 3(3).

45. *Id.*, s. 3(4).

46. Libel and Slander Act, R.S.B.C. 1969, c. 218, s. 2.

47. e.g., *Op. cit. supra*, n. 19, s. 4(1).

48. *Op. cit. supra*, n. 16, at p. 190.

49. *Id.*, at p. 191.

50. *Ibid.*

51. *Op. cit. supra*, n. 11, pp. 234-243.

52. *Op. cit. supra*, n. 3.

53. *Op. cit. supra*, n. 1, at p. 326.

54. *Op. cit. supra*, n. 11, at p. 232.

55. *Ibid.*

56. *Id.*, at p. 234.

57. *Op. cit. supra*, n. 19, s. 24.

58. *Slim* v. *Daily Telegraph Ltd.*, (1968), 1 All E.R. 497, at 503.

59. *Op. cit. supra*, n. 11, at pp. 715-716.

60. The Defamation Act, R.S.A. 1955, c. 243, s. 18(1).

61. Defamation Act, R.S.N.B. 1952, c. 58, s. 14.

62. Harry Street, *Freedom, The Individual and The Law*, (Hammondsworth: Penguin, 1967), p. 155.

63. Press Act, R.S.Q. 1964, c. 48, s. 11.

64. *Id.*, s. 9(b).

65. *Op. cit. supra*, n. 20, s. 19.

66. An apparent exception is to be found in the Quebec case, *Ortenburg* v. *Plamondon*, (1914), 35 Can.L.T. 262, 24 Que. K.B. 69. The Court of Appeal awarded damages to the plaintiff after the defendant had attacked the Jewish community of Quebec City. The judgment took note of the fact that, out of a total population of 80,000, there were only seventy five Jewish families. The Court also found that the plaintiff had suffered both in his person and in his business because of the libel.

67. A trade union or professional association is so entitled. See *Saskatchewan College Of Physicians & Surgeons* v. *Co-operative Commonwealth Federation Publishing & Printing Co. Ltd. et al.*, (1965), 51 D.L.R.(2d), 442.

68. The case is discussed interestingly by Alexander Stark in his paper, "Dangerous Words." The reference he cited for the case is 307 Illinois 595.

69. P. G. Osborn, *A Concise Law Dictionary* (London: Sweet & Maxwell, 1968), p. 101.

70. *Op. cit. supra*, n. 11, at p. 197.

71. *Op. cit. supra*, n. 1, at p. 79.

Chapter 6

Criminal Libel

1. The Criminal Code, R.S.C. 1970, c. C34, s. 262(1).

2. *Id.*, s. 262(2).

3. A. D. Yonge et al, *Halsbury's Statutes of England*, v. 19 (London: Butterworth, 1970), p. 7.

4. R. L. McEwen and P. S. C. Lewis, *Gatley on Libel and Slander* (London: Sweet & Maxwell, 1967), p. 10.

5. *Ibid.*

6. R. F. V. Heuston, *Salmond on Torts* (London: Sweet & Maxwell, 1969), p. 357.

7. *Op. cit. supra*, n. 1, s. 275.

8. *Op. cit. supra*, n. 6, at p. 357.

9. *Op. cit. supra*, n. 1, s. 274.

10. Section 269 of the Criminal Code says:

No person shall be deemed to publish a defamatory libel by reason only that he publishes defamatory matter

(a) in a proceeding held before or under the authority of a court exercising judicial authority, or

(b) in an inquiry made under the authority of an Act or by order of Her Majesty, or under the authority of a public department or a department of the government of a province.

11. Section 270 of the Criminal Code says:

No person shall be deemed to publish a defamatory libel by reason only that he

(a) publishes to the Senate or House of Commons or to a legislature, defamatory matter contained in a petition to the Senate or House of Commons or to the legislature, as the case may be,

(b) publishes by order or under the authority of the Senate or House of Commons or of a legislature, a paper containing defamatory matter, or

(c) publishes, in good faith and without ill-will to the person defamed, an extract from or abstract of a petition or paper mentioned in paragraph (a) or (b).

12. Section 271 of the Criminal Code says:

(1) No person shall be deemed to publish a defamatory libel by reason only that he publishes in good faith, for the information of the public, a fair report of the proceedings of the Senate or House of Commons or a legislature, or a committee thereof, or of the public proceedings before a court exercising judicial authority, or publishes in good faith, any fair comment upon any such proceedings.

(2) This section does not apply to a person who publishes a report of evidence taken or offered in any proceeding before the Senate or House of Commons or any committee thereof, upon a petition or bill relating to any matter of marriage or divorce, if the report is published without authority from or leave of the House in which the proceeding is held or is contrary to any rule, order or practice of that House.

13. Section 272 of the Criminal Code says:

No person shall be deemed to publish a defamatory libel by reason only that he publishes in good faith, in a newspaper, a fair report of proceedings of any public meeting if

(a) the meeting is lawfully convened for a lawful purpose and is open to the public

(b) the report is fair and accurate,

(c) the publication of the matter complained of is for the public benefit, and

(d) he does not refuse to publish in a conspicuous place in the newspaper a reasonable explanation or contradiction by the person defamed in respect of the defamatory matter.

14. Section 273 of the Criminal Code says:

No person shall be deemed to publish a defamatory libel by reason only that he publishes defamatory matter that, on reasonable grounds, he believes to be true, and that is relevant to any subject of public interest, the public discussion of which is for the public benefit.

15. Section 276 of the Criminal Code says:

No person shall be deemed to publish a defamatory libel by reason only that he publishes defamatory matter

(a) on the invitation or challenge of the person in respect of whom it is published, or

(b) that it is necessary to publish in order to refute defamatory matter published in respect of him by another person, if he believes that the defamatory matter is true and is relevant to the invitation, challenge or necessary refutation, as the case may be, and does not in any respect exceed what is reasonably sufficient in the circumstances.

16. Section 277 of the Criminal Code says:

No person shall be deemed to publish a defamatory libel by reason only that he publishes, in answer to inquiries made to him, defamatory matter relating to a subject-matter in respect of which the person by whom or on whose behalf the inquiries are made has an interest in knowing the truth or who, on reasonable grounds, the person who publishes the defamatory matter believes has such an interest, if

(a) the matter is published, in good faith, for the purpose of giving information in answer to the inquiries,

(b) the person who publishes the defamatory matter believes that it is true,

(c) the defamatory matter is relevant to the inquiries, and

(d) the defamatory matter does not in any respect exceed what is reasonably sufficient in the circumstances.

17. Section 278 of the Criminal Code says:

No person shall be deemed to publish a defamatory libel by reason only that he publishes to another person defamatory matter for the purpose of giving information to that person with respect to a subject-matter in which the person to whom the information is given has, or is believed on reasonable grounds by the person who gives it to have, an interest in knowing the truth with respect to that subject-matter if

(a) the conduct of the person who gives the information is reasonable in the circumstances,

(b) the defamatory matter is relevant to the subject-matter and

(c) the defamatory matter is true, or if it is not true, is made without ill-will toward the person who is defamed and is made in the belief, on reasonable grounds, that it is true.

18. Section 279 of the Criminal Code says:

No person shall be deemed to publish a defamatory libel by reason only that he publishes defamatory matter in good faith for the purpose of seeking remedy or redress for a private or public wrong or grievance from a person who has, or who on reasonable grounds he believes has the right or is under an obligation to remedy or redress the wrong or grievance, if

(a) he believes that the defamatory matter is true,

(b) the defamatory matter is relevant to the remedy or redress that is sought, and

(c) the defamatory matter does not in any respect exceed what is reasonably sufficient in the circumstances.

19. *Op. cit. supra*, n. 1, s. 280.

20. *Id.*, s. 261.

21. *Id.*, s. 263.

22. *Id.*, s. 267.

23. *Id.*, s. 268.

24. *Id.*, s. 421.

25. *Id.*, s. 281.

26. *Id.*, s. 266.

27. *Id.*, s. 266(3).

28. *Id.*, s. 264.

29. *Id.*, s. 265.

30. *Id.*, s. 60(2).

31. *Id.*, s. 60(4).

32. *Id.*, s. 61.

33. *Id.*, s. 62.

34. From *A Digest of the Criminal Law* by Sir James Stephen, as quoted in [1950] 1 D.L.R. 668.

35. (1938), 64 Quebec K.B. 270.

36. D. A. Schmeiser, *Civil Liberties in Canada* (London: Oxford, 1964), p. 211.

37. William H. Wickwar, *The Struggle For Freedom Of The Press, 1819-1832* (London: George Allen & Unwin, 1972), p. 25.

38. *Id.*, at p. 89.

39. Thomas Dawson, *The Law Of The Press* (London: P. S. King and Son, 1927), p. 89. He cites as authority for the Stephen statement, *Digest of Criminal Law*, Article 179.

40. (1883), 48 L.T. 733.

41. Quoted by Lord Chief Justice Coleridge as being on page 599 of the fourth edition of *Starkie on Libel*.

42. *Op. cit. supra*, n. 1, s. 260(2).

43. *Id.*, s. 260(3).
44. *Id.*, s. 260(1).
45. *Annotation*, (1927), C.C.C. 1.

Chapter VII

Obscenity and Censorship

1. *Ottawa Citizen*, November 17, 1967.
2. For a fuller development of this theme see also the opening pages of Kate Millett, *Sexual Politics* (Garden City, New York: Doubleday, 1970), pp. 3-22.
3. Sarel Eimerl, "The Trouble With Jeeves," *The Reporter*, March 7, 1968, p. 47.
4. Zena Cherry, "MacLennan says pornography signifies authoritarian trend," *The Globe and Mail*, March 29, 1968.
5. Some of the insistence, particularly by certain members of the underground press, on uttering the hitherto taboo words is comparable to the behavior of the four-year-old at the party. Little Johnny electrifies the adults by shouting the four-letter obscenity not because he prizes the liberty of speaking the obscenity, but because he has discovered a sure-fire way of gaining attention. Sarel Eimerl adverts to this sort of attention-seeking when he reviews *Why Are We In Vietnam?* by Norman Mailer ("Loaded for Bear," *The Reporter*, October 19, 1967).
Eimerl says:

Despite its self-conscious intellectual pretentiousness, this novel is blatantly anti-thought and anti-reason. This is shown most vividly in Mailer's use of obscenities. Perhaps he decided that by adopting the literary style of an illiterate G.I.—and exaggerating it, at that—he would be better able to portray the state of mind of a typical present-day teen-ager—or Texan, or American. Some reviewers have flattered this illusion by speaking with approval of the salutary shock that Mailer has just handed America. If they really believe this, they must be remarkably naive, for Mailer being obscene is about as shocking or salutary as a slum child would be bawling out the same old, weary words.

6. For a fuller discussion of this committee's work see W. H. Charles, "Obscene Literature and the Legal Process In Canada," *Canadian Bar Review*, May, 1966, pp. 250-252.
7. *The Report of the Commission on Obscenity and Pornograph* (Toronto: Bantam Books, 1970), p. 1.
8. *Id.*, at 196.
9. *Id.*, at 235.
10. *Id.*, at 277.
11. *Id.*, at p. x. And as Clive Barnes says (in his introduction to the *New York Times* publication of the report at page x) the two psychiatrists who made the quoted statement "were only, in effect, underlining the majority viewpoint of the Commission."

12. *Id.*, at 57.

13. *Id.*, at 63.

14. *Id.*, at 67.

15. *Id.*, at 54.

16. *Id.*, at xvi.

17. Longford Committee, *Pornography: Longford Report* (London: Coronet Books, 1972).

18. Prof. Jacques Fortin *et al*, *Obscenity* (Ottawa: Prohibited and Regulated Conduct Project, Law Reform Commission, 1972).

19. *Id.*, at 19.

20. *Ibid.*

21. *Ibid.*

22. *State* v. *Lerner*, (1948) 81NEed 282 (Ohio) at p. 286.

23. (1868) L.R. 3 Q.B. 360, at p. 371.

24. For a fuller account of the objections to the *Hicklin Test* see W. H. Charles, "Obscene Literature and the Legal Process In Canada," *Canadian Bar Review*, May, 1966, pp. 243-292, an article to which this part of this book is indebted.

25. The Criminal Code, R.S.C. 1970, c. C34, 159(8).

26. *Id.*, at s. 159(1)(a).

27. *Id.*, at s. 159(2)(a).

28. *Op. cit. supra*, n. 24, at 265-266.

29. J. C. Martin, Alan W. Mewett, and Ian Cartwright, *Martin's Annual Criminal Code, 1972* (Toronto: Canada Law Book Ltd., 1972), p. 109.

30. *Op. cit. supra*, n. 24, at 290.

31. *Op. cit. supra*, n. 25, s. 159(7).

32. D. A. Schmeiser, *Civil Liberties in Canada* (London: Oxford, 1964), pp. 251-253.

33. *Op. cit. supra*, n. 25, s. 160. An analysis of this section is given in J. L. K. Vamplew, "Obscene Literature and Section 150A", *The Criminal Law Quarterly*, 1964-65, Volume 6, pp. 187-192.

34. *Regina* v. *C. Coles Co. Ltd.*, (1964), 49 D.L.R.(2d) 34.

35. *Op. cit. supra*, n. 24, at 243.

36. Quoted in Schmeiser, *op. cit. supra*, n. 32, at 249-250. Schmeiser himself gives as reference 72F.2d705, at pp. 706-8.

37. In "Who Killed Censorship?" (*The Globe Magazine*, October 9, 1965) William French says:

> The unsung hero in the fight against book censorship, and in a way the major figure, is the late George Nowlan. As Minister of National Revenue in the Diefenbaker Administration, he was Canada's chief censor. Under a system in use since 1867, Customs officers at the border had the power to stop any book they thought might be obscene. They sent the book to Ottawa, where it was passed around to clerks and other workers in the department for their average guy opinion. The final decision rested with the minister.

> Nowlan's predecessor, Dr. J. J. McCann, a Catholic physician from Renfrew, was an assiduous book banner during his long term of office (1945-1957). In 1955, for example, he added 140 new titles to his list. In 1956, the year before the Liberals were defeated, 79 more books were prohibited from entering the country. The secret list included, in addition to

Peyton Place, such things as Mae West's *Diamond Lil,* books by James T. Farrell and Erskine Caldwell, the *Memoirs of Casanova,* sunbathing magazines.

Nowlan quietly took the decision to end this utterly indefensible system— which is still in use in such countries as Australia—in January, 1962. The list of prohibited books was abolished; instructions went out to border points not to stop any publication . . . .

38. *Regina* v. *Brodie Regina* v. *Dansky Regina* v. *Rubin,* (1962), 32 D.L.R.(2d) 507, at p. 526.

39. *Id.,* at p. 532.

40. *Op. cit supra,* n. 34, at p. 38.

41. *Regina* v. *Cameron,* [1966] 4 C.C.C. 273 at p. 312.

42. (1966), 58 D.L.R.(2d) 274, at p. 278.

43. (1970), 73 W.W.R. 221, at p. 232.

44. *Op. cit. supra,* n. 24, at p. 258.

45. *Op. cit. supra,* n. 38, at p. 513.

46. *Id.,* at p. 515.

47. *Id.,* at p. 520.

48. *Ibid.*

49. *Op. cit. supra,* n. 24, at p. 258.

50. *Ibid.*

51. *Op. cit. supra,* n. 38, at p. 517.

52. *Id.,* at p. 520.

53. *Ibid.*

54. *Id.,* at 527.

55. *Id.,* at pp. 527-528.

56. (1963), 42 W.W.R. 75.

57. *Op. cit. supra,* n. 34, at pp. 42 and 43.

58. *Id.,* at p. 34.

59. *Op. cit. supra,* n. 42, at p. 280.

60. (1970), 75 W.W.R. 585.

61. *Id.,* at p. 601.

62. *Op. cit. supra,* n. 24, at p. 290.

63. *Op. cit. supra,* n. 38, at p. 517.

64. *Id.,* at p. 521.

65. *Id.,* at p. 531.

66. *Op. cit. supra,* n. 43, at p. 230.

67. *Op. cit supra,* n. 6.

68. (1904), 9 C.C.C. 415.

69. *Id.,* at pp. 422 and 423.

70. *Op. cit. supra,* n. 32, at p. 249. Schmeiser cites *U.S.* v. *Kennerley,* 209 Fed 119 (1913).

71. James Joyce, *Ulysses* (New York: Modern Library, 1946). Pages ix to xiv of this edition provide the complete Judge Woolsey decision.

72. *Id.,* at p. xiii.

73. C. H. Rolph (editor), *The Trial of Lady Chatterley* (London: Penguin, 1961), p. 107. Miss Jones also gave evidence that: "In my experience girls are very good at knowing what they want to read, and they reject what is unsuitable

for them. If they should be a little prurient they may read the book, but I find the majority of the girls don't wish to read such books."

74. (1951), 100 C.C.C. 171.
75. *Id.*, at p. 172.
76. *Ibid.*
77. *U.S.* v. *Kennerley* (1913) 209 Fed. 119 at p. 121.
78. *Op. cit. supra*, n. 6, at p. 270 *et seq.*
79. *Op. cit. supra*, n. 38, at p. 521.
80. *Id.*, at pp. 528-529.
81. *Id.*, at p. 531.
82. *Ibid.*
83. *Id.*, at p. 54.
84. *Ibid.*
85. *Op. cit. supra*, n. 56, at p. 65.
86. *Id.*, at p. 66.
87. [1964] 3 C.C.C. 1, 42 C.R. 209.
88. (1968), 58 D.L.R.(2d) 274.
89. (1970), 13 D.L.R.(3d) 257.
90. [1966] 4 C.C.C. 273, 44 C.R. 49, [1966] 2 O.R. 777.
91. [1966] 4 C.C.C. 274.
92. (1970), 72 W.W.R.(N.S.) 354.
93. *Id.*, at p. 361.
94. *Op. cit. supra*, n. 47, at p. 221.
95. *Id.*, at p. 230.
96. *Op. cit. supra*, n. 89, at p. 257.
97. *Id.*, at p. 230.
98. [1971] 4 C.C.C.(2d) 191.
99. (1971), 75 W.W.R. 585.
100. *Id.*, at p. 599.
101. *Id.*, at p. 600.
102. [1971] 4 C.C.C.(2d) 241.
103. *Op. cit. supra*, n. 73.
104. The Criminal Code, R.S.C. 1970, c. C34, s. 159(3).
105. The Criminal Code, R.S.C. 1970, c. C34, s. 159(4).
106. *Op. cit. supra*, n. 28, at p. 508.
107. *Id.*, at p. 515.
108. *Id.*, at p. 516.
109. *Id.*, at p. 523.
110. *Ibid.*
111. *Id.* at p. 526.
112. *Op. cit. supra*, n. 34, at p. 34.
113. *Id.*, at p. 35.
114. *Op. cit. supra*, n. 41 at p. 273.
115. *Id.*, at p. 274.
116. *Ibid.*
117. *Ibid.*
118. *Op. cit. supra*, n. 88.
119. *Id.*, at p. 282.

120. *Op. cit. supra*, 92, at p. 354.

121. *Id.*, at p. 363.

122. [1971] 4 C.C.C.(2d) 187, [1971] 3 O.R. 323.

123. Acknowledgment of the role of the expert in helping to decide what is obscene and what is not is implicit in the establishment of the Ontario Indecent Literature Committee, more recently called the Obscenity Committee. This is a purely advisory body, first appointed in 1956. Among its members have been Ray C. Edwards, Arnold Edinborough, W. B. Common, deputy attorney-general of the province, David Coon, Toronto lawyer, Hans Mohr, sociologist, Bernard Jackson, McMaster English porfessor, and Bob Porter, Peterborough librarian. It is interesting to note that Edinborough said he would resign from the committee if it became a requirement that obscenity hearings had to be initiated by the attorney-general's office rather than by private individuals. Apparently his reasoning was that anyone seeking censorship action should be required to stand up and be counted. When David Coon was chairman of the committee he and other members found their work to be not only stultifying but also the cause of depressing criticism. Public attitude to their labors was that the committee was a narrow, bluestocking censorship board, whereas they regarded their tolerant advisory role as saving the province from the need to establish a true censorship board with *legal* power to impose far less liberal and far more coercive restraints. The Alberta Advisory Board on Objectionable Publications has had the reputation of being more censorious.

124. Ian Cartwright's *Martin's Criminal Code, 1972* (Agincourt, Ontario: Canada Law Book Ltd., 1972) at page 165 says:

It is stated at pp. 213-4 C.C.C.:

"That a person intends the natural consequences of his acts is not a presumption of law. Denning, L. J. dealt with the matter in HOSEGOOD *v.* HOSEGOOD (1950), 66 T.L.R. 735 at p. 738, which incidentally was a civil case, thus, when people say that a man must be taken to intend the natural consequences of his acts, they fall into error; there is no 'must' about it: it is only 'may.' The presumption of intention is not a proposition of law but a proposition of ordinary good sense. It means this: that, as a man is usually able to foresee what are the natural consequences of his acts, so it is, as a rule reasonable to infer that he did foresee them and intend them. But, while that is an inference which may be drawn, it is not one which must be drawn. If on all the facts of the case it is not a correct inference then it should not be drawn."
He referred to R. v. STEANE, [1947] K.B.997.

125. *Hulton* v. *Jones*, [1910] A.C., at p. 24.

126. *Op. cit. supra*, n. 71, at p. xi.

127. *Ibid.*

128. *Ibid.*

129. Certainly it was the spirit of this subsection which explains what happened to W. T. Stead in 1885. In order to help to get the Criminal Law Amendment Act passed and thereby combat "white slavery" in England, he sought to demonstrate, without actually committing the offence, the procure-

ment of a thirteen-year-old girl and then publish an exposé of the practice in his *Pall Mall Gazette*. Despite his high-minded purpose he was sentenced to two months in prison. See: H. Montgomery Hyde, *Cases That Changed The Law* (Toronto: Heinemann, 1951), at pp. 27-37.

130. *Op. cit. supra*, n. 60.
131. R.S.C. 1970, c. C41.
132. *Ibid.*
133. *Maclean's*, December 15, 1949.
134. *Op. cit. supra*, n. 99.
135. *Id.*, at p. 594.
136. *Id.*, at p. 595.
137. *Ibid.*
138. R.S.C. 1970, c. C34, s. 164.
139. R.S.C. 1970, c. P14, s. 7.
140. S.B.C. 1970, c. 27.
141. R.S.A. 1970, c. 18.
142. S.S. 1968, c. 76.
143. R.S.M. 1970, c. A70.
144. R.S.O. 1970, c. 459.
145. S.Q. 1966-7, c. 55.
146. R.S.N.B. 1952, c. 228.
147. R.S.N.S. 1956, c. 288.
148. R.S.Nfld. 1970, c. 30.
149. *Op. cit. supra*, n. 143, s. 22(1).
150. *Id.*, s. 22(4).
151. *Op. cit. supra*, n. 140, s. 3 and s. 6.
152. *Op. cit. supra*, n. 142.
153. *Op. cit. supra*, n. 145.
154. *Op. cit. supra*, n. 140, s. 9(2).
155. *Id.*, s. 9(3).
156. *Op. cit. supra*, n. 141, s. 29, ss. 19(1).
157. *Op. cit. supra*, n. 142, s. 8(2)(c).
158. *Op. cit. supra*, n. 144, s. 3(2)(e) and (f).
159. *Id.*, s. 21(4).
160. *Op. cit. supra*, n. 145, s. 10.
161. *Ibid.*
162. *Op. cit. supra*, n. 148, s. 4.
163. *Op. cit. supra*, n. 145, s. 10.
164. *Op. cit. supra*, n. 143, s. 23(2)(a).
165. *Id.*, s. 24(1).
166. *Op. cit. supra*, n. 142, s. 15(1).
167. R.S.C. 1970, c. C34, s. 159(2)(c).
168. *Id.*, s. 159(2)(d).
169. *R.* v. *Keystone Enterprises*, (1961), 133 C.C.C. 338, 37 C.R. 397, 38 W.W.R. 442.
170. *Ibid.*

171. In *Regina* v. *Brodie Regina* v. *Dansky Regina* v. *Rubin*, (1962), 32 D.L.R. 507 at p. 516 Mr. Justice Taschereau said "[a] nudity is not an obscenity" and other jurists have made the same point.

172. Over several months, the Ottawa *Citizen*'s regular column, "Action Line", has illustrated logophobia. In one letter a woman was too horrified by the word to write "bastard" although she was perfectly willing to speak of a person "born out of wedlock." Another recoiled from asking for a "ratchet" in a hardware store because she was repelled by what she considered to be the scatology of the second syllable of the word. A third correspondent condemned what for her was the distasteful word "sweat," preferring instead the mealy-mouthed euphemism, "perspire."

173. John Masefield, "Cargoes," in George B. Woods, Homer A. Watt, George K. Anderson (editors), in *The Literature of England* (Chicago: Scott Foreman, 1941), p. 1000.

174. John Kettle and Dean Walker, *Verdict!* (Toronto: McGraw Hill, 1968), pp. 49-66.

175. See also Renatus Hartogs with Hans Fantel, *Four Letter Word Games* (New York: Dell, 1968), p. 109.

176. Edward Sagarin, *The Anatomy Of Dirty Words* (New York: Paperback Library, 1962), p. 99.

177. Noel Perrin, *Dr. Bowdler's Legacy* (New York: Atheneum, 1969), pp. 216 and 217.

178. *Regina* v. *Prairie Schooner News and Powers*, (1970), 75 W.W.R. 585 contains reference to the 1968 amendment to the *Criminal Code* and relates it in an interesting way to the determination of obscenity. At page 588 Mr. Justice Freedman says that section 149A [now section 158]

> exempted from the scope of sec. 149 [now sec. 157] any act committed in private between husband and wife or between consenting adults. So whatever went on between husband and wife in their bedroom was nobody's business but their own. So too with consenting adults, be they one male and one female, or two males, or two females. But—and this is of special significance in the present context—sec. 149A [now 158] (2)(a) went on to state that "an act shall be deemed not to have been committed in private if it is committed in a public place, or if more than two persons take part or are present." Community thinking was not prepared to sanction an act so committed. What then shall we say of sexual conduct such as emerges from the photographs in these magazines? In many cases more than two persons appeared in the photograph. But even where there are only two persons there must in every case have been a third person present, namely the photographer. Can we justly say that Canadian opinion was ready to tolerate photographs of this character?

Chapter VIII

Copyright

1. Harold G. Fox, *The Canadian Law of Copyright and Industrial Designs* (Toronto: The Carswell Company, 1967).

2. *Id.*, at p. 1. Fox gives as his source: *Underwriters' Survey Bureau Ltd. et al* v. *Massie & Renwick Ltd.*, [1937] Ex C.R. 15 at 20, *per* Maclean J., [1937] S.C.R. 265, [1937] 2 D.L.R. 213.

3. *Ibid.* Fox gives as his source: *Chappel* v. *Purday*, (1845), 14 M & W 303 at 316, *per* Pollock C.B.

4. Hawley Black, "How U. S. 'manufacturing clause' is hurting Canadian printers," *Canadian Printer & Publisher*, May, 1963, 39.

5. Copyright Act, R.S.C. 1970, c. C30. Section 3(1) of the Act says:

for the purposes of this Act "copyright" means the sole right to produce or reproduce the work or any substantial part thereof in any material form whatsoever, to perform, or in the case of a lecture to deliver, the work or any substantial part thereof in public; if the work is unpublished, to publish the work or any substantial part thereof; and includes the sole right

(a) to produce, reproduce, perform or publish any translation of the work;

(b) in the case of a dramatic work, to convert it into a novel or other non-dramatic work;

(c) in the case of a novel or other non-dramatic work, or of an artistic work, to convert it into a dramatic work, by way of performance in public or otherwise;

(d) in the case of a literary, dramatic or musical work, to make any record, perforated roll, cinematograph film or other contrivances by means of which the work may be mechanically performed or delivered;

(e) in the case of any literary, dramatic, musical or artistic work, to reproduce, adapt and publicly present such work by cinematograph, if the author has given such work an original character; but if such original character is absent the cinematographic production shall be protected as a photograph;

(f) in case of any literary, dramatic, musical or artistic work, to communicate such work by radio communication;

and to authorize any such acts aforesaid."

6. *Op. cit. supra*, n. 1, at p. 1.

7. *Op. cit. supra*, n. 1, at pp. 7 to 40.

8. Philip Wittenberg, *The Protection of Literary Property* (Boston: The Writer, Inc., 1968), pp. 3 to 37.

9. P. F. Carter-Ruck, E. P. Skone James and F. E. Skone James, *Copyright, Modern Law and Practice* (London: Faber and Faber, 1965), pp. 28 to 34.

10. *Op. cit. supra*, n. 1, at p. 7.

11. *Ibid.*

12. *Id.*, at p. 9.

13. *Ibid.*

14. *Id.*, at p. 10.

15. *Id.*, at pp. 11-13.

16. *Id.*, at pp. 14-15.

17. *Id.*, at pp. 15-16.

18. *Id.*, at pp. 16-18.

19. *Id.*, at p. 18.

20. *Id.*, at p. 19.

21. *Id.*, at pp. 20-24.

22. *Id.*, at pp. 24-26.

23. *Id.*, at p. 26.

24. *Id.*, at p. 30.

25. *Ibid.*

26. *Ibid.*

27. *Ibid.*

28. *Id.*, at p. 31.

29. *Id.*, at p. 35.

30. *Ibid.*

31. *Id.*, at p. 29.

32. *Id.*, at p. 29 and p. 37.

33. *Id.*, at p. 37.

34. *Ibid.* Wittenberg (*Op. cit. supra*, n. 14, at pp. 98, 99) points out that those members are Australia, Austria, Belgium, Brazil, Bulgaria, Canada, Ceylon, Congo (Brazaville), Congo (Leopoldville), Czechoslovakia, Dahomey, Denmark, Finland, France, Gabon, Germany, Greece, Holy See, Hungary, Iceland, India, Ireland, Israel, Italy, Ivory Coast, Japan, Lebanon, Liechtenstein, Luxembourg, Mali, Monaco, Morocco, Netherlands, New Zealand Niger, Norway, Pakistan, Philippines, Poland, Portugal, Rumania, Senegal, South Africa, Spain, Sweden, Switzerland, Thailand, Tunisia, Turkey, United Kingdom, Upper Volta, and Yugoslavia. But the list is not unchanging, and readers will need to consult the most recent available information to be up-to-date.

35. *Op. cit. supra*, n. 1, at p. 37.

36. *Id.*, at p. 38.

37. "Copyright law would stifle writing: letter," *Globe and Mail*, March 28, 1973. *Copyright: Modern Law and Practice* (*Op. cit. supra*, n. 9 at p. 314) lists as members of the Geneva Convention Andorra, Argentina, Austria, Belgium (and Ruanda-Urundi), Brazil, Cambodia, Canada, Chile, Costa Rica, Cuba, Czechoslovakia, Denmark, Ecuador, Finland, France, Federal Republic of Germany (and Land Berlin), Ghana, Great Britain, Greece, Haiti, Iceland, India, Israel, Italy, Japan, Laos, Lebanon, Liberia, Liechtenstein, Luxembourg, Mexico, Monaco, New Zealand, Nicaragua, Nigeria, Norway, Pakistan, Panama, Paraguay, Peru, Philippines, Portugal, Republic of Ireland, Spain, Sweden, Switzerland, U.S.A. and Vatican City. Such a list takes no account of subsequent changes, of course.

39. *Op. cit. supra*, n. 8, at p. 102.

40. *Op. cit. supra*, n. 1, at p. 552.

41. *Ibid.*

42. *Op. cit. supra*, n. 4.

43. Marsh Jeanneret, "The United States Manufacturing Clause," *Quill & Quire*, September-October, 1961, Volume 27, No. 5.

44. *Op. cit. supra*, n. 1, at p. 547.

45. As of 1968, Philip Wittenberg (*Op. cit. supra*, n. 8, at pp. 103-104) listed those countries as: Andorra, Argentina, Austria, Belgium, Brazil, Cambodia, Canada, Chile, Costa Rica, Cuba, Czechoslovakia, Denmark, Ecuador, Finland, France, German Federal Republic, Ghana, Greece, Guatemala, Haiti, Holy See, Iceland, India, Ireland, Israel, Italy, Japan, Kenya, Laos, Lebanon, Liberia, Liechtenstein, Luxembourg, Malawi, Mexico,

Monaco, Panama, Paraguay, Peru, Philippines, Portugal, Spain, Sweden, Switzerland, United Kingdom, United States, Venezuela, Yugoslavia, Zambia. And, as has been indicated earlier, the U.S.S.R. has been recently added to the list.

46. *Op. cit. supra*, n. 4, at p. 39.

47. *Op. cit. supra*, n. 8, at p. 78. Wittenberg says:

It is important to note that at this time England is among the countries which have not adhered to the UCC, and that therefore works first published in England must still obtain protection in the United States by being manufactured therein after first procuring ad interim copyright.

48. *Op. cit. supra*, n. 1 at p. 39. Dr. Fox gives as authority *Louvigny de Montigny* v. *Cousineau*, [1950] S.C.R. 297 at 310-11, 10 Fox Pat. C. 161 at 172, 12 C.P.R. 45.

49. Universal Copyright Convention, Article IV. See *Op. cit. supra*, n. 1, at p. 777.

50. *Op. cit. supra*, n. 5, s. 8(1).

51. *Id.*, s. 9.

52. *Id.*, s. 10.

53. *Id.*, s. 11.

54. *Op. cit. supra*, n. 49, Article IV3.

55. *Op. cit. supra*, n. 1, at p. 6.

56. The Third Schedule, The Rome Copyright Convention, 1928. See *Op. cit. supra*, n. 1, at p. 739.

57. *Op. cit. supra*, n. 1, Article III 1.

58. *Id.*, Article III 4.

59. *Op. cit. supra*, n. 8, at pp. 75-76.

60. *Id.*, at p. 101.

61. *Op. cit. supra*, n. 5, ss. 37-41.

62. *Id.*, s. 52.

63. *Op. cit. supra*, n. 8, at pp. 38, 40.

64. *Op. cit. supra*, n. 1, at p. 560.

65. *Op. cit. supra*, n. 56, Article 4.

66. *Id.*, Article 5.

67. *Id.*, Article 6.

68. *Op. cit. supra*, n. 49, Article II.

69. *Op. cit. supra*, n. 5, s. 4.

70. *Op. cit. supra*, n. 1, at p. 44.

71. *Id.*, at p. 41.

72. *Ibid.*

73. *Id.*, at p. 43.

74. *Id.*, at p. 128 *et seq.*

75. W. H. Kesterton, *A History of Journalism in Canada*, The Carleton Library, No. 36 (Toronto: McClelland and Stewart, 1967), p. 5.

76. *Walter* v. *Steinhopff*, [1892] 3 Ch 489; *Blackie & Sons* v. *Lothian Book Publishing Co.*, (1921), 29 C.L.R. 396.

77. Revised Berne Convention, Article 9. See *Op. cit. supra*, n. 1, at p. 729.

78. *Ibid.*

79. *Ibid.*

80. *The Ottawa Citizen,* June 3, 1971.

81. *Op. cit. supra,* n. 1, at p. 46.

82. *Id.,* at p. 103. Fox gives as reference: *Exchange Telegraph Co.* v. *Gregory & Co.,* [1896] 1 Q.B. 147; *Exchange Telegraph Co.* v. *Howard,* (1906) 22T.L.R., 375; *Exchange Telegraph Co.* v. *Whale,* [1925] Macg. Cop Cas. 153.

83. 248 U.S. 215, 63 L. Ed. 211, 39 S. Ct. 68(1918) quoted in part in Gillmor and Barron, *Mass Communication Law* (St. Paul: West Publishing Co., 1969), at pp. 625-628.

84. *Id.,* at pp. 626-7.

85. *Id.,* at p. 627.

86. *Id.,* at p. 628.

87. *Ibid.*

88. *Op. cit. supra,* n. 5, s. 12(3).

89. *Id.,* s. (2)(e).

90. *Id.,* s. 18.

91. *Id.,* s. 12(7).

92. *Op. cit. supra,* n. 1, at p. 571.

93. *Id.,* at p. 49.

94. *Op. cit. supra,* n. 8, at p. 120. In his *Canadian Law of Copyright and Industrial Designs* at page 481, Dr. Fox says: "The deliberate introduction of errors into a compilation for the purpose of detecting infringers is a normal and legitimate practice which in no way affects the validity of the copyright or the relief that the owner of it is entitled to as against an infringer."

95. *Op. cit. supra,* n. 5, s. (1)(d).

96. *Id.,* s. 10.

97. *Id.,* s. 3(1)(e).

98. *Id.,* s. 9

99. *Id.,* s. 3(1)(f).

100. *Id.,* s. 2(g).

101. *Id.,* s. 19(1)(b) and 19(5).

102. For a consideration of the problems involved in assessing such payments see "Tariffs set for broadcasting recordings," *Ottawa Citizen,* May 20, 1971.

103. 14 Fox Pat. C. 114 at 127; [1954] Ex. C.R. 382 at 396; 20 C.P.R. 75.

104. *Op. cit. supra,* n. 1, at p. 140.

105. 392 U.S. 390, 20 L. Ed. 2d 1176, 88 S. Ct. 2084(1968) as reproduced in Gillmor and Barron, *Mass Cummunication Law* (St. Paul: West Publishing Co.), at pp. 634-639.

106. Erwin Knoll, "Our 'Model T' Copyright Law," *The Reporter,* March 10, 1966.

107. Roy C. Sharp, executive director of the Canadian Copyright Institute, quoted in Chris Braithwaite, "Publishers waging copyright battle against libraries' copying machines," *The Globe and Mail,* April 4, 1969.

108. *Op. cit. supra,* n. 5, s. 17(2).

109. Steven Allan, Sharon Green, Jerald Friedman, Bruce E. Harrington and Lawrence R. John, "New Technology and The Law of Copyright: Reprography and Computers," reprinted in George F. Bush, *Technology & Copyright* (Mt. Airy, Maryland: Lomond Systems, Inc., 1972), at p. 61.

110. R. C. Sharp, "Licensing the photocopier," *Scholarly Publishing*, April, 1970, pp. 245 and 246.

111. "Copyright Laws," *The Globe and Mail*, Toronto, May 20, 1969.

112. *Op. cit. supra*, n. 107.

113. "Copyright: The Canadian Authors Association," *In-Plant Repro-Graphics*, August, 1970.

114. *Op. cit. supra*, n. 109, at p. 66.

115. *Id.*, at p. 69.

116. *Op. cit. supra*, n. 110, at p. 248.

117. Quoted in J. S. Basmajian, "Saving the printed page from pirates," *The Globe and Mail*, February 25, 1973.

118. *Op. cit. supra*, n. 107.

119. *Ibid.*

120. *Ibid.*

Chapter IX

The Problem of Privacy

1. Various authorities have tried to analyze the concept of the right to privacy. Some of these include: Alan Westin, *Privacy and Freedom* (New York: Atheneum, 1967);
Hyman Gross, *Privacy: Its Legal Protection* (New York: Oceana, 1964);
Dr. Abraham Hoffer, "The Importance of Privacy," *Community Planning Review*, (Volume 19, No. 2, summer, 1969);
Task Force Report, *Privacy and Computers* (Ottawa: Department of Communications and Justice, 1972).
The Nordic Conference of 1967 of the Internationl Jurists Commission provided a more negative definition when it enumerated the enemies of an individual's privacy.

2. Anthony A. Thompson, *Big Brother In Britain Today* (London: Michael Joseph, 1970), at p. 67.

3. Harold G. Fox, *The Canadian Law of Copyright and Industrial Designs* (Toronto: Carswell, 1967), at page 67 has said that the right of privacy as such does not exist in Canada. Since he wrote these words (1967) privacy acts were passed in British Columbia (1968), Manitoba (1970), and Saskatchewan (1974), so that it now seems necessary to qualify this pronouncement. The three acts will be discussed later in this chapter.

4. Alan Westin, *Privacy and Freedom* (New York: Atheneum, 1967).

5. *Id.*, at p. 337.

6. The complete article is reproduced in Morris L. Ernst and Allan U. Schwartz, *Privacy: The Right To Be Let Alone* (London: MacGibbon and Kee, 1968), pp. 47-69.

7. In *Privacy and the Law*, (Seattle: University of Washington Press, 1972), Donald R. Pember disputes the claim of the two distinguished jurists that the press of Boston of that day was unduly sensational or intrusive.

8. (1849), 1 Mac. & G. 25, 2 DeG. & Sm. 652, 1 H. & Tw. 1, 18 L.J. Ch. 120.

9. Morris L. Ernst and Allan U. Schwartz, *Privacy: The Right To Be Let Alone* (London: MacGibbon and Kee, 1968), p. 57.

10. *Ibid.*

11. *Id.*, at p. 64.

12. *Id.*, at p. 66.

13. *Id.*, at p. 67.

14. *Ibid.*

15. *Ibid.*

16. *Id.*, at p. 68.

17. *Id.*, at p. 69.

18. For texts of these statutes see Donald R. Pember, *Privacy and the Press* (Seattle: University of Washington Press, 1972), at pp. 268-270.

19. Donald M. Gillmor and Jerome A. Barron, *Mass Communication Law: Cases and Comment* (St. Paul: West Publishing Co., 1969), at p. 485.

20. *Op. cit. supra*, n. 18, at pp. 264-266.

21. *Id.*, at p. 266.

22. *Id.*, at p. 265.

23. *Id.*, at pp. 264-266.

24. *Id.*, at pp. 231-232.

25. *Op. cit. supra*, n. 19, at p. 485.

26. Stig Strömholm, *Right of Privacy and Rights of the Personality* (Stockholm: P. A. Norstedt & Söners, 1967), at p. 46. It should be noted that not every legal authority agrees with this classification. Professor Edward Bloustein is one expert who disagrees. See *op. cit. supra*, n. 19, at p. 486. Gillmor and Barron cite Professor Bloustein's article, "Privacy As An Aspect of Human Dignity," in *39 N.Y.U. Law Review*, 962 at 963 (1964).

27. *Op. cit. supra*, n. 2, at p. 132.

28. H. Phillip Levy, *The Press Council: History, Procedure and Cases* (London: Macmillan, 1967), at pp. 243-244.

29. *Ibid.*

30. S.C. 1974, c. 50.

31. Harry Street, "Privacy and the Law," *Queen's Quarterly*, Volume LXXVII, No. 3, Autumn, 1970, pp. 323-324.

32. *Id.*, at p. 324.

33. R.S.C. 1970, c. C34, s. 38-42.

34. *Id.*, s. 173.

35. *Id.*, s. 381.

36. Privacy Act, S.B.C. 1968, c. 39.

37. The Privacy Act, S.M. 1970, c. P125.

38. The Privacy Act, S.S. 1974, c. 80.

39. e.g. *op. cit. supra*, n. 36, s. 2(1).

40. e.g. id., s. 2(3).

41. e.g. *op. cit. supra*, n. 37, s. 3(a).

42. e.g. *op. cit. supra*, n. 38, s. 3(c).

43. e.g. *op. cit. supra*, 37, s. 3(c).

44. e.g. *op. cit. supra*, n. 38, s. 3(d).

45. e.g. id., s. 7.

46. e.g. id., s. 9 and s. 10.

47. Sheila Ascroft, "Privacy, The Law And The Journalist," unpublished honours research project report, Carleton School of Journalism, Ottawa, Ontario, p. 37.

48. *The Daily Colonist.*, Victoria, June 15, 1973.

Chapter X: Government Secrecy and the Press

1. Hugh Lawford, "Privacy versus Freedom of Information," *Queen's Quarterly*, LXXVIII, No. 3, Autumn, 1971, p. 371.

2. Donald C. Rowat, "How Much Administrative Secrecy?" *The Canadian Journal of Economics and Political Science*, XXXI, No. 4, November, 1965, Footnote, p. 486.

3. *Op. cit. supra*, n. 1, p. 370.

4. Quoted in Rowat *op. cit. supra*, n. 2. Rowat gives as authority: C. P. Stacey, "Some Pros and Cons of the Access Problem," *International Journal* 20 (1964-65), p. 52.

5. *Op. cit. supra*, n. 1, p. 371.

6. For an excellent analysis of the legal issues involved in this case see: Leonard B. Boudin. "The Ellsberg Case: Citizen Disclosure," in Thomas M. Franck and Edward Weisband (editors), *Secrecy and Foreign Policy* (New York: Oxford University Press, 1974), pp. 291-311.

7. Representative William S. Moorhead, "Operation and Reform of the Classification System in the United States," in Thomas M. Franck and Edward Weisband (editors), *Secrecy and Foreign Policy* (New York: Oxford University Press, 1974), pp. 100-101.

8. *Op. cit. supra*, n. 2, p. 488.

9. *Op. cit. supra*, n. 1, p. 370.

10. For the difference between the two Official Secret Acts see Maxwell Cohen, "Secrecy in Law and Policy: The Canadian Experience and International Relations," in Thomas M. Franck and Edward Weisband (editors), *Secrecy and Foreign Policy* (New York: Oxford University Press, 1974), pp. 357-358.

11. *Op. cit. supra*, n. 1, pp. 368-370.

12. *House of Commons Debates*, May 1, 1969, p. 8199.

13. *Id.*, at p. 8200.

14. James Eayrs, "Ottawa's obsession with secrecy leaves our history to foreigners," *Ottawa Citizen*, February 2, 1971.

15. *Ibid.*

16. *Ibid.*

17. *Ibid.*

18. Leslie Katz, (letter to the editor), "Federal Court Act," Toronto *Globe and Mail*, November 20, 1970.

19. *Op. cit. supra*, n. 1, p. 368.

Postscript: The Changing Media Law

1. See page 57.

2. Charles Rembar, *The End of Obscenity* (New York: Random House, 1968). His concluding sentences (at page 493) are: "So far as writing is concerned, I have said there is no longer any law of obscenity. I would go farther and add, so far as writing is concerned, that not only in our law but in our culture, obscenity will soon be gone."

Bibliography

I. Books

Advisory Committe on Fair Trial and Free Press, *Standards Relating to Fair Trial and Free Press* (New York: American Bar Association, 1968).

Blanshard, Paul, *The Right To Read* (Boston: Beacon Press, 1955).

Busch, George P., *Technology & Copyright* (Mt. Airy, Maryland: Lomond Systems, Inc., 1972).

Carter-Ruck, P.F., Skone James, E.P., and Skone James, F.E., *Copyright, Modern Law and Practice* (London: Faber and Faber, 1965).

Clor, Harry M., *Obscenity and Public Morality* (Chicago: University of Chicago Press, 1969).

Committee on Obscenity and Pornography, *The Report of the Committee on Obscenity and Pornography* (Toronto: Bantam, 1970).

Cook, Sir Edward, *The Press In War-Time* (London: Macmillan, 1920).

Dean, Joseph, *Hatred, Ridicule or Contempt* (New York: Macmillan, 1954).

Ernst, Morris L. and Schwartz, Allan U., *Privacy: The Right To Be Let Alone* (London: McGibbon and Kee, 1968).

Ernst, Morris L. and Steagle, William, *To The Pure: A Study of Obscenity And The Censor* (New York: The Viking Press, 1929).

Felsher, Harold and Rosen, Michael, *The Press In The Jury Box.* (New York: Macmillan, 1966).

Fortin, Prof. Jacques et al, *Obscenity* (Ottawa: Prohibited and Regulated Conduct Project, Law Reform Commission, December, 1972).

Fox, Harold G., *The Canadian Law of Copyright and Industrial Designs* (Toronto: The Carswell Company, 1967).

Franck, Thomas M. and Weisband, Edward (editors), *Secrecy and Foreign Policy* (New York: Oxford University Press, 1974).

Friendly, Alfred and Goldfarb, Ronald L., *Crime and Publicity* (New York: Vintage Books, 1968).

Gavin, Clark, *Famous Libel and Slander Cases of History* (New York: Collier, 1950).

Gillmor, Donald M. and Barron, Jerome A., *Mass Communication Law: Cases and Comment* (St. Paul: West Publishing Co., 1969).

Gross, Hyman, *Privacy: Its Legal Protection* (New York: Oceana, 1964).

Hartogs, Renatus with Fantel, Hans, *Four Letter Word Games* (New York: Dell, 1968).

Heuston, R.F.V., *Salmond on Torts* (London: Sweet & Maxwell, 1969).

Hyde, H. Montgomery, *Cases That Changed The Law* (Toronto: Heinemann, 1951).

Inbau, Fred E., *Free Press - Fair Trial* (Chicago: Northwestern University School of Law, 1964).

Jackson, E. Hilton, *Latin For Lawyers* (London: Sweet & Maxwell, 1960).

Joyce, James, *Ulysses* (New York: Modern Library, 1946).

Kettle, John and Walker, Dean, *Verdict!* (Toronto: Mc Graw Hill, 1968).

King, John, *The Law of Defamation in Canada: Slander and Libel in Canada* (Toronto: The Carswell Company, 1907).

Koop, Theodore F., *Weapon of Silence* (Chicago: University of Chicago Press, 1946).

Lang, O. E. *Contemporary Problems of Public Law in Canada* (Toronto: University of Toronto Press, 1968).

Levy, H. Phillip, *The Press Council: History, Procedure and Cases* (London: Macmillan, 1967).

Lewis, J. R., *Civil and Criminal Procedure* (London: Sweet & Maxwell, 1968).

Martin, J. C., Mewett, Alan W., and Cartwright, Ian, *Martin's Annual Criminal Code, 1972* (Toronto: Canada Law Book Ltd., 1972).

McCormick, John, and MacInnes, Mairi, *Versions of Censorship* (Garden City, New York: Anchor Books, Doubleday and Company, 1962).

McEwen, R. L., and Lewis, P. S. C., *Gatley on Libel and Slander* (London: Sweet & Maxwell, 1967).

McRuer, The Hon. J. C., *Royal Commission Inquiry Into Civil Rights, Report Number One, Volume 2* (Toronto: Queen's Printer, Ontario, 1968).

Members of Longford Committee Investigating Pornography, *Pornography: The Longford Report* (London: Coronet Book, Hodder Paperbacks, 1972).

Millett, Kate, *Sexual Politics* (Garden City, New York: Doubleday, 1970).

Nizer, Louis, *My Life In Court* (New York: Pyramid Books, 1968).

Osborn, P. G., *A Concise Law Dictionary* (London: Sweet & Maxwell, 1964).

Parker, Graham (editor), *Collision Course? Free Press and the Courts* (Toronto: Communications Department, Ryerson Polytechnical Institute, 1966).

Pember, Donald R., *Privacy And The Law* (Seattle: University of Washington Press, 1972).

Perrin, Noel, *Dr. Bowdler's Legacy* (New York: Atheneum, 1969).

Rembar, Charles, *The End of Obscenity* (New York: Random House, 1968).

Rodgers, R. S., *Sex and Law in Canada* (Ottawa: Policy Press, 1962).

Rolph, Dr. C. H., *The Trial of Lady Chatterley* (London: Penguin, 1961).

Sagarin, Edward, *The Anatomy of Dirty Words* (New York: Paperback Library, 1962).

Schmeiser, D. A., *Civil Liberties In Canada* (London: Oxford, 1964).

Siebert, Fredrick Seaton, *Freedom Of The Press In England* (Urbana, Illinois: The University of Illinois Poress at Urbana, 1952).

Street, Harry, *Freedom, The Individual and The Law* (Hammondsworth: Penguin, 1967).

Strömholm, Stig, *Right of Privacy and Rights of the Personality* (Stockholm: P. A. Norstedt & Söners, 1967).

Task Force Report, *Privacy and Computers* (Ottawa: Department of Communications and Justice, 1972).

Thompson, Anthony A. *Big Brother in Britain Today* (London: Michael Joseph, 1970).

Vamplew, J. L. K., "Obscene Literature and Section 150A," *The Criminal Law Quarterly*, v. 6, 1964-65, p. 187.

Wallace, Irving, *The Seven Minutes* (Richmond Hill, Ontario: Pocket Book Edition, Simon & Schuster of Canada, 1970).

Westin, Alan, *Privacy and Freedom* (New York: Atheneum, 1967).

Wickwar, William H., *The Struggle For Freedom of the Press, 1819-1832* (London: George Allen & Unwin, 1972).

Williams, Glanville, *Learning The Law* (London: Stevens and Sons, 1969).

Wittenberg, Philip, *The Protection of Literary Property* (Boston: The Writer Inc., 1968).

Yonge, A. D. et al, *Halsbury's Statutes of England, v. 19* (London: Butterworth, 1970).

II. Magazine and Periodical Articles and Notes

Atkey, Ronald G, "The Law of the Press in Canada (1) and (2)," *Gazette: International Journal for Mass Communication Studies*, v. 15, nos 2 and 3, 1969, p. 105 and p. 185.

Black, Hawley, "How U. S. 'manufacturing clause' is hurting Canadian printers," *Canadian Printer & Publisher*, May, 1963, p. 39.

Brewin, F. A., "Cases and Comment," *Canadian Bar Review*, v. 30, 1952, p. 614.

Charles, W. H. "Obscene Literature and the Legal Process in Canada," *Canadian Bar Review*, v. 44, 1966, p. 243.

Eimerl, Sarel, "Loaded for Bear," *The Reporter*, October 19, 1967.

———"The Trouble With Jeeves," *The Reporter*, March 7, 1968.

Fraser, Blair, "Our Hush Hush Censorship," *Maclean's*, December 15, 1949.

French, William, "Who Killed Censorship?" *The Globe Magazine*, October 9, 1965.

Hoffer, Dr. Abraham, "The Importance of Privacy," *Community Planning Review*, v. 19, no. 2, summer, 1969.

Housser, Kathie, "Protecting Sources: A Basic Right," *Content*, March, 1973, p. 7.

Jeanneret, Marsh, "The United States Manufacturing Clause," *Quill & Quire*, v. 27, no. 5, September-October, 1961.

Knoll, Erwin, "Our 'Model T' Copyright Law," *The Reporter*, March 10, 1966.

Lawford, Hugh, "Privacy versus Freedom of Information," *Queen's Quarterly*, v. 78, no. 3, Autumn, 1971, p. 371.

McRuer, Hon. J. C., "Criminal Contempt of Court Procedure: A Protection To The Rights Of The Individual," *Canadian Bar Review*, v. 30, p. 225.

Powe, L. A. Jr., "*The Georgia Straight* and Freedom of Expression in Canada," *Canadian Bar Review*, v. 48, 1970, p. 433.

Rowat, Donald C., "How Much Administrative Secrecy?" *The Canadian Journal of Economics and Political Science*, v. 31, no. 4, November, 1965.

Sharp, R. C., "Licensing the photocopier," *Scholarly Publishing*, April, 1970.

Street, Harry, "Privacy and the Law," *Queen's Quarterly*, v. 77, no. 3, Autumn, 1970.

Waters, David, "Toward A Responsible Media," *Content*, July, 1973, p. 8.

(unsigned) "An Act To Protect The Public's Access To The News," *Content*, April/May, 1974.

(unsigned) "A Voice From Watts," *Newsweek*, June 20, 1966.

(unsigned) "Copyright: The Canadian Authors Association," *In-Plant ReproGraphics*, August, 1970.

(unsigned) "Newsmen v. the Courts," *Time*, January 1, 1973.

III. Newspaper Items

Basmajian, J. S., "Saving the printed page from pirates," *Globe and Mail*, February 25, 1973.

Cherry, Zena, "MacLennan says pornography signifies authoritarian trend," *Globe and Mail*, March 29, 1968.

Eayrs, James, "Ottawa's obsession with secrecy leaves our history to foreigners," *Ottawa Citizen*, February 2, 1971.

Katz, Leslie (letter to the editor), "Federal Court Act," *Globe and Mail*, November 20, 1970.

Sharp, Roy C., "Publishers waging copyright battle against libraries' copying machines," *Globe and Mail*, April 4, 1969.

(letter to editor), "Copyright law would stifle writing: letter," *Globe and Mail*, March 29, 1973.

(unsigned) "Copyright laws," *Globe and Mail*, May 20, 1969.

(unsigned) Editorial, *Globe and Mail*, March 20, 1969.

(unsigned) "Jailed over story in defunct paper," *Globe and Mail*, October 10, 1972.

(unsigned) "Press On Trial," *The Economist*, October 29, 1966.

(unsigned) "Tariff set for broadcasting recordings," *Ottawa Citizen*, May 20, 1971.

IV. Book Chapters

Allan, Steven; Green, Sharon; Friedman, Jerald; Harrington Bruce E; and John, Lawrence R., "New Technology and The Law of Copyright: Reprography and Computers," in Bush, George F. (editor) *Technology & Copyright* (Mt. Airy, Maryland: Lomond Systems, Inc., 1972), p. 61.

Boudin, Leonard B., "The Ellsberg Case: Citizen Disclosure," in Franck, Thomas M., and Weisband, Edward (editors), *Secrecy and Foreign Policy* (New York: Oxford University Press, 1974), p. 291.

Cohen, Maxwell, "Secrecy in Law and Policy: The Candian Experience and International Relations," in Franck, Thomas M., and Weisband, Edward (editors), *Secrecy and Foreign Policy* (New York: Oxford University Press, 1974), p. 355.

Curry, W. E., "The Import of the U. S. Manufacturing Provisions," in Government of Ontario, *Royal Commission on Book Publishing, Background Papers* (Toronto: The Queen's Printer and Publisher, 1972), p. 143.

Moorhead, Representative William S., "Operation and Reform of the Classification System in the United States," in Franck, Thomas M., and Weisband, Edward (editors), *Secrecy and Foreign Policy* (New York: Oxford University Press, 1974), p. 87.

Sharp, Roy C., "Some Copyright Concerns of Canadian Authors and Publishers," in Government of Ontario, *Royal Commission on Book Publish-*

ing, Background Papers (Toronto: The Queen's Printer and Publisher, 1972), p. 111.

V. Speeches and Seminars

Robinette, J. J., *Libel, Defamation, Contempt of Court and the Right of the People to be Informed* (Newspaper-legal seminar held in the Royal York Hotel, Toronto, March 27, 1962).

Stark, Alexander, *Dangerous Words* (paper delivered to Canadian Managing Editors' Conference, Niagara Falls, Ontario, January 28, 1950).

VI. Unpublished Material

Ascroft, Sheila, *Privacy, The Law And The Journalist* (unpublished honors research project report, School of Journalism, Carleton University, Ottawa, Ontario, 1973).

VII. Television Programs

Something Else, CBC Public Affairs Program, March 20, 1969.
The Way It Is, CBC Public Affairs Program, April 27, 1969.

Appendix:

Cases Discussed in this Book

Case No. 1

See: *R.* v. *The Vancouver Province, sub nom. Re Nicol*, [1954] 3 D.L.R. 690

In 1954, in British Columbia, a 19-year-old youth named William Gash was sentenced to be hanged for the murder of a man named Frank Pitsch. Eric Nicol, Vancouver *Province* columnist, used the occasion to write in opposition to capital punishment. In his column, which appeared two days after the sentence was pronounced, Nicol pictured himself as being tried after death before God for the murder of Gash. In his imaginary trial Nicol pleaded guilty to killing Gash by hanging. His article said, "Although I did not myself spring the trap that caused my victim to be strangled in cold blood, I admit that the man who put the rope around his neck was in my employ. Also serving me were the 12 people who caused the victim to suffer the exquisite torture of anticipation." Nicol blamed society for Gash's plight, asking, "What did he owe to us that we should drive him to murder, then commit him to the hell of the death chamber?" Nicol and the *Province* were found guilty of contempt, the columnist being fined $250 and the publishers and proprietors of the newspaper being fined $2500. After *dicta* emphasizing the fact that the jury had no part in deciding the punishment meted out to Gash, and the fact that the interval between sentence and execution of the verdict had nothing to do with torture but was designed to give the convicted man time to appeal his sentence, Justice Cline said, "To refer to the jurors in this case as criminals and to describe the judge as causing exquisite torture is calculated to lower the dignity of the court and to destroy public confidence in the administration of justice, and a practice of this kind must be stopped and stopped immediately in the public interest." (Case cited, page 699)

Case No. 2

See: *R.* v. Glanzer, [1963] 2 O.R. 30

In 1962, in Ontario Philip Glanzer wrote, in the *Division Court Reporter*, of which he was editor and publisher:

> His Honour Judge McDonagh presided over the 1st Division Court, York County, during the month of March, and again displayed his ruthless contempt for the court and all who came before him.
> The learned Judge apparently makes up his own rules and regulations in District Court, to suit his own convenience—the public be damned! These new rules and regulations are not necessarily concurred in by Judge

McDonagh's colleagues—not by a long shot. These same colleagues are precluded from publicly expressing their own displeasure at Judge McDonagh's handling of Division Court matters, and will therefore restrain themselves from making any public issue in the matter.

The article was but one of several articles critical of York County Court judges who presided over the Court before which Glanzer was frequently an agent. Characterizing the Glanzer strictures as vulgar abuse, Chief Justice J. C. McRuer sentenced Glanzer to pay a fine of $4,000. In passing judgment Chief Justice McRuer termed the contempt charge the most serious in the history of Ontario.

Case No. 3

See: *R.* v. *Murphy*, [1969] 4 D.L.R.(3d) 289

In 1968 the University of New Brunswick brought suit against Norman Strax, a professor of the institution. Tom Murphy, writing in the *Brunswickian*, a U. N. B. Student publication, commented on the case. He said:

A short while ago, I testified in the Supreme Court of New Brunswick on the Strax case. That court was a mockery of justice . . .

Take for instance the attitude of Judge Barry. I am in no position to accuse a man of being biased; his manners have been self-convicting . . .

The courts in New Brunswick are simply the instruments of the corporate elite. Their duty is not so much to make just decisions as to make right decisions (i.e. decisions which will further perpetuate the elite which controls and rewards them.) Court appointments are political appointments. Only the naive would reject the notion that an individual becomes a justice or judge after he proves his worth to the establishment.

In convicting the defendant of contempt, the New Brunswick Supreme Court found that Murphy had exceeded the limits of fair criticism in his malignment of Mr. Justice Barry and that he had made "a most uncalled for attack on the integrity of the Courts of New Brunswick." (Case cited, page 295)

Case No. 4

See: F. A. Brewin, *Case and Comment*, [1952] 30 Can. Bar Rev. 614.

During 1951 a Mrs. Sullivan was tried—and acquitted—on a charge of murdering her husband. On February 13, during the course of the trial, the Chief Justice of Ontario imposed a fine of $3,000 on the Journal Publishing Company of Ottawa. The cause of the contempt citation was the fact that the newspaper had carried, under the very large headline "Mrs. Sullivan to Tell Own Story," a news account which said that the accused, "whose own story of how her husband came to his death has been locked in secrecy since her arrest last September," would take the witness stand in her own defence. Summoned before the Chief Justice, the *Journal* editor apologized and explained that there had been no intention to prejudice the conduct of the trial. In passing judgment the Chief Justice pointed out the shocking nature of the report. He was not concerned with the prestige of the court but with the treatment of the accused. He said she was entitled to be heard on evidence given in court, and, without comment, to remain out of the witness box (as indeed she did so remain). He considered that the question to be determined was not whether the article interfered but whether it had a tendency to interfere with the course of justice. The Chief Justice found that there had been such a tendency. The fact that the *Journal* was well known and widely circulated increased the seriousness of the offence. But the moderateness of the fine, by comparison with fines levied in similar cases in England, was due, said the Chief Justice, to the excellent reputation of the newspaper and to the editor's apology. Had it not been for these considerations, he said, committal to jail would have resulted.

Case No. 5

See: *Meriden Britannia Co.* v. *Walters re Lewis*, (1915), 24 C.C.C. 364

The contempt motion grew out of a law suit over the paving of a street in front of the plaintiff's premises, a suit in which Mayor Walters of Hamilton was made a defendant. John Lewis Lewis, publisher of *The Hamilton Herald*, published an editorial, entitled "An Action At Law," commenting on the case. The plaintiff company objected that the newspaper and its editor were "making misleading and incorrect statements as to the facts involved in the action, and suppressing important and material facts, and commenting on the case adversely to the plaintiff company's claim and contention." Ruling on the motion, the Court said: "The words of Cottenham, L. C. quoted by Blackburn, J., in *Skipworth's Case* (1873), L.R. 9 Q.B. 219, 230, 235, are apposite: Comments in a pending case must be such as to manifest that 'the object is to taint the source of justice, and to obtain a result of legal proceedings different from that which would follow in the ordinary course.' If the tenour of the article is such as to be likely to prejudice the proper conduct of the case, to create a feeling against the litigant, and so to affect the minds of those who may be charged with the trial, then the disciplinary power of the Court should be exercised. This arbitrary jurisdiction, from which there is no appeal, should be sparingly and carefully exercised." (Case cited, page 369) The Court found that the Lewis editorial did not offend in the manner just described, and the motion to commit for contempt was refused.

Case No. 6

See: *R.* v. *Hamilton Spectator R.* v. *Globe & Mail*, [1966] 2 O.R. 503

In 1966 Rudy Platiel found himself, as a *Globe and Mail* reporter, doing double duty in the courts of Halton County Courthouse. This was because a colleague was sick and Platiel was required by his paper to handle his friend's assignments as well as his own. Platiel was responsible for reporting a trial before Mr. Justice E. G. Moorhouse of four men charged with criminal negligence. While Platiel was away from the court attending to his colleague's assignment the judge heard evidence given in a *voir dire*. The consideration of evidence in *voir dire* proceedings is really "a trial within a trial." The jury was sent out of the room, and the judge heard counsels' representations to decide whether a certain piece of the evidence but neglected to say that the evidence had been heard in a *voir* it. Mr. Justice Moorhouse ruled that the matter in question was *not* admissible. Presently Platiel returned to the court and asked what had happened during his absence. Another reporter (not from the *Globe and Mail*) told him the substance of the evidence but neglected to say that the evidence had been heard in a *voire dire*. The result of Platiel's failure to realize the confidentiality of the contentious evidence was a story carried by the *Globe and Mail* under the headline, "Four Accused Visited Bootlegger, Jury Told"—a headline dealing with the very matter ruled out as evidence. The story also attributed to one of the accused a statement which had actually been made by a constable in the case. The Canadian Press picked up the *Globe and Mail* story. The Hamilton *Spectator* used the Canadian Press account. But in early February Mr. Justice Moorhouse cited the *Globe and Mail*, the Hamilton *Spectator*, R. J. Doyle (*Globe and Mail* editor), and Rudy Platiel for contempt. The two newspapers were fined $1,500 each, Doyle was fined $500 and Platiel fined $100. The sentences were appealed. In May the Ontario Court of Appeal reduced the fine against the *Globe and Mail* to $500 and set aside the fines levied against the *Spectator*, Doyle and Platiel. In passing judgment, Mr. Justice Walter Schroeder said, "The publishing company must itself shoulder responsibility for misreporting the proceedings in question." (Case cited, page 503) He also said that the *Globe and Mail* "should not have imposed double duty upon the reporter . . ."(Case cited, page 505)

Case No. 7

See: *Re Sommers* v. *Sturdy*, [1956] 19 W.W.R. 583

In 1956 the Hon. R. E. Sommers brought a defamation suit against David Sturdy following accusations that Sommers had accepted bribes while he held a seat in the recently dissolved B. C. legislature. While the case was pending the writ for a provincial election was issued and Sommers and Deane Finlayson were nominated as candidates. On August 20, 1956, Finlayson made a campaign speech in North Vancouver in which he referred to the Sommers-Sturdy case. The Vancouver *Sun* and Vancouver *Herald* reported the speech. In proceedings before Mr. Justice Wilson of the British Columbia Supreme Court Sommers complained that Finlayson's statements and the consequent newspaper reportage was prejudicial to a fair trial of the defamation case. Respondents in the appeal were Finlayson, the Thomson Company (owner of the Vancouver *Herald*), Mr. Gerald Brown (editor and publisher of the Herald), the Sun Publishing Company (owner of the Vancouver *Sun*), Donald C. Cromie (publisher of the *Sun*), and Frank Walton (staff reporter of the *Sun*).

The justice dismissed the appeal, ruling that what the respondents had done was not, under existing circumstances, a contempt. He found that republication of the speech would not be prejudicial to a fair trial, since the charge of bribery had been widely disseminated, notably by Sommers himself.

There is no evidence here to suggest that any of the respondents intended to taint the source of justice or prejudice a fair trial . . .

The plaintiff stands as a candidate for the legislature and does so with the full knowledge that his character must be publicly discussed and the knowledge that his libel action is pending. He has put himself in the public eye and while this does not justify any act which may be construed as contempt of court, it makes inevitable some exploration of his conduct as a member and as a minister.

Mr. Finlayson's speech was not an attack on the plaintiff but on the premier for having, as Mr. Finlayson alleges, unnecessarily called an election before the serious charges against a former member of his government had been aired in the courts." (Case cited, page 592)

A noteworthy point made by the B. C. Supreme Court justice was that the newspapers had presented a fair and accurate report of the speech, and, like Finlayson, had not gone outside of the context of Premier Bennett's election call. The justice was also careful to point out that his conclusion was "not to be taken as a general absolution in respect of any future reference to the matters *sub judice* in *Sommers* v. *Sturdy*." (Case cited, page 584)

Case No. 8

See: *Re Tilco Plastics Ltd.* v. *Skurjat et al. Attorney-General for Ontario* v. *Clark et al.*, [1966] 2 O.R. 547

In the 1966 trial held before Chief Justice G. A. Gale of the Ontario High Court of Justice, it was ruled that no valid objection could be taken to the use of summary proceedings under the then Section 108 of the Criminal Code. (The number given to this section in the 1970 revision of the Code is 116.) According to the headnote of the case, Chief Justice Gale found:

The Court has a time-honoured inherent power to punish summarily for contempt and such power may be invoked by the Attorney-General where anything has taken place which may tend to interfere with the fair administration of justice. The procedure adopted gave the defendants all the rights they would have had in any other trial except the right to elect trial by jury. (Case cited, page 548)

Chief Justice Gale made it clear that:

because of the large number of persons involved and the public nature of the defiance of the Court order, the public depreciation of the authority of the Court and of the administration of justice was a criminal contempt, as distinguished from a civil contempt, requiring proof of all essential elements of the offence beyond a reasonable doubt, and, on the evidence, such proof has to be shown. (Case cited, page 549)

Case No. 9

See: *Wismer* v. *Maclean-Hunter Publishing Co. Ltd. and Fraser, No. 1,* (1952-53), 7 W.W.R. (N.S.) 514

Wismer v. *Maclean-Hunter Publishing Co. Ltd. and Fraser, Nos. 2 and 3,* (1953), 10 W.W.R. (N.S.) 625.

Wismer v. *Maclean-Hunter Publishing Co. Ltd. and Fraser, No. 2,* [1954] 1 D.L.R. 501.

This case originated in a February 15, 1952 *Maclean's* magazine article entitled, "B. C. Coalition Commits Suicide." In it Blair Fraser discussed the disintegration of the Liberal-Conservative government headed by Premier Byron Johnson. He implied that the attorney-general of that government, Gordon Wismer, had been involved in a questionable real estate transaction and had used his position to do "favors" for his friends in the granting of liquor licences.

The following month Wismer filed a libel suit against the magazine and Fraser. Acting on the advice of his counsel, the Ottawa editor declined to answer 36 out of 443 questions asked him on "examination for discovery" in Toronto. The case was taken to the Supreme Court of British Columbia, where Mr. Justice Whittaker exempted Fraser from answering 18 of the 36 questions, but directed him to answer the remaining 18. Seven of these concerned his intention or opinion and 11 had to do with the names of people who had given Fraser information upon which the offending article had been based. Grounds for insisting that sources be divulged were that, because Fraser was pleading both fair comment and privilege, malice was an ingredient of the case, and determination of malice was dependant on the nature and character of the informants who had furnished the information on which he had based his article. Fraser still refused to answer questions related to his sources. The British Columbia Court of Appeal upheld Mr. Justice Whittaker's ruling. The defendants were refused the right to appeal their case to the Supreme Court of Canada, and the defendants had their defence in the libel action struck out. Later in the year the case was settled out of court, with *Maclean's* publishing an apology and the defendants making a cash settlement. It is to be noted that whereas in England a defendant journalist is not required, except in exceptional cases, to name sources at an "interrogatory" (which roughly corresponds to the Canadian "examination for discovery") in the Wismer-Fraser case he was. In neither country, however, may confidentiality of sources be claimed at a trial proper.

Case No. 10

See: *Reid* v. *Telegram Publishing Co. Ltd. and Drea* (1961), 28 D.L.R.(2d) 6

In 1960 Weir Reid launched libel actons against the Toronto *Telegram* and reporter Frank Drea after Drea had written articles claimed to be libellous of the plaintiff and after the newspaper had republished those articles in pamphlet form. Very heavy damages were sought. In examinations for discovery Drea answered 1,439 questions and *Telegram* managing editor J. D. MacFarlane answered 182. Notwithstanding this, a motion was brought before the Senior Master to compel Drea and MacFarlane to reattend before the special examiner at Toronto and to divulge further information. In the event the defendants failed to comply, the plaintiff sought to have them jailed for contempt and to have their defence struck out.

What Weir asked for, among other things, was that Drea should reveal the author and supplier of words used in his stories and the identity of other sources of information, and should produce the transcript and alternatively the transcript and tape recording on which Drea had based his articles. Similar information was sought of MacFarlane.

The motion to compel reattendance was adjudicated by Mr. Justice Dalton Wells of the Ontario High Court in 1961. The defendants opposed the granting of an order on the grounds that: the reporter had promised that he would not disclose the name of the informant who had provided the information on which his articles were based, and that to surrender tapes and transcripts would be to reveal that informant's identity; releasing the tape recordings and transcripts would make the plaintiff aware of the names of persons the defendants intended to call as witnesses in their defence; the R.C.M.P. had requested Drea not to make the tapes available on the grounds that national security would be jeopardized, in addition to which much of the material contained in the tapes was irrelevant to the case.

In making his judgment, Mr. Justice Wells took into account that:

> In the statement of defence there is a denial of malice and the assertion that the defendants published what they did in respect of the matters raised in the articles complained of as a matter of journalistic duty under circumstances raising qualified privilege and that the publication constituted fair comment made in good faith without malice and that in fact the words complained of in their natural and ordinary meaning are true. (Case cited, page 9)

The justice cited several cases, some of them English, in which there had been no requirement, during the examination for discovery or interrogatory stages of proceedings, to divulge. Citing the Fraser case, he rejected the majority decision, but adverted approvingly to the dissenting opinion of O'Halloran, J. A. He saw the plaintiff's tactics in seeking disclosure as a "fishing expedition" whereby Weir sought to gather evidence supportive of his suit which he could not obtain by other means. Conversely he ruled that the privilege of confidentiality would work no undue hardship on the plaintiff for the simple reason that *when it came to the trial proper* the defendants would have to disclose sources in order to support their defence arguments against the plaintiff's allegations of libel. Furthermore, Mr. Justice Wells cited a case which threw light on the differences with respect to the malice that the plaintiff complained a newspaperman had shown and the malice which was attributable to his informants.

During the course of his judgment, the justice pointed out:

> It would appear that normally the information sought by the plaintiff should be made available to him but it also appears from the cases when the defendant is a newspaper or journal of some description or reporter thereof, there has, over a long time, developed a rule of practice which is based substantially on grounds of public policy, which has led to the refusal of such information as the plaintiff is now seeking in discovery. (Case cited, page 10)

His conclusion was that in examinations for discovery involving actions against newspapers disclosure was to be required only in exceptional circumstances. Therefore the application by the plaintiff was dismissed.

Case No. 11

See: *Knox* v. *Spencer* [1923] D.L.R. 162

The suit originated with an aritcle by a reporter named Spencer, of the Saint John *Daily Telegraph.* In his story he wrote about three children, without actually naming them, declaring them to be children of a drunkard. He stated that as a result of their father's drunkenness they had been placed in a charitable institution by the court. A photograph of the three children accompanied the story. As next friend, William Knox brought suit on behalf of the children against Spencer. It was Knox's contention that since the children were recognized through the photograph and designated in the story as children of a drunkard they had been deprived of a happy home and been greatly injured and defamed. The plaintiffs claimed $20,000 in damages. Chief Justice McKeown of King's Bench Division ruled that it could become a matter for a jury to decide whether or not the plaintiff's claim of special damages be granted. New Brunswick Supreme Court Justice White upheld the defendant's appeal from the verdict, thereby accepting the defence contention that the alleged libels, if any, referred only to the father of the plaintiffs, and the libel of a father only cannot give a cause of action to his children.

Case No. 12

See: *Tedlie* v. *Southam et al.,* [1950] 4 D.L.R. 415

The case involved a serious collision which had occurred on September 1, 1947, at Dugald when a westbound C.N.R. train from Minaki crashed head-on into the regular eastbound passenger train standing on the main track waiting for the other train to take the siding. The Board of Transport Commissioners for Canada held a public inquiry into the causes of the wreck. The Winnipeg *Tribune* reported the Board's proceedings. A front page news story appeared under the seven column heading: "SPECIAL HAD GREEN LIGHT, OPERATOR TELLS HEARING." A following deck and lead paragraph said, "Train Reported 'Under Control'," and "The Minaki campers' special had a green light, or 'proceed' signal in its favor, at the time of the Dugald train wreck, according to testimony given today at the Board of Transport Commissioners inquiry in the law courts building." The Dugald railroad operator mentioned in the headline, a man named Tedlie, brought suit against the Southam Company, publisher of the *Tribune.* In his statement of claim Tedlie alleged that the headlines and lead paragraphs quoted above were falsely and maliciously published and that they had imputed that he had displayed the wrong signal, which misled the Minaki Campers' special train, resulting in the accident and that therefore the plaintiff Tedlie was incompetent and negligent in the performance of his work and duties. Among other pleadings, the defendants claimed the protection of section 11(1) of the Manitoba *Defamation Act,* which says, "A fair and accurate report, published in a newspaper or by broadcasting, of proceedings publicly held shall be absolutely privileged if (a) the report contains no comment . . . .'' In giving judgment Manitoba King's Bench Justice Montague found:

> that he [the plaintiff Tedlie] had faithfully and strictly complied with the rules and regulations of his employment and had properly performed his duties on the night in question. He was not in any way responsible for the negligence in the switch being thrown or the train stopped.
>
> I find that the headline report "Special Had Green Light, Operator Tells Hearing" was not true in itself and that the operator did not make that statement. His evidence, and that of other witnesses, was that the special was not operating on signal lights but train orders. The published heading was not fairly or substantially accurate; it was a voluntary statement and *comment* [italics mine] by the paper; it was not a fair and accurate report . . .
>
> As I have found that the above headline and lead paragraphs complained of were not fair and accurate reports, the defendants are not within the protection accorded by s. 11 of the act. The report in question was not privileged. (Case cited at pages 423, 424)

The Southam Company was found liable and the plaintiff was awarded $2,000 and costs of his action.

Case No. 13

See: *Banks* v. *Globe and Mail Ltd. et al.*, (1961), 28 D.L.R. (2d) 343

Qualified privilege was an ingredient of the defence when Hal Banks sued the *Globe and Mail* in 1961. The case followed publication in the Toronto *Globe and Mail* of an editorial entitled "Mission Accomplished." It accused Harold C. Banks, Canadian director of the Seafarers' International Union, of being brought to Canada for the specific purpose of scuttling Canada's deep-sea fleet. It referred to his record of offences in the United States and said that he had extended and diversified that record before coming to this country. It claimed that Banks had put almost all of Canada's deep-sea fishermen out of work. And it suggested that the union leader should be sent back to the United States. Banks sued for libel. Part of the *Globe and Mail*'s defence was a plea of qualified privilege. The newspaper claimed that, to serve the public interest, it had a duty to publish information about a strike called by Banks which had resulted in the transfer of eight vessels from Canadian to Trinidadian registry and that news and comments on the subject were privileged. Banks opposed the claim and contended that even if the situation was one otherwise justifying the privilege plea, the *Globe and Mail* had shown malice, thereby negativing privilege. The trial judge ruled that the *Globe and Mail* could claim qualified privilege, and the jury to whom the question of privilege was referred ruled that there had been no express malice. After dismissal of Bank's action, the action was taken on appeal to the Supreme Court of Canada. In rendering the judgment of the court, Supreme Court Justice Cartwright found that the trial Judge had "confused the *right* which the publisher of a newspaper has, in common with all Her Majesty's subjects, to report truthfully and comment fairly upon matters of a public interest, with a *duty* of a sort which gives rise to an occasion of privilege." (Case cited, pages 349 and 350) This meant the denial of the plea of qualified privilege. The question of malice became therefore relevant and Banks was awarded $3500.

Case No. 14

See: *Murphy* v. *LaMarsh et al.*, (1970), 73 W.W.R. (N.S.) 114

This case arose after the former Liberal cabinet minister, Judy LaMarsh, wrote a book of political reminiscences entitled *Memoirs of a Bird in a Gilded Cage.* In it she described the reporting, by Ed Murphy, a radio newsman in the press gallery of Ottawa, of an instance involving Maurice Lamontagne, former secretary of state. In her account, Miss LaMarsh termed Murphy a "brash young radio reporter" and referred to him parenthetically as "heartily detested by most of the Press Gallery and the members." It was not argued that the word "brash" was defamatory but the claim that he was detested was. Weight was attached to the fact that the detestation was not given as the defendant's own opinion. British Columbia Supreme Court Justice Wilson said of the matter: "If, in this case, Miss LaMarsh had expressed her own detestation of the plaintiff I would have thought little of it but it is a different matter when she attributes, without foundation, detestation of Mr. Murphy to his associates." (Case cited, page 121) That a plea of fair comment must be based on true facts was implicit in the chief justice's rejection of the defence of fair comment. "One may properly ask, 'fair comment on what?' " he said. "The comment is not an opinion on the quality of his reporting, in the nature of fair literary criticism, it is a bald statement, irrelevant to the subject under discussion." (*ibid*) Murphy was awarded damages of $2,500. It is to be noted that the award was lessened because Murphy gave publicity to his libel action, and, contemporaneously with his trial, his employer radio station advertised that "Murphy stirs things up."

Case No. 15

See: *MacKay et al.* v. *Southam et al.*, (1956), 2 D.L.R. (2d) 1

Case No. 2 dealt with the citation of Eric Nicol and the Vancouver *Province* for contempt of court. That offence also caused Nicol and his employers to be found liable for a civil defamation. Trial Judge McInnes, sitting without jury, had dismissed the action, but the Alberta Court of Appeal allowed the appeal. The higher court took note of the fact that the Nicol column had specifically charged the jurymen with moral turpitude in carrying out their sworn duties and found the plea of fair comment untenable. (Case cited, page 4) The eight jurymen who filed the suit for libel were awarded damages of $500 each, $100 nominal damages augmented by $400 so the damages might be regarded as substantial but not exemplary. In making the award the Court took account of three mitigating factors: the jurors had not been mentioned in the Nicol column by name; the columnist and newspaper had already been found guilty of contempt; the defendants had tendered an apology three months before the libel action but on the eve of the contempt hearing.

Case No. 16

See: *Mack* v. *North Hill News Ltd. McIntosh* v. *North Hill News Ltd. et al.*, (1964), 44 D.L.R. (2d) 147

Three actions, consolidated for trial, were commenced after the the Calgary *North Hill News*, in its June 16, 1960 issue, published a news story and editorial condemnatory of seven Calgary aldermen. The news item was headlined ''Resign Now,'' with a deck which said ''Seven Aldermen Found Guilty.'' In bold face body type the story read:

Seven Aldermen may be disqualified from holding public office on Calgary City Council following last week's court judgment on the Sarcee Triangle.

The seven aldermen, acting as a majority on council, have been found guilty of:-

1. Voting a bonus to commerical promoters;
2. Voting to lose the citizens at least $25,000 by land sale;
3. Failing to act in the best interests of the city;
4. Failing to act in good faith after previous warning about the Sarcee Triangle by Judge Sherman Turcotte last year.

On any of these counts, the seven aldermen should resign forthwith.

Then there were listed the names of the seven aldermen who had voted for the sale of the Sarcee Triangle.

The editorial read in part:

. . . Seven aldermen voted to sell the Sarcee Triangle to Warner Holdings Ltd. for less than its fair actual value. If they have any moral fibre at all, they should resign now.

. . . [T]hey were given a warning. Judge Turcotte told them the proposed direct sale was wrong and called it, somewhat mildly, 'an error of judgment' . . .

The City Act says that any alderman who attempts to vote a bonus to a private company is automatically disqualified from office. Furthermore, he is liable to a jail sentence.

Aldermen C. F. Mack and D. F. McIntosh brought suit against the *North Hill News*. In giving judgment Alberta Supreme Court Justice Kirby asserted:

The words appearing in the subheading ''Seven Aldermen Found Guilty'' would in themselves, in my view, convey to readers of common and reasonable understanding that the plaintiffs who were afterwards named among the seven aldermen had been charged and found guilty in some Court of acts which constitute a crime, and were therefore of a defamatory nature. (Case cited, page 156)

Justice Kirby found that the ''rolled-up plea'' had failed because the ''facts'' on which the defence claimed its comment was based were not true facts.

Damages were assessed to the plaintiff, Mack, in the sum of $1,000, and to the plaintiff, McIntosh, in the sum of $1,500.

(*Toronto Star Ltd.* v. *Globe Printing Co.*, [1941] 4 D.L.R. 113 furnished an example of a similar failure of a "rolled up plea." Here the *Globe and Mail* proposed to plead that its comment was based on such facts as appeared in the alleged libel "together with what has appeared from time to time in the Toronto Daily Star." The plea was disallowed on the grounds that if it were permitted to stand, "the defendant would be able to adduce at the trial without the plaintiff knowing what it has to meet anything that may have appeared in the Toronto Daily Star since it commenced publication." See case cited at pages 115 and 116.)

Case No. 17

See: *New Era Home App. Ltd.* v. *Toronto Star Ltd.*, [1963] 1 O.R. 339

The suit was caused by a story in the *Toronto Star* in which the names of Jack and Murray Blustein were misspelled "Bluestein" and it was erroneously indicated that the two men were related to Max Bluestein, a principal in a crime probe, described as "a man of some notoriety." (See case cited, page 339) The newspaper issued an apology and a retraction. In examination for discovery the defendants proposed to plead justification and publication of the apology. The plaintiffs claimed the defence could not say, "I justify and I apologize." But the master of the Ontario High Court ruled that the defence could do so. He indicated the rationale for this ruling when he noted:

> Counsel for the defendants points out the quandary in which a newspaper finds itself when given notice under s. 5(1) of the Libel & Slander Act, in that in order to obtain the benefit of the statute it must publish a retraction within three days of receipt of the said notice giving it only that very limited time to investigate the facts, and that therefore it would be unfair to deprive it of the alternative plea of justification if subsequently such a plea were found to be available. (See case cited, page 342)

Case No. 18

See: *Bonham* v. *Pure Water Association*, (1970), 14 D.L.R. (3d) 749

In November 1968, before certain parts of the lower mainland of British Columbia were to vote on the question of fluoridation, an informal panel discussion on the subject was conducted on Vancouver radio station CJOR, with listeners phoning in their questions to the panellists. One caller asserted that there were compulsive water drinkers who will drink 20 to 35 litres of water a day and thereby consume more than a safe amount of fluorine. To this Dr. G. H. Bonham, Vancouver Medical Health Officer and an advocate of fluoridation, answered, "Your kidneys won't take that 25 to 30 litre business." By this he meant that the kidneys did not have the capacity to pass that quantity of water. But the Pure Water Association, which was opposed to fluoridation, published an advertisement in which they knowingly misinterpreted Bonham's statement, presenting it as an admission that some people would suffer kidney damage if fluoridation was introduced. Dr. Bonham wrote to the defendant association, explaining the meaning of his remark, but the defendant officers of the Association refused to apologize or retract. The Association persisted in its defence of fair comment at its trial before the British Columbia Supreme Court. The Court found that the advertisement was defamatory of Dr. Bonham. It ruled that the words at issue "could convey the innuendo complained of to ordinary people in the community concerned with this issue and such innuendo would bring into discredit the plaintiff in his capacity as a public health officer amongst ordinary people in the community. They would convey to the ordinary reasonable man . . . that the plaintiff had advocated as a public measure a proposal which he knew would cause kidney damage to some people." (Case cited, page 754) It was also the Court's judgment that "[s]ince the words complained of purported to be a statement of fact, the defence of fair comment could have no application." (*Idem*, 749)

Case No. 19

See: *Brannigan* v. *Seafarers' International Union of Canada*, (1964), 42 D.L.R. (2d) 249

The defendant was the publisher of a newspaper named *Canadian Sailor*. In its issue of August 23, 1961, it published a picutre of a placard-carrying parade marcher whom it identified as William Brannigan. The caption on the photograph was "C.B.R.T. Official Waves Red Flag." The accompanying story cited the picture as positive proof that the Canadian Brotherhood of Railway and Transport Workers was "Commie tinged." Brannigan filed suit for libel. The defendant newspaper pleaded that the statement was not defamatory, that it was true in substance and in fact, that it was fair comment, and that the matter had been rectified by public apology in a subsequent edition of the newspaper.

In 1963 the Supreme Court of British Columbia rejected all four contentions. The apology referred to had been printed on page 12 of the December 31, 1961 issue. It read:

WE HAVE BLUNDERED

In the August 23rd, 1961 edition of the "Canadian Sailor", we published a photograph of the May Day, 1960 Communist parade in Vancouver, in which we erroneously identified a Communist banner holding Canadian Brotherhood of Railway and Transport Worker as one, William Brannigan. The standard bearing Communist supporter however was William Mozdir, Vice-President of Local 400, Canadian Brotherhood of Railway and Transport Workers. In order to set the record straight we apologize to Mr. William Brannigan for confusing two pictures and thereby embarrassing Mr. Brannigan by not showing him as he also proudly held aloft a placard in support of the policies of the Communist Party—in the same parade, but a few squads back.

In a further effort to placate the ruffled feelings of Mr. Brannigan we publish below both pictures, with the proper identification. Again, to Mr. Brannigan, we tender our sincerest apologies and make this retraction with the hope that he will feel that satisfaction has been achieved.

There followed two pictures, one of them the original picture but with a new caption identifying Mozdir. To its left was a new picture accompanied by the cutlines:

PICTURE THAT SHOULD HAVE APPEARED

The picture on left shows Mr. Brannigan, former Financial Secretary of Local 400, Canadian Brotherhood of Railway and Transport Workers, (Arrow) as he proudly carries a placard in support of the Communist party in the same Communist May Day Parade in Vancouver of 1960.

The placard carried by the plaintiff was completely undecipherable. Brannigan did not recall the wording of his sign, which had been made by someone else. He believed that it was to the effect that "Canada Needs More Ships" or "Canada Needs More Jobs." He was "definite in his sworn testimony that the wording on the sign had nothing to do with Red countries or Communist countries and that he was not nor to his knowledge was anyone in his group giving support to the Communist party." (Case cited, page 253)

Justice Hucheson of the B. C. Supreme Court gave it as his opinion that "it is also evident from the form and wording of the so-called apology that it is a deliberate and intended reiteration or emphasizing of the statements made in the earlier issue of the Canadian Sailor, the truth of which the defendant has asserted throughout but has failed to establish. That apology, rather than mitigating the damages caused to the plaintiff, as urged on behalf of the defendant, would, in my opinion, tend to aggravate the damage done by the libel." (*Idem*, 258) In spite of the fact that there was no evidence of special damage, the Court ruled that the plaintiff was entitled to damages in the amount of $5,000.

Case No. 20

See: *Platt* v. *Time International of Canada Ltd.*, (1964), 44 D.L.R. (2d) 17

In 1962 the Canadian section of *Time* had carried a story under the headline "Smugglers' Reward." It wrongly associated Major W. A. Platt with a group of other ranks convicted of smuggling opium between Viet Nam and Laos, and falsely implied that the officer was about to be court-martialed on the same charge. The editors of *Time*'s Canadian edition disregarded its staffers' warnings against linking Major Platt's name with the opium smuggling trials. When Platt's solicitors served notice of his intention to launch a libel suit against the magazine and called on its editorial staff to print a retraction of the statements injurious to their client, the defendant magazine declined to do so. Instead it invited the plaintiff's lawyers to submit a "corrective" letter to *Time*'s "letters to the editor" section. This, Platt's lawyers, in their turn, refused to do. Later *Time*'s Canadian edition published a letter signed by John M. Scott pointing out that Platt's court-martial (on a lesser charge of which he was subsequently acquitted) was in no way related to the earlier opium courts-martial. The latter was buried among 21 other letters, almost all of which were from the U. S. A. and were concerned with American topics. The fact that Scott was the editor of the Canadian section of *Time* was not disclosed. Of the magazine's behavior, the Court's opinion was:

> The article was written with full knowledge that there was no suggestion that the plaintiff was in any way involved in dope trafficking and both before and throughout the trial the defendant displayed an attitude of defiant arrogance and persistently refused to give a proper apology . . . Not only did defendant impute conduct of a most revolting and reprehensible nature to the plaintiff, but its own conduct indicated such a reckless, if not deliberate, disregard for any injury that might be done to the good name of the plaintiff as to constitute malice in law and properly deserved the imposition of punitive damages. (*Ibid*)

The award was $35,000.

Case No. 21

See: *R.* v. *Unwin*, [1938] 1 W.W.R. 339, 69 C.C.C. 197 and
R. v. *Powell*, [1938] 1 W.W.R. 347, 69 C.C.C. 205.

The case involved two prominent Social Creditors. What precipitated the prosecution was a Social Credit leaflet entitled, "Bankers' Toadies." Its text read:

> My child, you should Never say hard or unkind things about Bankers' Toadies. God made Bankers' Toadies, just as He made snakes, slugs, snails and other creepy-crawly, treacherous and poisonous things. NEVER therefore, abuse them—just exterminate them,
>
> and to prevent all evasion
>
> Demand the *Result* you want
>
> $25.00 a month
>
> and a lower cost to live.

The reverse side of the leaflet contained the names of nine prominent businessmen and repeated the adjuration, "Exterminate them." "Bankers' Toadies" had been produced by G. F. Powell, imported Welsh adviser to the Aberhart government, and J. L. Unwin, government whip, the two men who had caused the leaflet to be distributed. The publication caused Unwin and Powell to be charged with counselling to murder, seditious libel and defamatory libel. After the first two charges were dropped, Unwin was sentenced to three months' imprisonment and Powell to six on the third charge. Of the "breach of the peace" concept the Alberta Court of Appeal stated:

It is also urged that the trial Judge should have directed the jury that they should not convict unless satisfied that the libel was by reason of its terms, or the circumstances, calculated to cause a breach of the peace. It is sufficient to say that there is no law that warrants the view implied in this objection. It has been said that defamatory libel has been made a crime because such libels may have a tendency or be liable or calculated to cause breaches of the peace but that is a wholly different thing from declaring that any particular libel must have such an effect and whether it has or has not is not in any way material. (Case cited, page 343)

The justices indicated as rationale for their decision that they felt it necessary to protect bankers from a hostile populace, asserting that ''it is shown by the evidence that the state of feeling throughout the Province was such that the broadcasting of such a libel might have disastrous consequences.'' (Case cited, page 353)

Case No. 22

See: *R.* v. *Georgia Straight Publishing Ltd.*, *McLeod and Cummings*, (1969), 4 D.L.R. (3d) 383

This was one of the rare cases of defamatory libel in Canada. The chain of events which led to the criminal proceedings against the hippie newspaper, *Georgia Straight*, and its principals started after a number of hippies began frequenting the grounds in front of the Vancouver courthouse. In March 1968 police arrested a number of persons among the approximately 200 loiterers there. One of these, a University of British Columbia student named Stanley Perskey, was tried and convicted by Magistrate Lawrence Eckhardt under a British Columbia order-in-council which the magistrate said was discriminatory but which he felt bound to apply. The *Georgia Straight* reacted by awarding Magistrate Eckhardt the Pontius Pilate Certificate of Justice. The citation read:

Eckhardt, Magistrate Lawrence—The Pontius Pilate Certificate of Justice—(Unfairly maligned by critics, Pilate upheld the highest tradition of a judge by placing law and order above human considerations and by helping to clear the streets of Jerusalem of degenerate non-conformists.) . . . To Lawrence Eckhardt, who, by closing his mind to justice, his eyes to fairness, and his ears to equality, has encouraged the belief that the law is not only blind, but also deaf, dumb and stupid. Let history judge your actions—then appeal.

The author of these words, Robert Cummings, and the editor and publisher of the *Georgia Straight*, Daniel McLeod, were prosecuted under (the then) Section 251 (now Section 265) of the Criminal Code and convicted of publishing a defamatory libel. The paper was fined $1,000 and Cummings and McLeod were fined $250 each.

In a perceptive analysis of the legal troubles of *Georgia Straight* (L. A. Powe Jr, ''The Georgia Straight and Freedom of Expression in Canada,'' *Canadian Bar Review*, Volume XLVIII, 1970, 410) L. A. Powe Jr. characterized the "crime" with which the newspaper was charged as an anachronism in modern law. (*Op. cit. supra*, 428) Pointing out that, at different times in Anglo-Canadian legal history, the Pontius Pilate satire might have constituted defamatory (criminal) libel, seditious libel or constructive contempt of court by scandalizing (*idem*, 426), he felt that history had demolished the rationale for using criminal law to deal with the sort of offences of which the *Georgia Straight* was convicted. (*idem*, 428) To this result Professor Chafee has contributed by demonstrating that if words become criminal only when they have an immediate tendency to produce a breach of the peace then a law of sedition would be redundant. (*ibid*) Affirming that defamatory libel had outlived its rationale, he declared that "[d]efamatory libel has been even less frequently used than seditious libel in the twentieth century, probably not so much from the judicial caveats about its use which are present in cases of conviction as from the obvious fact that the civil remedy for defamation is not only equally effective in inhibiting borderline statements, but more likely to be successful and often more rewarding." (*ibid*)

Case No. 23

See: *R. v. Boucher*, [1950] 1 D.L.R. 657

The prosecution was the outcome of distribution by a Jehovah's Witness named Boucher of a religious pamphlet in Quebec. Its title was "Quebec's Burning Hate for God and Christ and Freedom is the Shame of all Canada." Parts of the pamphlet read:

> Before the hot denials and protests and false counter-charges boom out from the priestly keepers of Quebec Province and whip up an unreasonable frenzy, calmly and soberly and with clear mental faculties reason on the evidence presented in support of the above-headlined indictment . . .
>
> Did the parish priests that have stood by and approvingly witnessed such outrages show regard or disregard for Christian principles? And what about Quebec's law-making bodies that frame mischief by law to "get" those not favored by the ruling elements? and her police forces that allow mobsters to riot unchecked while they arrest the Christian victims, sometimes for no more than distributing Bibles or leaflets with Bible quotations . . . and what of her judges that impose heavy fines and prison sentences against them and heap abusive language upon them, and deliberately follow a malicious policy of again and again postponing cases to tie up tens of thousands of dollars in exorbitant bails and keep hundreds of cases pending? . . .
>
> In a torrential downpour all the foregoing violences and injustices rain down daily upon Jehovah's witnesses in Quebec province . . . Such deeds are the outgrowth of burning hate, and cause the finger of shame to point to Canada . . . Not satisfied with throwing tomatoes and potatoes and rocks, this time the Catholic hoodlums added to the bombardment cucumbers, rotten eggs and human excrement . . .
>
> All the French Canadian courts were so under priestly thumbs that they affirmed the infamous sentence, and it was not until the case reached the Supreme Court of Canada that judgment was reversed . . .

All well informed persons in Canada grant that Quebec province with its 86-percent-Catholic population is under church-and-state rule. In the Quebec legislature the crucifix is placed above the Speaker's Chair, and in the Quebec Parliament buildings alongside the throne of the lieutenant-governor of Quebec is installed a throne for the cardinal. It was reportedly the cardinal who instituted the notorious Padlock Act, supposedly against a mere handful of Communists, but which Act left 'Communist' undefined so that anyone not suiting the priests and their puppet politicians could be prosecuted. The Act was used against Jehovah's Witnesses . . .

Quebec Catholics will show love for God and Christ and freedom not only by words but also by righteous deeds. They will join with the many thousands of other Quebec people, Catholic and Protestant and non-religious, that have vigorously protested the wicked treatment meted out to Jehovah's Witnesses in that benighted, priest-ridden province . . .

Quebec, Jehovah's Witnesses are telling all Canada of the shame you have brought on the nation by your evil deeds. In English, French and Ukrainian languages this leaflet is broadcasting your delinquency to the nation. You claim to serve God; you claim to serve freedom. Yet if freedom is exercised by those who disagree with you, you crush freedom by mob rule and gestapo tactics . . . Quebec, you have yielded yourself as an obedient servant of religious priests, and you have brought forth bumper crops of evil fruits. (Case cited, pages 672-673)

Boucher was found guilty at St. Joseph de Beauce, P.Q. The Court of Appeal confirmed the trial court decision with two of the five judges dissenting. The defendant next appealed to the Supreme Court of Canada. By a five-four vote the appeal was upheld and the accused was acquitted. All but Chief Justice Rinfret held that, for there to be sedition, not only must the writings complained about raise discontent or disaffection among subjects or provoke ill-will or hostility between different classes, but it must be intended to produce disturbance of or resistance to established authority. Justices Kerwin, Kellock, Estey and Locke found that, in addition to bringing the administration of justice into hatred or contempt, or inciting disaffection against it, there must be an intention to incite people to violence against or to defeat the functioning of the administration of justice. Justices Taschereau, Cartwright and Fauteux held that an intention to bring the administration of justice into hatred and contempt was alone sufficient to constitute a seditious intention. Chief Justice Rinfret and Justice Rand expressed no opinion on the question.

Case No. 24

See: *Annotation*, "Blasphemy," (1927) 48 C.C.C. 1

As reported by E. J. Murphy in his Annotation, what gave rise to the case, *Rex* v. *Sterry*, was the following passage in the *Christian Enquirer*, published in Toronto by Ernest V. Sterry:

Read your Bible, if you have not done it before, and you will find in it hundreds of passages relative to the Divine Being which any moral and honest man would be ashamed to have appended to his character . . .

The God of the Bible is depicted as one who walked in the Garden of Eden, talked with a woman, cursed a snake, sewed skins together for clothes, preferred the savour of small roast cutlets to the odours of boiled cabbage, who sat in a burning bush or popped out from behind the rocks, this irate Old Party who thunders imprecations from the mountain or mutters and grouches in the Tabernacle and whom Moses finds so hard to tame, who in his paroxysms of rage has massacred hundreds of thousands of His own Chosen People, and who would have slaughtered the whole lot if cunning old Moses hadn't kept reminding Him of 'What will the Egyptians say about it.' This touchy Jehovah whom the deluded superstitionists claim to be the creator of the whole universe, makes one feel utter contempt for the preachers and unfeigned pity for the mental state of those who can retain a serious countenance as they peruse the stories of His peculiar whims, freaks and fancies and His frenzied megalomaniac boastings.

For his offence Sterry was tried, convicted and sentenced to sixty days in jail. He appealed, but the Appelate division of the Supreme Court of Ontario dismissed the appeal, thereby confirming the conviction.

Commenting on the state of the law of blasphemy in Canada at the time of the Sterry case, Murphy wrote:

It is blasphemy to publish any profane words vilifying or ridiculing God, Jesus Christ, the Old or New Testament, or Christianity in general with intent to insult and shock believers or to pervert or mislead the ignorant or unwary. This intent is an essential element in the offence, though it may be presumed wherever such a result is the natural and necessary consequences of the publication. The defendant is not allowed to plead any justification or to argue at the trial that his blasphemous words are true. (Case cited, page 1)

At the same time he was quick to point out:

The arm of the law is not stretched out to protect the character of the Almighty; the Courts do not assume to be protectors of our God but to protect the people from indecent language." (*Ibid*)

Case No. 25

See: *R.* v. *Rahard*, (1935), 65 C.C.C. 344.

This is one of the most recent if not most recent blasphemous libel prosecutions to take place in Canada. The case followed the 1933 action of Rev. Victor Rahard, an Anglican minister, in putting up posters outside his Montreal church. The posters included the following words:

. . . Judas sold Christ for a large sum of money; the Roman priests sell Him every day and even three times.
. . . Judas repented and threw his money away; the Roman priests do not

repent and even keep the money. Now what do you think of the papist religion?

. . . The Roman Church is not content with the commandments of God. She wishes to have her own commandments for the satisfaction of her ambition and the prosperity of her shop.

. . . These human commandments are not an act of God nor of universal morality nor of conscience. They bind no one and their transgressions may be considered an act of enfranchisement in regard to usurped authority.

Rahard was tried under what was then section 198 of the Criminal Code. The defence maintained that blasphemy is a crime under English common law which exists only in an attack on God or Christianity generally and that the writings did not make such an attack. However, the Court of Sessions of the Peace, Montreal, ruled that: "The expression in writing of an opinion on a religious question in bad faith and injurious to the religious convictions of those who do not share those convictions and of such a nature that it might lead to a disturbance of the peace, constitutes blasphemous libel." (Case cited, page 344)

Case No. 26

See: *Regina* v. *Brodie Regina* v. *Dansky Regina* v. *Rubin*, (1962), 32 D.L.R. (2d) 507

In November 1959 copies of *Lady Chatterley's Lover* were seized under the newly enacted section 150A (now section 160) of the Criminal Code. The Court of Sessions of the Peace for the District of Montreal declared the book to be obscene and forfeited to Her Majesty in accordance with the new section. In the lower court oral evidence was given by Hugh MacLennan and Morley Callaghan on the literary and artistic merit of the book and the position of Lawrence in the world of English literature. Mr. Harry T. Moore, a teacher and critic, gave evidence as well, and many reviews by outstanding literary critics in the United States were also filed. But the Court did not consider such defence evidence persuasive. Brodie, Dansky and Rubin, who had been occupants of the premises from which copies of the book had been seized, appealed from the lower court decision to the Court of Queen's Bench. The Queen's Bench Court dismissed the appeals in 1961. Then Brodie, Dansky and Rubin carried their appeals to the Supreme Court of Canada.

In March 1962 the Supreme Court handed down its decision. This was delivered in terms of the Brodie case since the Court considered that each of the appeals raised the same question. It marked the first time in history that the Supreme Court of Canada had to deal with the legal definition of obscenity. (W. H. Charles, "Obscene Literature and the Legal Process in Canada," *Canadian Bar Review*, May 1966, 263). The Supreme Court upheld the appeal, declared *Lady Chatterley's Lover* was not obscene within the statutory definition of the then s. 150(8) of the Criminal Code, ordered the seized copies of the book returned and the ban lifted.

The case was a landmark one in that it dealt with a multiplicity of issues and crystallized them so that they became the subject matter in innumerable subsequent cases. Some of such issues were later to be resolved while others still await solution.

For the majority, Justices Cartwright, Judson, Abbott, Martland and Ritchie found the book not obscene. Chief Justice Kerwin and Justices Taschereau, Locke and Fauteux, for the minority, found the book obscene. Only Justices Fautuex and Ritchie applied the *Hicklin Test*, [in addition to the new s. 150(8),] in their determinations. Justices Judson, Abbott and Martland for the majority and Chief Justice Kerwin for the minority concluded that the *Hicklin Test* was no longer to be applied. Justice Cartwright for the majority and Justice Taschereau, dissenting, reserved judgment on the point. Justice Locke expressed no opinion but applied s. 150(8).

On the question of expert evidence, Justice Ritchie found such evidence admissible under both s. 150(8) as related to the determination of community standards and under the *Hicklin Rule* with reference to the tendency of the matter alleged as obscene to corrupt and deprave. Justice Fauteux considered the evidence of literary excellence to have always been excluded under the Hicklin jurisprudence and saw no reason to admit it under s. 150(8). Although Chief Justice Kerwin found that expert evidence was competent in the determination of the merits of the book as a work of art he held that it was not conclusive on the questions of "dominant characteristic" and "undue exploitation of sex." Justice Taschereau did not expressly decide the question but indicated his thinking on the matter when he said he thought that art can co-exist with obscenity and does not exclude it.

Justice Judson, with Justices Cartwright, Abbott and Martland concurring, considered it necessary to read the book as a whole, to inquire into the purpose and sincerity of the author and the literary and artistic qualities of his work. He focussed attention on "dominant characteristic" and "undue exploitation," the latter in terms of base purpose and in terms of offending community standards. Justice Ritchie agreed with Justice Judson in finding *Lady Chatterley's Lover* inoffensive to community standards, and found the defence of "public good" under s. 150(3) of the Criminal Code acceptable in the case.

By contrast Chief Justice Kerwin, while allowing that the numerous adulterous episodes of the Lawrence novel might be appropriate to Greece and Rome of ancient times, in the context of *contemporary* community standards, found it did have as *a* dominant characteristic the undue exploitation of sex. Justice Taschereau took a comparable stand in designating as obscenity "the brutally frank detailing of more than fifteen adulterous scenes which leave nothing to the imagination and the use of words that no decent person would dare speak without offending the ordinary standards of decency, self-respect and dignity, which words and passages are entirely unnecessary to the purposes claimed for the book." (Case cited, page 509) Justice Fauteux held that: " 'Lady Chatterley's Lover' may be accurately described as replete with descriptions in minute detail of sexual acts which utilize filthy, offensive and degrading terms. Any literary merit the book may have is far outweighed by the pornography and smutty passages so that the book, taken as a whole, is an obscene and filthy publication and comes within the ban of both the Hicklin rule and s. 150(8) as a work tending to corrupt, especially juveniles, and exploiting sex to a shocking and disgusting extent." (Case cited, page 509)

The judicial disagreements of this case gave a foretaste of the diversity of issues which were to require decision in subsequent obscenity cases.

Case No. 27

See: *Regina* v. *C. Coles Co. Ltd.*, (1964), 49 D.L.R.(2d) 34

Early in 1964 copies of John Cleland's *Fanny Hill—Memoirs of a Woman of Pleasure* were seized from the Toronto bookstore, C. Coles Co. Ltd., under s.150A (now s. 160) of the Canadian Criminal Code. On February 27, Judge Weaver, of the County Court of the County of York, ordered all copies previously seized be forfeited for disposal by the Ontario Attorney-General. This was in spite of the sympathetic expert evidence on behalf of the book given by Robertson Davies and Arnold Edinborough. The lower court judgment was appealed by the accused bookstore to the Ontario Court of Appeal, which handed down its decision on December 2, 1964.

Chief Justice Porter and Justices Gibson and MacKay, for the majority, found *Fanny Hill* to be not obscene; and Justices Roach and McLennan found the book to be obscene. All the members of the Court agreed that the statutory definition [then s. 150(8), now s. 159(8)] had superseded the *Hicklin Test* in determining obscenity.

Members of the Court who found *Fanny Hill* not obscene agreed that, as might be expected of a book taking such a theme, a dominant characteristic of the novel was the exploitation of sex but that that exploitation was not undue. Chief Justice Porter (Justices Gibson and MacKay concurring) felt that the book should be viewed as a whole to assess the purpose of the author, whether it was a base purpose or a serious literary purpose. The literary merit of the work therefore became relevant, even though such merit was not to be taken as cancelling out a base purpose. Chief Justice Porter also addressed himself to "community standards" as a yardstick for measuring undue exploitation and cited the definition of Mr. Justice Freedman in the *Dominion News Gifts* case. (See Case No. 32) Chief Justice Porter found the evidence of Robertson Davies and Arnold Edinborough helpful in the determination of undueness.

For the minority, Justice Roach gave definitions of "sex," "exploitation" and "undue." In respect to the latter he considered the critical question to be the contemporary standard of decency and morality, that is, how a particular publication would be regarded by the well intentioned, moderate individual. The minority did not disregard artistic merit of the book but felt that it did not override the obscenity the book contained. Unlike the majority of the Court, Justices Roach and McLennan felt that candor was not an elixir capable of transmitting obscenity into decency. Although not irrelevant in terms of the literal and historical attributes of the book, the opinions of experts as to its moral qualities should not be allowed, according to Justice Roach. In characterizing *Fanny Hill* as obscene he used such descriptive phrases as "composed of nothing but a chronological succession of venereal adventures, wallowing in sex and dripping with sensuality and lewdness" and "plain *unvarnished* dirt for dirt's sake." (Case cited, 35)

Case No. 28

See: *Regina* v. *Cameron*, [1966] 2 O.R., 777

Early in 1965 Miss Dorothy Cameron offered an exhibition of drawings entitled "Eros 65" in her Toronto art gallery, known as the Dorothy Cameron Gallery. On May 21 Detective Sergeant Quennel and another member of the Toronto Morality Bureau visited the gallery and prevailed on Miss Cameron to remove one picture, "Lovers I Tempera" by Robert Markle, and place it in a store room at the back of the gallery on the grounds that the picture was obscene. Evidence was that the picture would not be displayed again until the police were notified. But apparently Miss Cameron felt rather strongly about the picture and thought that the gallery had no alternative but to display it again. It was restored to its former place. On May 26 the Morality Squad again visited the gallery, this time with a search warrant authorizing seizure of "obscene pictures." Seized in addition to the original drawing were: Lovers I—The Kiss, Charcoal, by Robert Markle; Lovers VI—The Kiss, Tempera, by Robert Markle; Paramour, Tempera, by Robert Markle: Lovers VII—The Kiss, Tempera, by Robert Markle; Lovers, by Lawrence Chaplin; Lovers, in Red Pencil, by Fred Ross. The accused elected trial by magistrate, proceedings being under s 150(2)(a) of the Criminal Code. The defence called five expert witnesses in the field of art. They testified to the artistic merit of the seven drawings. Some of the witnesses were teachers of art with or without actual experience, some were connected with well-known art galleries, one was described as an art critic. On November 25, 1965, despite their evidence, Magistrate C. F. Hayes convicted the accused on seven counts of exposing obscene pictures to public view, and she was fined $50 in respect of each of the seven counts.

Miss Cameron appealed her conviction to the Ontario Court of Appeal. Justices Aylesworth, MacKay, Schroeder and McLennan dismissed the appeal, thereby confirming the lower court finding that the pictures were obscene. Justice Laskin, dissenting, favored the appellant and considered the pictures not to be obscene.

The majority of the justices, denying the appeal, took into account the fact that each of the seven pictures had a strong sexual connotation, that four of them portrayed two or more nude female figures, that, of the four, three portrayed acts of lesbianism, and that one portrayed a single nude figure "in an attitude of sexual invitation," and that two purported to show a male and a female figure engaged in sexual acts or positions. These justices upheld the magistrate's view that such presentations constituted an undue exploitation of sex. They supported his opinion that there had been an excessive emphasis on the sex theme for a base purpose having regard to the internal necessities of each drawing and to community standards. The justices adopted the Freedman definition of community standards. (See Case No. 32) They held that while artistic merit is relevant in determining obscenity or the purpose of the artist, where there is a clear and unequivocal offence against community standards, artistic merit would not obliterate the obscenity thereby established. And according to the headnote of the case, "the defence under s. 150(3) of the *Code*, that the public good was served by the exposing of the drawings to public view, was not made out by the accused. The argument that the pictures conferred a benefit on art students by depicting with artistic merit the human form, and on the public by educating them in the appreciation of art failed because to accomplish these ends the exposure of obscene drawings was unnecessary." (Case cited, 778)

Mr. Justice Laskin dissented. He did not find the exploitation of sex to be "undue." Expert evidence, he thought, was relevant to the question of "undueness'' and ''community standards.'' Determination of ''community standards'' required experience of art, so that expert evidence became indispensable to assist the Court. Justice Laskin felt that the magistrate should not have relied on the pictures themselves to make his appraisal of the drawings in the light of community standards. He thought that the magistrate was not entitled to supply the evidence that should have come from witnesses for the Crown.

Case No. 29

See: *Regina* v. *Duthie Books Ltd.*, (1966), 58 D.L.R.(2d) 274

The book, *Last Exit to Brooklyn*, consists of a collection of seven short stories, novelettes, sketches or vignettes having as a unifying theme sex, degradation, crime, violence, misery and hate in the Brooklyn slums, and emphasizing the deplorable living conditions and mores of the characters depicted therein. In early 1966 this book was on sale in the British Columbia bookstore, Duthie Books Ltd. Copies were seized pursuant to section 150A (present section 160) of the Criminal Code. In the subsequent hearing before County Court Judge Remnant, five expert witnesses gave evidence on behalf of the defendant. These were a freelance writer and literary critic, a prominent local writer and magistrate, a teacher of literature at the University of British Columbia, an assistant professor of literature at the University of Hawaii and a psychiatrist. After proceedings lasting three days the Judge found the book obscene and issued a forfeiture order.

Duthie Books Ltd. appealed from the trial court decision to the British Columbia Court of Appeal, which gave its ruling July 13, 1966. Justice Bull, with Justices Davey and Maclean concurring, gave the unanimous judgment of the Court. Result was confirmation of the obscenity finding and dismissal of the appeal. Conceding that the expert evidence was persuasive in a finding that the book was a serious one with some degree of literary merit and that it was treated with technique and skill, Justice Bull nevertheless concluded that, because a finding that the work in question had literary and artistic merit and that the author's purpose was of a high standard did not preclude a conclusion that the work was obscene. Mr. Justice Bull said, ''It is equally 'base' to treat sex in a vulgar, repulsive and ugly manner for the purpose of encouraging people to think of it and treat it as something less than beautiful and normal, and to sweep it from one's consciousness and under the rug. I am convinced that an exploiting purpose to bestialize and vilify sex is as base as to use it as an aphrodisiac or aid to pruriency.'' (Case cited, 280) In applying the ''community standards test,'' the justice referred approvingly to the Justice Freedman reasoning. (See case No. 32)

Case No. 30

See *Regina* v. *Salida*, [1969] O.R. 1, 203

On August 20, 1968 Sgt. Podolsky of the Windsor City Police visited the Book Centre at 340 Ouellette in the City of Windsor. There he found a 15-year-old boy in charge of the store. He was the nephew of the proprietor, a man by the name of

Salida. There were books and magazines in the store's small alcove, at the entrance of which was a sign, "you must be 21 and prove same. The Management." When Salida returned, Sgt. Podolsky produced a search warrant which authorized him to search the premises for obscene pictures, books or other obscene literature and to seize these for Court purposes. He seized *Fetish In Films*, specific issues of *Touch, Sapho, Barracuda, Lezo, Shocker, Fun in The Sun, Nudist Omnibus, Outdoor Nudist, Sun Era, My Secret Life* as well as *The Greek Touch, Miss M., A Man With A Maid, Autobiography of a Flea, Gymn* and *The Pearl*.

Mr. Salida was charged under s. 150(1)(a) of the Criminal Code [now s. 159(1)(a)] and tried by Magistrate Jasperson under summary proceedings. Mr. Salida pleaded guilty to the charge, but his counsel contended that before the Court made its finding the Magistrate should consider each of the 17 publications separately and rule on their obscenity. In examining the accused's literature, Magistrate Jasperson decided that they all depicted one or more of pornography, deviate behavior such as homosexuality, masochism, voyeurism, lesbianism and *fellatio*. The Magistrate said: "No one publication has all these elements . . . but every publication has at least one of them and some have several." (Case cited, 209) The Court found the accused guilty with reference to each item seized, seventeen titles in all.

Case No. 31

See: *Regina* v. *Georgia Straight Publishing Ltd.*, (1970) 73 W.W.R. 221

In its issue dated April 25-May 1, 1969 the *Georgia Straight* newspaper of Vancouver carried, among others, the following three items: an article entitled "Penis De Milo created by Cynthia Plaster Caster"; an advertisement, "Young man wants to meet woman to 30 yrs. old for Muffdiving, etc.;" and an illustration humanistically depicting a dog urinating against a fire-plug, and a male person known as "Acid Man" naked from the waist down and with an enlarged penis prominently displayed. These led to summary proceedings under s. 150(1)(a) of the Criminal Code against the Georgia Straight Publishing Company and Dan McLeod, sole director and editor-in-chief of the publication. Trial was before Provincial Judge Isman in the Provincial Court in Vancouver. On September 23, 1969, he dismissed the information laid against the defendants. In his judgment on the first count he held that "Penis De Milo" was not an undue exploitation of sex considering the publication as a whole. Since the judge felt there was a dearth of evidence as to the meaning of "muffdiving" he refused to consider the advertisement obscene. As for the illustrations, Judge Isman held that the dog picture was of no significance in an obscenity case, and that the Crown had failed to prove that the Acid Man illustration was obscene.

The case was then appealed by the Crown, and came before County Court Judge Darling by way of a trial *de novo* pursuant to the then s. 727 (present s. 755) of the Criminal Code. Judge Darling dismissed the appeal. He took note of the fact that evidence was given that "muffdiving" was a slang word understood to mean cunnilingus or oral intercourse. He characterized as "opinion evidence, but of considerable weight" (Case cited, 225) the testimony given for the respondent defendants by Dr. Frederick Bowers, associate professor of English at the University of British Columbia. Dr. Bowers gave evidence related to the community tolerance and acceptance of sexually-oriented reading material. He said there had been a marked rise in the usage of such words and expressions as had been complained about in the *Georgia Straight*, and he testified that the respondents' exhibits were a true reflection of public tolerance. One possible interpretation of the Penis De Milo article was that it was a satirical comment on the phallus-adulation by the fanatic worshippers of contemporary rock stars. It is notable that in his judgment, Judge Darling treated the *Georgia Straight* issue in question as a whole, found that it did not offend against community standards, pronounced that the statutory definition of obscenity had superseded the *Hicklin Test*, and adverted to the Freedman definition of community standards. (See Case No. 32)

Case No. 32

See: (1) *Regina* v. *Dominion News & Gifts (1962) Ltd.*, (1963), 42 W.W.R. 65

   (2) *Dominion News & Gifts (1962) Ltd.* v. *The Queen*, [1964] 3 C.C.C. 1

The September 1962 issue of *Dude* magazine and the December 1962 of *Escapade* magazine were seized and their distributor was prosecuted under the then s. 150(8) of the Criminal Code on information laid by Inspector Webster of the morality department of the Winnipeg police force. Despite evidence by Arnold Edinborough for the defence, County Court Judge Macdonell declared the publications obscene and ordered their forfeiture by the Crown. The ruling was appealed to the Manitoba Court of Appeal. The appeal was dismissed, Manitoba Chief Justice Miller and Justices Monnin, Schultz and Guy finding against the book. In a minority judgment Justice Freedman held that the magazines were risqué but not obscene and favored allowance of the appeal and the setting aside of the orders of forfeiture. In his judgment Justice Schultz furnished an excellent historical note on obscenity jurisprudence, particularly with reference to the applicability of the *Hicklin Test*. He did find s. 150(8) [now s. 159(8)] to be exhaustive. He found Arnold Edinborough's evidence with respect to community standards to be inconclusive. He concluded that the community standard of what is or is not obscene is not necessarily the same in every metropolitan area in Canada. Relying therefore on the evidence provided by an examination of the particular issues of the magazine before the court, he found that a dominant tendency of the magazine was undue exploitation of sex. Justice Monnin reached the same conclusion as Justice Schultz by a somewhat different route.

Justice Freedman dissented, agreed with Arnold Edinborough, and found the magazines not obscene. But his most memorable words were:

Those [community] standards are not set by those of lowest taste or interest. Nor are they set exclusively by those of rigid, austere, conservative, or puritan taste and habit of mind. Something approaching a general average of community thinking and feeling has to be discovered. Obviously, this is no easy task, for we are seeking a quantity that is elusive. Yet the effort must be made if we are to have a fair objective standard in relation to which a publication can be tested as to whether it is obscene or not. The alternative would mean a subjective approach, with the result dependent upon and varying with the personal tastes and predilections of the particular judge who happens to be trying the case.

Community standards must be contemporary. Times change, and ideas change with them. Compared to the Victorian era this is a liberal age in which we live. One manifestation of it is the relative freedom with which the whole question of sex is discussed. In books, magazines, movies, television, and sometimes even in parlour conversation, various aspects of sex are made the subject of comment, with a candour that in an earlier day would have been regarded as indecent and intolerable. We cannot and should not ignore these present-day attitudes . . .

Community standards must also be local. In other words, they must be Canadian. In applying the definition in the *Criminal Code* we must determine what is obscene by Canadian standards, regardless of attitudes which may prevail elsewhere, be they more liberal or less so. [Case cited, (1), 80]

That the foregoing reasoning is significant was illustrated when Dominion News & Gifts appealed from the Manitoba Appeal Court decision to the Supreme Court of Canada. In overturning the lower court's decision and allowing the appeal, all seven justices of the Supreme Court unanimously approved and adopted the reasons of Justice Freedman.

Case No. 33

See: *Regina* v. *O'Reilly and Four Others*, (1970), 13 D.L.R.(3d) 257

A presentation, "An Evening With Futz," was given in a small Toronto theater in March, 1969. The offering consisted of a prologue and a one-act play by Rochelle Owens. The prologue contained unscripted audience participation and cameo performances by the actors which used sexuality as a theme and spoke in scatalogical terms. The performers referred in poetry and jokes to sexual activity. Sexual intercourse was simulated on stage. The play itself dealt with the relationship between a farmer, Futz, and his pig, Amanda, the pig never appearing on stage.

As a result of the presentation the lessee, manager and agent in charge of the theater were charged with presenting or giving or allowing to be presented or giving an obscene theatrical performance contrary to (the then) s. 150 of the Criminal Code. Miles Dewar O'Reilly, Arthur Carson Pennington, William Marshall, James Garrard and Trio Productions Ltd. were convicted and sentenced on June 30, 1969 in the Provincial Court (Criminal Division) in the Municipality of Metropolitan Toronto. The conviction was appealed by way of a trial *de novo* before County Court Judge Lyon of the County Court of York, Toronto.

The conviction was quashed. In giving his judgment, Judge Lyon noted that a sign erected near the box office had restricted attendance at the play to those over 18 years of age, and that a review of the play had been posted near the box office indicating the nature of the performance. He decided that the prologue had not been presented for its shock value but that its purpose was to set the mood of the evening for the play that was to be enacted. Judge Lyon determined that the play had been written with serious purpose and that it had artistic merit. He pointed out that it had won the Off Broadway Best Play Award for 1967. He also examined the author to find that she was a well-known writer with a good reputation. The judge concluded that the play was an allegory, a symbollic presentation, and since the symbols enabled the author to convey her ideas, those symbols were justified.

Although, as the judge decided, there was as a dominant characteristic exploitation of sex, this exploitation was not undue having regard to the internal necessities of the production itself. Nor did the performance, in his judgment, exceed the limit of acceptability or tolerance as tested by the contemporary Canadian community.

An original and interesting recommendation made by Judge Lyon was:

> Since the standard of acceptability or tolerance is contemporary and Canadian, those charged with the enforcement of this aspect of the law should receive special training in terms of their understanding, knowledge and appreciation of contemporary Canadian standards of acceptability and tolerance. They should also not be hesitant to consult with those in the field who have the expertise, experience and knowledge to give advice with respect to areas of contemporary Canadian culture and arts. (Case cited, 258)

Case No. 34

See: *Regina* v. *Prairie Schooner News Ltd. and Powers* (1970), 75 W.W.R. 585

Charged under s. 150 (now s. 159) of the Criminal Code for having in possession obscene written matter for the purpose of publication, distribution or circulation, Prairie Schooner News Ltd. and Powers were fined $10,000 and $500 respectively by Senior County Court Judge Keith in Winnipeg. The matter in question consisted of 227 paperback books and 29 magazines largely pictorial in nature. They were described as heavily imbued with sex. The defendants appealed from the conviction and sentence to the Manitoba Court of Appeal. Although Justice Freedman moved to reduce the fines to $2,000 and $200 respectively, he held that the appeal from the conviction should be dismissed, and Justices Dickson and Monnin, for the majority, held that both conviction and sentence should be allowed to stand.

Justice Freedman found that what was offered in the magazines went beyond what the Canadian community was prepared to tolerate. He explored the distinction between hard-core pornography and books like *Lady Chatterley's Lover* and *Portnoy's Complaint.* He found that

> It was not a defence to plead that even though the publication was found to be obscene the defendants were entitled to be acquitted because they acted under a *bona fide* mistake of fact in believing that, since the material had been admitted to this country through the Canadian Customs Department, it was not of an immoral or indecent character. It was for the courts, and not for the Customs department, to determine whether or not a publication was obscene

and to hold otherwise would be to deprive the court of its proper function. (Case cited, 586)

Justice Dickson directed attention to survey results that the defence had sought to introduce before the trial judge. There witness R. G. Carbert, a graduate of the Faculty of Law of the University of Manitoba in conjunction with Dr. Morrison, teacher of criminology and sociology of the University of Winnipeg, sought to introduce evidence of a survey they had conducted to determine reaction of people to the type of material presented in the case. Subjects had been an adult evening class of 43 persons at the University of Winnipeg and 25 persons employed at the C.N.R. shops in the City of Transcona. Although the survey was rejected at the trial, the trial judge allowed Mr. Carbert to give in evidence the results or conclusions emerging from it. Judge Dickson held that the trial Judge rightly ruled as inadmissible the report of the public-opinion survey. He discussed at length the various rigid and exacting tests that would have to be met if such survey results were to be acceptable, but he did not find the Carbert opinion survey had met the required conditions. Moreover, Justice Dickson found that the Judge had erred in his finding that guilt [that is, in terms of *undue exploitation*] was to be determined by reference to the fact that the appellants had made a financial profit out of the exploitation of sex. He said there was no support in authorities for such a proposition.

Case No. 35

See: *Regina* v. *Goldberg and Reitman*, (1971), 4 C.C.C.(2d) 187

In August, 1969, two McMaster students, Goldberg and Reitman, showed two films running side by side, accompanied by a tape recording, all under the general heading, ''Columbus of Sex.'' Each of the films portrayed a series of sex acts or simulated sex acts including nude males and females in various positions of sexual intercourse. There was a beach orgy in which six naked couples, male and female, participated in various positions, males upon males, females upon females, and males upon females. There were scenes in which the actors' faces were in contact with the genitals of others. There were scenes in which couples appeared to be having oral intercourse. There was a rape scene. As a result the two students had four charges brought against them under s. 150 (now s. 159) of the Criminal Code. County Court Judge McCombs of the County of Wentworth found them guilty on all four counts despite the fact that Pierre Berton, experienced film critic Joan Fox, the curator of the Canadian Film Archives in Ottawa, a member of the Ontario Board of Obscenity, a curator from the Art Gallery of Ontario, and three McMaster University professors testified that the presentation had artistic merit and that they did not consider it obscene.

The verdict was appealed to the Ontario Court of Appeal. Justice McGillivray, who gave the judgment for the Court, found himself fully in accord with Judge McCombs' decision and the reasons he adduced for it, thereby ruling that the appeal should be dismissed. He directed particular attention to the appellant's contention that the trial judge had erred in not giving proper weight to the fact that the film was viewed only by a predominantly

University audience and not shown indiscriminately to all segments of the community. Pointing out that the question to be answered was not "What does the University approve?" but rather "Has Parliament by its legislation made it illegal to act in the manner charged against the appellants?", he held that no exception is to be made for those in the university community even if it be viewed as having standards differing from those of the Canadian community about it. (Case cited, 191)

Case No. 36

See: *Regina* v. *Times Square Cinema Ltd.*, [1971] 4 C.C.C.(2d) 229

As a result of the showing of the videotape "Vixen" in Toronto in February 1970, Times Square Cinema Ltd. was tried by a York County Judge and jury under s. 150 (present s. 159) of the Criminal Code. During their trial the accused sought to introduce expert testimony as to community standards of tolerance or acceptance of the tape. As a preliminary to the experts' evidence, the defence sought also to introduce two public opinion polls or surveys through two witnesses. Both the survey evidence and the opinions of the experts were rejected by the trial Judge. He found the defendants guilty of the charge. The verdict was appealed to the Ontario Court of Appeal.

The Appeal Court agreed to allow the appeal, set aside the conviction, and ordered that a new trial be directed. Chief Justice Gale and Justice McGillivray agreed that in the new trial expert evidence so far as it was based upon the polls in question should be refused. Taking into account the fact that one group of persons polled had responded to an invitation in Toronto newspapers and that the other had been "randomly selected from the Toronto telephone directory" he found questionnaire results to be based on a sampling too small, too local and too unscientifically chosen for the surveys to have any probative value. As a general question he found it unnecessary to decide whether opinion polls or surveys were admissible in their own right.

Justice McGillivray was not prepared to say that expert evidence based upon a poll should in no case be received. He adverted to the increasing acceptability of such surveys in the United States. He gave a useful dissertation on the conditions that needed to be fulfilled if surveys were to have legal validity.

Justice Jessup found that experts might testify as to community standards of tolerance in an obscenity case and must be allowed to state the premises of their opinion, whether or not such premises were hearsay. Therefore opinion surveys or polls became acceptable to the court. He believed that when an opinion survey or poll is put forward simply as a foundation of the expert's opinion no question of inadmissible hearsay arises because the survey or poll is not offered to prove the truth of the statement it contains but merely to show the foundation of the expert's opinion. He stressed the need to prove the credibility of expert witnesses. He gave it as his opinion that:

If the survey is made in only one locality of the country the expert called should be prepared to justify, on the basis of science and reason, the use of such a purely local poll as the basis of his opinion on the standard of tolerance in the whole community of Canada and a trial Judge should instruct the jury that the expert's opinion is entirely without weight and is to be disregarded if the expert cannot do so. (Case cited, 231)

Case No. 37

See: *Deeks* v. *Wells*, [1930] 4 D.L.R. 513, [1931] O.R. 818, [1931] 4 D.L.R. 533, [1933] 1 D.L.R. 358

The plaintiff in the suit was Miss Florence Deeks of Toronto. In a four year period she had written a manuscript entitled *The Web*. Its theme was feminism in history. It was a large work, world-wide in the geographic area of its subject matter, and in time span dating before the appearance of man on earth. In August 1918 she submitted the finished manuscript to Macmillan Company of Toronto to help determine whether she might use some material in which Macmillan held copyright and also to see whether Macmillan was interested in publishing her work. The book publishing company had that manuscript in its possession or under its control for about six months. (The D.L.R. accounts of the cases before the Supreme Court of Ontario and the appellate division of the Supreme Court of Ontario use the spelling "MacMillan" but the D.L.R. account of the appeal to the judicial committee of the Privy Council uses the spelling "Macmillan.")

About the time of Miss Deeks' submission, H. G. Wells began to write *The Outline of History*. He offered publication rights for Great Britain to the Macmillan Company of England, but that company rejected his offer. But he was more successful with Newnes Company for England and Macmillan Company of New York for North America. It is to be noted that Macmillan Company of England was the parent company of Macmillan of Canada and Macmillan of New York.

Miss Deeks brought suit against Wells and Macmillan Company of Canada. Her claim was that between August 1918 and February 1919 Macmillan of Toronto had sent her manuscript to England for Wells to read, after which it was returned to Toronto. She maintained that the English author had committed literary piracy and that Macmillan of Canada was an accessory before the fact and a co-conspirator with Wells. She made no claim that there had been direct copying but alleged that the general plan of *The Outline of History* was the same as that of *The Web*, and that Wells had borrowed many ideas and words from her manuscript.

Mr. Justice Raney of the Ontario Supreme Court characterized the matter in the following terms:

> The plaintiff's charges against the MacMillan [sic] Company of Toronto and Mr. Wells are obviously of the most serious character. If they were well founded then Mr. Wells was not only guilty of plagiarism, but of receiving stolen goods, and of a peculiarly despicable form of literary piracy, and the MacMillan Co. of Canada was guilty of theft, and both these defendants were guilty of conspiracy within the definition of the criminal law. But if the plaintiff's charges are proved to be groundless then she is guilty of the offence

of defamation of these defendants, an offence scarcely less serious than that of which she accuses them, and none the less so in a moral sense though the libel is published in a privileged pleading filed in Court. ([1930] 4 D.L.R. 514)

The plaintiff called three witnesses to testify that the similarities between the two works could not be the result of coincidence and reliance on common sources, but rather could only have come about as a result of literary plagiarism. Two of the witnesses made their submissions somewhat tentatively but the third, Mr. William Irwin, associate professor of Oriental languages at the University of Toronto (in the case heard by the judicial committee of the Privy Council he was described as a professor at the University of Chicago) was more positive in his claims. The Ontario Supreme Court Justice dealt extensively with the Irwin testimony and rejected the plaintiff's pleading. He said: "But the extracts I have quoted, and the other scores of pages of Prof. Irwin's memorandum are just solemn nonsense." ([1930] 4 D.L.R. at 522) He dismissed the plaintiff's action.

The D.L.R. account of the trial was accompanied by an interesting Annotation on "Literary Piracy and Common Sources of Information." It considered the distinction between copyrighted and uncopyrighted material or manuscript submitted for publication in respect to literary plagiarism and damages awarded therefor. It also made the point that:

Copyright creates no monopoly in the subject matter. All human events are equally open to all who wish to add to or improve the materials already collected by others making an original work . . . A work may be produced identically the same as the protected work provided the author goes to the common source of information and does not merely copy the protected work. He must, however, do the work of research and compilation for himself. He may, however, made "fair use" of former copyright works. ([1930] 4 D.L.R. at 525)

It said further that "it is no infringement to take the general scheme or idea of another book or the theories therein." ([1930] 4 D.L.R. at 526.)

Mr. Justice Raney gave his opinion that Miss Deeks' suit should never have been brought to trial. Nevertheless, she appealed the decision to the appellate division of the Ontario Supreme Court, where she pleaded her own case. In considering the appeal, Chief Justice Latchford enunciated the test for plagiarism: "Leaving aside the ideas underlying the two works which would admittedly necessitate great similarity in treatment and often in terminology, the evidence of plagiary may fairly be said to consist in (1) similarity of language (2) common inclusions (3) common omissions (4) common mistakes (5) physical impossibility of the "Outline" being written independently of the "Web" in the time [Wells actually took to write the book]." ([1931] 4 D.L.R. 538.) He found that the plaintiff's submission did not satisfy the test, and dismissed the appeal. So too did Justices Riddell, Masten and Orde.

The plaintiff next carried her appeal, again in her own person, to the judicial committee of the Privy Council. Lord Atkin gave the findings for the Court. Except that he found that the lower courts had allowed the plaintiff's expert witnesses too great a leeway in their evidence, he agreed with their findings. He said:

> that in the opinion of their Lordships not only did Miss Deeks fail to make out her case, but that it was definitely established that the manuscript in this case did not leave Canada and that Mr. Wells did not have any access to it and did not use it in the preparation of his work. ([1933] 1 D.L.R. 358)

Case No. 38

See: *Pasickniak* v. *Dojacek*, [1928] 1 W.W.R. 865, [1928] 2 D.L.R. 545

The case arose after a Mr. Pasickniak wrote and published a book entitled, "The Great Dream Book." It was in the Ukrainian language and interpreted dreams in terms of central European folklore. In 1926 a Mr. Dojacek and others printed, published and sold a large number of copies of the same book. With the exception of the cover, title page and certain typographical errors the Dojacek book was an exact copy of the Pasickniak book. The author brought suit against Dojacek and his associates for infringement of copyright. The defendants made the defence that because the book was of an obscene and immoral nature it was not copyrightable and therefore no copyright could be infringed. They translated for the Court 88 of the 3,892 dreams interpreted in the book and cited them in support of their case. Typical were the following:

Dream of lime means dishonest gain
To see a woman's breasts: betrayal
Human excrement: misfortune
Nude buttocks: quarreling and enmity
To lie with a person of a different sex: difficulties in your intentions
To lie with a handsome man: delusion
To lie with wife: joy
To lie with daughter: scandal
To lie with sister: journey

Mr. Justice Curran, the trial judge, accepted the defence argument and dismissed the action.

Pasickniak appealed the judgment to the Manitoba Appeal Court and that judgment was reversed. Although the Court was of the opinion that a small part of "The Large Dream Book" was indelicate, it did not find the book obscene. Mr. Justice Fullerton was of the opinion that unless there was something in the book that made its sale a legal offence the plaintiff had the right to sell it and therefore to protect his copyright. ([1928] 1 W.W.R. 868) Mr. Justice Dennistoun said:

> There is nothing in this Act to deny an author his copyright upon the grounds that his work is indecent, obscene or immoral. That the Courts will refuse to give an author damages when his work is of such a character that the law would not permit him to publish it is frequently held. If an author cannot sell his work he cannot prove damages. But apart from damages I can see no

reason why the pirating of an author's original work should not be restrained by injunction, provided it is honest work and not a fraud upon the public. ([1928] 1 W.W.R. 875)

The justice also disposed of the suggestion that the book was fraudulent in a way that tended to deceive the public. He said:

It is argued that this book plays on the weakness of credulous people, which may be true, but there is in it no false statement of existing fact, and ignorant people may accept the folklore as authoritiative or not, as they see fit, there is no pretence that it is anything else. ([1928] 1 W.W.R. 874)

Case No. 39

See: *Robbins* v. *Canadian Broadcasting Corp. (Que.)*, (1958) 12 D.L.R.(2d) 35

The circumstances leading up to the action involved the televising and broadcasting, in the early days of CBC television, of a program entitled "Tabloid." According to the statement of its producer, Ross McLean, it was of a "provocative" nature. One response it provoked was a letter, written January 16, 1956 by a Dr. E. E. Robbins of Montreal and addressed to Producer McLean in Toronto. It said:

I am enclosing a clipping from the Montreal Star which I trust you will read and in turn pass it along to the Easy M.C. and his partners on *Tabloid*.

It is indeed fortunate that Mr. W. O'Hearn did not see some of the past performances in which the script called for MacDougal and Saltzman to put on the most infantile acts one could imagine.

It would be interesting to know what our American Viewers think of this production, but they probably do as many here do, Shut it off as soon as the weather is over.

The weather is the one redeeming feature of the show and I must congratulate Mr. Saltzman on his clear talks on·this subject.

Our only hope is that *Tobloid* like *Living* in the past will die a natural death.

I wonder if the Tabloid Quartette will read this letter with some of the others they get from Viewers.

The clipping referred to was an article written by Walter O'Hearn, drama and television critic of the *Montreal Star*. The article was critical of the Tabloid program.

On February 8, 1956, the program broadcast and televised the newspaper article and Robbins letters. Master of Ceremonies Dick MacDougal (who was to die before the suit was tried by the Quebec Superior Court) invited viewers and listeners to write Dr. Robbins to "cheer" him up. The doctor's name and address were then flashed twice on the television screen so viewers could copy them down. The Court accepted the plaintiff's contention that MacDougal also suggested that members of the audience in the Montreal area might telephone their comments to Dr. Robbins.

As a result the doctor's phone began to ring soon afterwards, rang well into the evening, and continued to ring for the three days following until he had his telephone number changed. He received abusive mail. Hostile practical jokes, such as the sending of taxicabs and C.O.D. food parcels to his home, were played on him.

Dr. Robbins brought action for damages against the CBC under articles 1053 and 1054 of the Quebec Civil Code. Article 1053 states:

Every person capable of discerning right from wrong is responsible for the damage caused by his fault to another whether by a positive act, imprudence, neglect, or want of skill.

Article 1054 says:

[H]e is responsible not only for the damage caused by his own fault, but also for that caused by the fault of persons under his control and by things he has under his care . . .
Masters and employers are responsible for the damage caused by their servants and workmen in the performance of the work for which they are employed.

The Court awarded the plaintiff damages in the amount of $3,000 with interest from date of service of the action and costs. The grounds specified for granting the award were diminution of income, impairment of health by reason of emotional disturbance, humiliation and invasion of privacy. (Case cited, page 35)

Case No. 40

See: a. *Krouse* v. *Chrysler Canada Ltd. et al.*, [1972] 2 O.R. (2d) 134
     b. *Krouse* v. *Chrysler Canada Ltd. et al.*, [1973] 1 O.R. (2d) 225

The case came about as the result of the publication, as a Chrysler Company Canada promotional offering, of a picture of Bobby Krouse, Hamilton Tiger-Cat football player. Krouse, who maintained that he had not authorized the use of the picture for any purpose, alleged that his privacy had been invaded and that he had lost the saleable value of the photo. It is to be noted that although Krouse's name had not been attached to the picture his Hamilton Tiger-Cat number was visible. The numbers of the other players had been blotted out or were not visible because they were out of focus. By an ingenious device known as the "Spotter," which was part of the promotional offering, it was easy to use his number to identify Krouse. The football player sued for damages.

The plaintiff's case, Mr. Justice Haines of the Ontario High Court of Justice noted, broke down into distinct and severable elements, even though it was presented under the rubric of "invasion of privacy." He considered those elements to be:

(a) Invasion of privacy *per se* . . .

(b) Appropriation of the plaintiff's identity for commercial purposes without his consent or compensation.

(c) Breach of confidence.

(d) The actions of the defendants put the plaintiff in breach of his contract and subjected him to potential litigation.

(e) Unjust enrichment. (a case cited, page 138)

The justice declined to rule on whether there was a common law right of privacy in Ontario. He did rule that the plaintiff's action for breach of confidence (which was not raised in the pleadings) also failed. He attached greatest weight to the claim of appropriation of the plaintiff's identity and, lacking evidence that Krouse's ability to get rival endorsements had been diminished, relied on the consideration of unjust enrichment in assessing damages. According to the headnotes of the case it was

> *Held*, defendants had associated plaintiff with the automobiles being sold and had thus seriously affected his chances of advertising for any other automobile manufacturer. This constituted a misappropriation of something of commercial value and injury to the plaintiff's rights of property. Furthermore, it amounted to a passing off as defendants were attempting to take advantage of the plaintiff's popularity by using his name to sell their goods and since plaintiff was engaged in the business of promoting the sales of goods there was a common field of activity. (a case cited, page 134)

Bobby Krouse was awarded $1,000 and costs. The defendants appealed from the decision to the Ontario Court of Appeal. The appeal was allowed with costs and the judgment of the lower court was set aside.

Mr. Justice Estey delivered the judgment of the Appeal Court. He called attention to the fact that Krouse's contract with the Hamilton Tiger-Cats Football Club stipulated that the Club had the exclusive right to permit the display, for publicity or commercial purposes, of pictures of the player without the player receiving remuneration. The justice found there had been no passing off. That doctrine had been traditionally restricted by the Courts to proceedings in which plaintiffs and defendants were competing in a common trade, and clearly the doctrine did not apply: the buying public would not be led to believe that the manufacturer's products or the advertising device had been manufactured by the player. Nor was there an implication that Krouse had endorsed Chrysler of Canada's automobiles. Inasmuch as exposure of athletes through publication of photographs and information is the life-blood of professional sport, some minor loss of privacy is to be expected, but the Court found that the defendants had not committed the wrong of appropriating Krouse's personality for commercial purposes. As the headnote of the case stated,

> Appellant manufacturer had sought a trade advantage through association with the game of football generally, and it was the game of professional football rather than the personality of the respondent which had been deliberately incorporated in the advertising device. (b case cited, page 225)

Index

Table of Cases Mentioned

Table of Statutes, Conventions and Treaties Cited

Evidence Act, R.S.N.S., 1967, с. 94, 35
Theatres and Amusements Act, R.S.N.S., 1956, c. 288, 105

ONTARIO

Evidence Act, R.S.O., 1960, c. 125, 35
The Libel and Slander Act, R.S.O.; 1970, c. 243, 46, 52, 53, 64-65
Public Inquires Act, R.S.O., 1960, c. 323, 35
Theatres Act, R.S.O., 1970, c. 459, 105; Section 3 (2) 106; Section
   21(4), 106

PRINCE EDWARD ISLAND

The Defamation Act, R.S.P.E.I., 1952, c. 41, 46
The Evidence Act, R.S.P.E.I., 1951, c. 52, 35
The Public Inquiries Act, R.S.P.E.I., 1951, c. 130

QUEBEC

Cinema Act, S.Q., 1966-7, c. 55, 105, 106, 107, Section 10 (Amendment
   1967), 106-7, 107
Fire Investigations Act, R.S.Q., 1964, c. 188, 35
Newspaper Declaration Act, R.S.Q., 1964, c. 49, 46
Press Act, R.S.Q., 1964, c. 48, 46, 59
Public Inquiry Commission Act, R.S.Q., 1964, c. 11, 35

SASKATCHEWAN

The Libel and Slander Act, R.S.S., 1965, c. 107, 45
The Privacy Act, S.S., 1974, c. 80, 147, 148
The Public Inquiries Act, R.S.S., 1965, c. 19, 35
The Saskatchewan Evidence Act, R.S.S., 1965, c. 80, 35
The Theatres and Cinematographs Act, S.S., 1968, c. 76, 105, Section
   8(2) (c), 106, Section 15 (l), 107
The Village Act, R.S.S., 1965, c. 149, 157

UNITED KINGDOM

Copyright Act, 1709, 8 Anne, c. 19, 115
Defamation Act, 1952, 15 & 15 Geo. 6 and 1 Eliz. 2, c. 66, 50
Fox's Libel Act, 1792, 32 Geo. III, c. 60, 3-4, 60, 69
Imperial Copyright Act, 1911, 1-2 Geo. V, c. 46, 116
International Copyright Act, 1844, 117
International Copyright Act, 1886, 117
Law of Libel Amendment Act, 1888, 51 & 52 Vict. c. 64, 4
Licensing Act, 1662, 13 and 14 Car. 2, c. 33, 115
Licensing Act, 1692, 4 William and Mary, c. 24, 115
Literary Copyright Act, 1842, 5-6 Vic., c. 45, 116

THE CARLETON LIBRARY